'Who?'

The most remarkable people you've never heard of

'Who?'

The most remarkable people you've never heard of

Donough O'Brien

Foreword by
Frederick Forsyth

LIB
ERT
IES

First published in 2013 by
Liberties Press
140 Terenure Road North | Terenure | Dublin 6W
Tel: +353 (1) 405 5701
www.libertiespress.com | info@libertiespress.com
Trade enquiries to Gill & Macmillan Distribution
Hume Avenue | Park West | Dublin 12
T: +353 (1) 500 9534 | F: +353 (1) 500 9595 | E: sales@gillmacmillan.ie

ISBN: 978-1-907593-84-0
2 4 6 8 10 9 7 5 3 1

Cover design: Ian Hughes – Mousemat Design Ltd
Cover image: © freshidea
Text design: Ian Hughes, Prue Fox, Tony Hannaford
Printed in China on behalf of Latitude Press Limited

CONTENTS

THANKS

Thank you to the innumerable people and organisations who have helped to make this book possible, suggesting stories and verifying them, and helping me to fill the pages with photographs, paintings and illustrations. Sincere apologies if anyone has been left out.

Dr Peter Ackroyd
Aeroplane magazine
After the Battle magazine
The Hon. Brian Alexander
Earl Alexander of Tunis
Mary Berry
The late John Blake
Bletchley Park
Mark Buckingham
Brooklands Motor Museum
Reggie Boyle
Paul Buckett, Volkswagen Group
Gordon Burns
Mark ('Woody') Campbell
Churchill War Rooms
Sir Anthony Cleaver
Nicholas Courtney
The late Sir John Cowley
Tony Cowland
Robert Corbishley, Xerox
Barry Dinan
Pam Easton, Baker Hughes
Edison National Historic Site
Edwards Air Force Base
Professor Malcolm Elliot
The Earl of Erroll
Eton College
Timothy ffytche
Ford Motor Company
French Foreign Legion
Teresa Fry
Michael Grimsdale
Hamburg, New York, Chamber of Commerce

Charles Douglas-Hamilton
Tim von Halle
The late Richard Holmes
Imperial War Museum, Duxford
Lord Inchiquin
Indianapolis Motor Speedway
Irish Guards
Holly James, Mattel
Lord Kakkar
Lori Kupec, Carrier
The late Earl of Lichfield
Danny Litani
Tricia Lord
Louisiana State Museum
Joanna Lumley
Phil Liggett
Sir William McAlpine Bt
Laurence McDonnell
David McDonough
Moët & Chandon
Phil Mooney, Coca-Cola
Professor Vivian Moses
Sir Stirling Moss
Jon Mostyn
Florence Nightingale Museum
National Army Museum, London
National Civil Rights Museum, Memphis
National Maritime Museum, Greenwich
New York Historical Society
Ed O'Brien
Murrough O'Brien

Murrough O'Brien Jr
O'Brien Trust
The Parachute Regiment
Nicole Payne
Henry Poole & Co
Portsmouth Historic Dockyard
The late David Rattray
Dawn Roads, AGA
Royal Aeronautical Society
Royal Air Force Club
Royal Botanic Gardens, Kew
Royal Military Academy, Sandhurst
Royal Observatory, Greenwich
Thomas Ryan, RHA
Chris Samuel
Society of the Monument to the Children's Casualties of War, Prague
Hugh Synge
The Hon. Michael Spring-Rice
Victoria Thai, Otis
Charles Thompson
J. Walter Thompson
Josefin Thorell, IKEA
US National Park Service
John Utley
Tom Waldrop, Intel
Anthony Weldon
Stuart Wheeler
Bob Wills Museum, Texas

ACKNOWLEDGEMENTS TO AUTHORS

So many books have helped this book that it is easier to list the authors:

Peter ACKROYD, Constance BABINGTON SMITH, Anthony BEEVOR, A. Scott BERG, Mary BERRY, John BLAKE, William BODDY, A.E.C BREDIN, Piers BRENDON, Dee BROWN, Bill BRYSON, Ron CHERNOW, Winston CHURCHILL, J A COLE, S J CONNELY, Tim Pat COOGAN, Nicholas COURTNEY, John COWLEY, Len DEIGHTON, Larry DOBROW, Stephen DORRIL, James DUNNIGAN, Erik DURSCHMIED, James DURNEY, Harold, EVANS, Roger FORD, Nick FRENCH, David FROST, Edward GIBBON, Daniel GOLDHAGEN, Linda GUTTSTEIN, Salisbury HARRISON, Peter HART, Jim HASTINS, Max HASTINGS, Maureen HILL, Ian HOGG, Richard HOLMES, Stephen HOWARTH, John HUGHES-WILSON, Robert, JACKSON, Roy JENKINS, Paul JOHNSON, R.V, JONES, David KAHN, Christine KEELER, Thomas KENEALLY, Ian KNIGHT, and John LABAND, H.W KOCH, Spiro KOSTOF, Mark KURLANSKY, Bruno LAGRANGE, Christian LAMB, Richard LAMB Michael LANNING, Edward LAXTON, Patrick LICHFIELD, Lord LONGFORD, Yigal LOSSIN, Douglas MACARTHUR, John MACDONALD, James MACKAY, Harold MACMILLAN, Norman MAILER, William MANCHESTER, Ben McINTIRE, Larry McMURTY, Giles MILTON, Gerry MULLINS, Emmett MURPHY, Jay Robert NASH, Ulick O'CONNOR, David OGILVY, Dr David OWEN, Matthew PARKER, Lawrence REES, Geoffrey REGAN, Anthony RHODES, Jasper RIDLEY, Mark ROSEMAN, Anthony SAMPSON, Simon SCHAMA, Simon SEBAG MONTEFIORI, Michael SETH-SMITH, William SHIRER, Arthur SIFAKI, Kate SIMON, Antoine de ST EXUPERY, Anthony SUMMER, Adrian SYKES, Colin TAYLOR, Peter TAYLOR, Rich TAYLOR, Margaret THATCHER, Gordon THOMAS, Alvin TOFFLER, Blanche TOUHILL, Masanobu TSUJI, Tim TRAVERS, Miranda TWISS, Mark URBAN, Peter VERNEY, Edgar VINCENT, Christian WALMER, Geoffrey WARD, John WARRY, Keith WATERHOUSE, Hugh WIER, Harold WILSON, Derek WOOD, Cecil WOODMAN-SMITH, Brock YATES, Chuck YEAGER, Adam ZAMOYSKI.

PICTURE CREDITS

Where possible, picture credit have been given on the appropriate page next to individual images. Where this is impractical, additional credits are acknowledged below. Every effort has been made to acknowledge all sources. If any sources have, in error, not been credited, please contact the publisher.

After the Battle: 100
AGA Ltd: 48 top
Baker-Hughes: 104
Bletchley Park: 70 bottom. 71
Bundesarchiv: 30
Cerebos Pacific: 29 top
Corbis: 15
Tony Cowland: 74
Ellis Island Immigration Museum: 156

Imperial War Museum: 130 top
Indianapolis Speedway: 67
Irish Guards: 106
Bob Gibbons: 167
Michael Grimsdale: 20, 45, 58, 61, 83, 138 bottom, 146, 159, 163, 174, 181
Josh Hallet: 52 bottom
Lichfield Studios: 191 bottom right

Liberties Press: 140, 141
National Museums of Scotland: 86
Tate London: 33
Charles Thompson: 56
Paul Wright: 78 top
United States Air Force: 203
Chuck Yeager Inc: 129 top

AUTHOR'S NOTE

In a world dominated by often shallow celebrity, many remarkable people have remained unknown and unlauded. This book brings the unrecognised to recognition, with over 200 names that should trip off the tongue – but don't.

In the title, I claim that readers have never heard of the people described. But I admit there will be those with specialised knowledge who will have heard of some of them.

I would be surprised, for instance, if doctors did not know about Howard Florey, Frederick Banting or William Harvey, but probably not of Henrietta Lacks who gave the world her immortal 'HeLa cells'. Military buffs may be familiar with William Brydon or Constance Babington Smith, and film fans may well know of Reginald Denny, Hedy Lamarr and John Loder – but will they know of their significance beyond acting? Irish people will probably know all about Michael Collins, but may be much less familiar with John Boyle O'Reilly, James Hoban or Eliza Lynch. At the same time, some readers will recognise and relate to just one area of a character's importance – like Davy with his safety lamp, Leotard with his costume, or Whitney and his 'Cotton Gin' – but not for other excellent reasons to include them.

Of course, 'remarkable' can be interpreted in many ways. Here, too, are individuals who were remarkably deceitful, dangerous, crooked or cruel, but are also worth remembering, in the hopes that we never see the likes of them again.

So often we only remember people who have affected our lives directly, or are increasingly in the public view. Above all, I hope this book redresses the balance and gives credit where credit is due – or overdue.

Donough O'Brien
www.quirkyhistory.com

SPECIAL THANKS

To my wife, editor, proof reader and greatest supporter, Liz
To my designers: Ian Hughes, Prue Fox and Tony Hannaford
To Ian Hughes of Mousemat Design for the striking cover

FOREWORD

Most of us are intrigued by the question 'Whatever happened to . . .?' followed by the details about a now long-forgotten personage of whom we used to know a lot.

Donough O'Brien has hit on another splendid idea: 'Whoever was . . .?' listing and describing scores and scores of extraordinary people who played an important but hidden task in the story of our times, but whom we probably never heard of in the first place.

Definitely a book to dip into from time to time for an hour or more's remarkable details.

FREDERICK FORSYTH

Frank **ABAGNALE**

At a hotel conference in 1995 in Seville, we were impressed with the silver-haired speaker warning us of the frauds that threatened our industry. And more amazed by Frank Abagnale's credentials, because before becoming a respected security consultant and an advisor to the FBI, Frank had been one of the world's most daring fraudsters – and been jailed for it. Later, the world knew him from Spielberg's film *Catch me if you can*, with Frank portrayed by Leonardo DiCaprio.

Frank grew up in the New York suburb of Bronxville, and the first person he conned was his own father, who forgave him. His mother did not, and sent him to a monastic school. Frank decided to leave both school and home. A girl on a beach asked him, 'Who are you?' 'Anyone I want to be,' he replied. An ability to learn like lightning, mature looks and attractiveness to women would prove him right.

A revelation came outside New York's Commodore Hotel. A flight crew emerged. The men in their uniforms were handsome and confident, the stewardesses lovely.

Deciding 'to become an airline pilot' he stole a Pan Am uniform and wing badges, forging an identification card and FAA licence. He then started to 'dead head', whereby pilots can travel for nothing in the cockpit of other airlines all over America. In each city, he cashed many small dud cheques, becoming an ace 'paperhanger', and in his pilot's uniform, nobody suspected or checked until he was long

Leonardo DiCaprio learns from the master

gone. 'The FBI was now looking for a cool, well-dressed con man of twenty nine. I was seventeen.' Only when his identity was questioned by airline officials in Miami did he decide to lie low.

In Atlanta, he then put 'Doctor' on a resident's form, and incredibly was offered a job as the local hospital's Supervising Paediatrician, which 'Frank Conners' held down for eleven months until becoming scared that his ignorance might kill a child. Then as Harvard Law School graduate 'Robert Black', he was recruited on to the Louisiana Attorney General's staff of prosecutors for nine months, before decamping to become 'a teacher' in Utah.

A child in danger?

Now he forged Pan Am pay cheques, and starting to fly again, complete with a TWA identity to supplement his Pan Am one, covering a million miles and 26 countries. His rented safe deposit boxes soon held bulging suitcases of money. Frank then fell in love, and felt he must tell his fiancée that he was not a twenty-eight year old pilot, but a crook of nineteen – only to find police cars in her parent's driveway. In Washington, FBI Inspector Joe Shea was taking a special interest in this elusive young man.

Another girl, a cheque designer, now set him on a seriously ambitious course – counterfeiting cheques on an industrial scale. He left Las Vegas $39,000 richer after two days. Noticing that people often forgot to put their account number on the deposit slips left on the counter, he stole some, entered his own account number, put them back and found $43,000 had been transferred by the bank's computer to his 'temporary' account.

A millionaire by twenty, and with things hot in the US, a girl in France then gave him another opportunity. Her father was a printer in Paris, and Frank, as a 'purchasing agent', persuaded him to print 10,000 Pan Am cheques, duly showering Paris with them, and then America, nearly caught by Shea.

The crook who became a crime fighter

But in provincial France, now in retirement, 'Robert Monjo' was cornered at last by armed police in a supermarket and sentenced to a year in prison. A lenient sentence? No, because for six months he lay naked and unwashed in a bare, stone cell completely without light. When he emerged, two Swedish female police inspectors were appalled by the half-blind, bearded, filthy and emaciated figure they had to fly to Malmo.

He was horrified to hear about the queue of twelve countries waiting to jail him, but just in time was extradited to the United States. Amazingly, as his plane landed, he squeezed through a toilet hatch to drop to the ground, and ran off across a darkened JFK airport – to the fury of Shea awaiting the plane. He was arrested, but bluffed his way out of another jail and then from a motel surrounded by police.

His luck did not last, and five years in jail finally brought him to some lateral thinking. With his unique knowledge of white-collar crime, why not put it to legitimate use? For years, Frank has been one of the world's experts on beating such crime, working with the FBI, lecturing to the world's police and helping 14,000 financial institutions.

Which is why he came to talk to us in Seville.

Claude de Jouffroy d'**ABBANS**

America is rightly proud of Robert Fulton, the 'father of the steamboat'. But the first steamboat came from a more unlikely source, a French aristocrat – and twenty years before Fulton was to succeed.

Marquis Claude de Jouffroy d'Abbans built his first steamboat in 1776, and seven years later his paddle steamer, the *Pyroscaphe*, sailed on the river Seine. But his efforts were blocked by rivals and then delayed by the French Revolution. So it was the American Robert Fulton who turned from his first interest, submarines, and plied a steamboat up and down the Seine. Soon he had the world's first commercial steamboat line running, in New York. He also suggested to Napoleon that he could invade Britain by towing invasion barges across the Channel when the winds were unfavourable for the blockading Royal Navy.

Napoleon, one of the world's innovators, lost his chance with the memorable rebuff: 'What sir, would you make a ship sail against the winds and currents by lighting a bonfire under her deck? I pray you excuse me, I have no time for such nonsense.'

Frederick **ABBERLINE**

The slums of 19th century Whitechapel in London's East End would defy modern imagination – poor, filthy, over-crowded, racially tense, blighted by violence, robbery, drink, and riddled with prostitution. On 31st August 1888, one of Whitechapel's hundreds of prostitutes, Mary Anne Nicolls, was found with her throat cut and her stomach ripped open.

Because he knew the area so well, recently promoted Scotland Yard Inspector Frederick Abberline was quickly sent back to Whitechapel. Described as 'sounding and looking like a bank manager', Abberline was recognised as a fine detective, but even he was overwhelmed by events. Within days another prostitute, Annie Chapman, was found with a severed throat and her abdomen slashed open, her uterus removed. Three weeks later, two more girls were butchered on the same night, and in early November Mary Kelly's mutilated body revealed an abdomen emptied of organs and with her heart missing.

Several letters were received by the police and the newspapers, one signed 'Jack the Ripper'. The name stuck, and there was a worldwide media frenzy. The hundreds of suspects investigated included butchers, slaughterers, doctors and even aristocrats. Recently a Spanish 'expert' claimed in the *Daily Mail* that Abberline's handwriting was the same as in the letters, concluding that he must have been the villain.

In spite of his excellent record and other successes, Abberline and his huge team of detectives never solved the case, and it remains the most written and talked about crime in history. Abberline himself went on to be Chief Inspector, receiving 84 commendations and awards before retiring to spend twelve years as European head of Pinkerton's famous detective agency. The only good to come of the horrible murders was that the appalling East End conditions were revealed to a shocked Victorian society and the worst of the slums were pulled down.

Abberline has been portrayed in films by Michael Caine as a reformed drunk, and by Johnny Depp as a young clairvoyant who died of a drug overdose in his thirties – whereas Frederick Abberline actually died peacefully in his Bournemouth retirement home aged 86.

But then, showbusiness is no business for getting the facts right.

Eliza **ACTON**

Most of us will have heard of Mrs Beeton. Even today, 140 years after her death, she remains an icon and a household name. But there was someone before her who deserved far more recognition, and without whom Mrs Beeton would not have been nearly as famous: shy, retiring Eliza Acton, much of whose work was disgracefully poached for Beeton's sensational and best-selling *Book of Household Management*.

Britain's great contemporary chef, Delia Smith, once described Eliza Acton as 'the best writer of recipes in the English language'. Born in Sussex, Eliza briefly ran a girls' school near Ipswich and had gone to France where she had an unhappy love affair. She then published her *Poems* in 1826, followed by a book of longer ones.

Eliza Acton was advised by her publisher to abandon her poetry and try something more commercial. In 1845 the result was her *Modern Cookery for Private Families*. Compared with the vagueness of previous writers, Eliza was to provide exact measurements and cooking times and set the scene for all cookery books ever since. A masterly work, it remained in print for years.

In 1861, Mrs Isabella Beeton used her husband's publishing house to launch *Mrs Beeton's Book of Household Management*. This was an extraordinary success – appealing to the emerging middle-classes created by the wealth of the Industrial Revolution and the British Empire. She gave the impression that she was dispensing her copious advice from the lofty viewpoint of an experienced middle-aged matron, whereas she was just twenty-three when she started the book. It actually had only 23 pages on household management, and 900 pages devoted to cooking, though incredibly Isabella Beeton did not like cooking much, rarely visiting her kitchen at all. Most of the recipes were either submitted by her readers, or outrageously, stolen straight from Eliza Acton.

'The best writer of recipes in the English language'

Mrs Beeton treated everyone with unshakeable confidence 'As with the commander of an Army, or the leader of any enterprise, so it is with the mistress of the house'. A bit rich for a young housewife born in Cheapside's market. But it worked, and that's why in Victorian England her work and fame overshadowed the more deserving Eliza Acton.

Roscoe **ARBUCKLE**

Roscoe 'Fatty' Arbuckle was remarkable in many ways – yet anyone who has heard of him probably only remembers the 'Keystone Kops' and something about a rape case.

He was one of the most successful and highly-paid actors in cinema history and yet an unfortunate accident led to his ruin – thanks to an unholy triple alliance of a disreputable woman seeking to extort money, an unscrupulous District Attorney seeking to become State Governor and a newspaper baron seeking to boost circulation.

Fatty Arbuckle certainly had the right nickname, nearly twenty-one stone, although amazingly acrobatic for his size. Actor Max Sennett described him 'skipping up the stairs as lightly as Fred Astaire and, without warning, doing a backward somersault as graceful as a girl tumbler.' And ironically for a silent movie star, Arbuckle had such a wonderful voice that Caruso thought he should have changed career to be an opera singer. He was liked, respected and generous, mentoring three actors who would go on to illustrious comedy careers – Charlie Chaplin, Buster Keaton and Bob Hope.

In September, 1921, and now at the height of his career, Arbuckle had just signed a $1 million contract with Paramount and decided to celebrate by giving a party at a

hotel. A guest, a small-time actress called Virginia Rappe, became ill, but the hotel doctor thought she was merely drunk. Then she died four days later of a ruptured bladder and Arbuckle was accused of rape by her companion, Maude Delmont, a noted procuress and blackmailer. Ambitious San Francisco District Attorney Matthew Brady jumped on the bandwagon and charged Arbuckle with murder, while William Randolph Hearst's newspapers created a frenzy of yellow journalism (people today still quote the disgusting false claim that Arbuckle raped Virginia with a bottle).

There were three trials, two with hung juries. But the third acquitted him in six minutes, the last five spent by the jury writing a statement of apology. (See panel). But the damage was done. Cinemas banned his films, producers – fearful of the pressures that several other Hollywood scandals had created – refused to employ him, and his legal expenses ruined him. He eventually started work as a director under the pseudonym 'William Goodrich'.

Ten years later Warner Brothers at last signed up Fatty Arbuckle for a full-length feature film. 'The best day of my life', he said. But he tragically died that very night, aged just forty-six, the sad victim of one of the most unfair vilifications in American history.

VERDICT: 'Acquittal is not enough for Roscoe Arbuckle. We feel that a great injustice has been done to him. There was not the slightest proof adduced to connect him in any way with the commission of a crime. He was manly throughout the case and told a straightforward story which we all believed. We wish him success and hope that the American people will take the judgment of fourteen men and women that Roscoe Arbuckle is entirely innocent and free from blame.'

Vasili **ARKHIPOV**

It was long after the event that the terrifying details emerged about how an unknown Soviet naval officer, Vasili Arkhipov, was, in the words of a top American, the 'guy who saved the world.'

In 1962, at the height of the Cold War, the Soviet Premier Nikita Khrushchev did something very risky. America still had an overwhelming superiority in nuclear weapons, and had placed some rockets in Turkey capable of destroying Moscow in minutes, adding to Soviet paranoia. To counteract this move, Khrushchev, thinking that President John F. Kennedy was a weak man, smuggled medium-range nuclear missiles into his ally Castro's Cuba. These were soon detected by the Americans, who were horrified

Submarine B-59

to find that their key cities could be taken out in a Soviet first-strike attack. President Kennedy responded carefully by imposing a 'quarantine zone', and the world waited with bated breath to see if the Soviet freighters carrying new missiles would turn back.

What nobody knew was that 700 feet under water, four Soviet diesel submarines were lurking in the Sargasso Sea. What is more, each was armed with a nuclear torpedo of Hiroshima power, and each Captain had the discretion to use it. Conditions inside the submarines, designed for cold Arctic waters, were terrible. After a week submerged, electric power was failing, the air-conditioning had stopped and the temperature had reached a boiling 60°C (140°F), with the crew rationed to one glass of water a day.

Then an American fleet of 11 destroyers and the planes of an aircraft carrier detected submarine B–59, and began to harass her by dropping small practice depth-charges to frighten her into surfacing. In the conning tower were the Captain Valentin Savitsky and Vasili Arkhipov, who was of equal rank, but crucially, also the Flotilla Commander.

With no orders or news from Moscow for a week, under tremendous strain and in the appalling conditions, Captain Savitsky suddenly succumbed to the strain and announced that he was going to use the 'Special Weapon'– the nuclear torpedo. 'We are going to blast them now! We will die, but we will sink them all. We disgrace our navy.' His political officer agreed, and both reached for their keys. Arkhipov knew that the other three submarines had agreed to launch their own nuclear weapons if B-59 did, and that nuclear 'mutual destruction' with America was imminent. (The US had indeed gone to Defcon-2, the condition just short of war, but in fact the Soviets were actually in the process of backing down).

In a dramatic confrontation, Arkhipov over-ruled Savitsky and, moreover, ordered the submarine to surface, which it did unmolested, and sailed home to less than a hero's welcome.

Only years later did other officers reveal what went on in those few frightening moments. The Intelligence Officer admitted, 'We thought – that's it – the end.'

Vasili Arkhipov was to become a Rear-Admiral and died

Olga with Vasili Arkhipov

in 1998 from the radiation he had absorbed when exposed to a nuclear accident. His wife, Olga, is in no doubt about his crucial role, 'The man who prevented a nuclear war was a Russian submariner. I was proud, and I am proud of my husband – always.'

? Inga **ARVAD**

Who made it possible for John F. Kennedy to become President? Curiously, it was not someone powerful. It was none other than the first of his 'unsuitable girlfriends' – Inga Arvad. She was certainly not to be the last.

The affair happened a long time before Jack Kennedy became famous, but his family was certainly well-known enough – as well as controversial. Jack's father, Joe Kennedy, bootlegger, film tycoon and multi-millionaire, had been Ambassador to

Britain in her darkest hour in 1940, so defeatist about her prospects that he was known as 'Jittery Joe'.

In 1941, John F. Kennedy was an ensign in the US Navy's Office of Intelligence in Washington when he started an affair with Inga, a beautiful but married Danish journalist who in 1935 had interviewed Hitler. *'His eyes, showing a kind heart, stare right at you'*, she wrote of him, rather naively. A year later she had been photographed at the Berlin Olympics with Hitler, who publicly called her 'a perfect example of Nordic beauty'. Back in Washington, J. Edgar Hoover's FBI suspected she was a spy, found out that 'Ensign Jack' was a Kennedy and began photographing the couple and recording their bedroom activities. Kennedy's boss, Captain Seymour Hunter, sensing danger in a new 'Mata Hari', suddenly posted Kennedy to seagoing duties just before Hoover could pounce and use the affair to ruin all the Kennedys. Without this sudden move, Jack Kennedy might have been disgraced or stayed in Washington in obscurity. Instead, his PT boat was rammed by a Japanese destroyer and he saved his men, transforming him into a hero and Presidential material.

Inga, who was never a spy and actually despised Hitler, was to marry Tim McCoy, filmstar and army officer, and even have a movie career. Jack Kennedy married Jackie Bouvier and they became the golden couple in the White House. But Jack was an insatiable sexual adventurer – who today would not have survived the media.

Notable among his 'unsuitable' girlfriends was Marilyn Monroe, whom he casually passed on to his brother Robert. More dangerous was Judith Exner, introduced by Frank Sinatra, whom Jack shared with Sam Giancana, the head of the Mafia (a bit like Winston Churchill having an affair with a girlfriend of the Krays). There are many who think that when Robert Kennedy, as Attorney General, started to harass the Mafia, to stop him, they decided to assassinate his brother, the President.

And only years later did Jack Kennedy's image become really tainted by revelations about his unsuitable girlfriends – of whom Inga Arvad was merely the first.

Constance **BABINGTON SMITH**

A young Flight Officer suddenly looked up from the photograph she was studying. She had discovered something that would alter the course of World War II.

It is a little-known fact that Britain led the world in aerial photographic intelligence. By 1944, a superb organisation had been built up using the cameras of the RAF's special Spitfires and Mosquitoes, joined by American P-38 Lightnings. All the evidence was sifted at a large house and building complex near Henley – 'RAF Medmenham'. It was here that a young WAAF called Constance Babington Smith became one of the most

(Medmenham Collection)

Sharp eyes with low-tech equipment

watchful, sharp-eyed and highly successful interpreters of the streams of photographs coming in.

She and her team had detected the dispersed German fighter factories. They were duly bombed, after which the Luftwaffe became short of planes, and then short of fuel, thanks to the detection and bombing of the synthetic oil plants.

Peenemunde was bombed following Constance's discoveries. (Courtesy: Frank Wootton)

All this time, an obscure place called Peenemünde on the Baltic had been under suspicion, and photographic missions revealed the V-2 supersonic rockets, the Messerschmitt Me-163 rocket fighter and the fearsome twin-jet Me-262. Bombing had set these developments back by critical weeks.

Now Constance reported something else; a tiny cruciform shape on the lower end of inclined rails – a midget aircraft actually in position for launching. She revealed that the real danger would not be the Germans' complex V-2 rockets, but their thousands of simple, cheap V-1 flying bombs.

Thanks to Constance, the Allies now knew the purpose of the mysterious buildings and ramps going up all over Northern France. Their bombers were quickly diverted to flatten the mushrooming launch sites, and when in June 1944 the droning, menacing V-1 'Doodlebugs' came rumbling towards London, the defences were ready for them and only 20% got through. 6,000 civilians died, but it could have been very much worse.

Constance Babington Smith starred in a film, *Target for Tonight*, went off to help the Americans with their photo-reconnaissance in the Pacific, wrote several books including one on the aviatrix Amy Johnson, worked for *Life* magazine and was made an MBE. She died at the age of 88 in July 2000, a largely unsung heroine.

Johannes **BADRUTT**

How many winter sports enthusiasts have ever heard of Johannes Badrutt? Yet he is vital to the sports they love.

The Swiss villages of Davos and St Moritz were obscure until local doctor Alexander Spengler confirmed that Davos was free of tuberculosis, and that infected people soon recovered from the disease. In 1869 he advocated the bizarre thought that invalids should not only spend the summer there, but the winter as well.

In St Moritz, Dr Peter Berry agreed.

The first iced run. 1884.

His sister Maria married Johannes Badrutt, and the couple bought a local hotel. Soon after, Johannes made a bet with four Englishmen that the climate in winter was marvellous,

and to convince them, he even offered them free accommodation. That December they arrived in blazing sunshine, to be greeted by Johannes Badrutt in his shirt. So delighted were his guests with their winter stay that the word spread and hundreds of visitors began arriving every year.

One gentle activity that the doctors did allow for invalids was tobogganing down the snowy slopes. The toboggans (an American Indian word) were, at first, adaptations of the local Schlitten, normally used as handcarts. Soon, the enthusiastic English had lengthened them, and competitions began between the Davos hotels. St Moritz was not to be outdone, and Johannes Badrutt hired the geometrician, Peter Bonorand, to lay out a special curved and banked course between St Moritz and the village of Cresta. Because the toboggans' runners were cutting into the snow, someone suggested deliberately icing the course. Speeds shot up, as they did again when the first competitor decided not to sit on the sled, but to lie down and go headfirst.

Soon Badrutt's 'Cresta Run' was one of the fastest and most exciting sports anyone could undertake, and St Moritz and Davos became leading centres of the new craze of 'winter sports'.

Every year, when the snow falls, the run is lovingly rebuilt with its 85 mph straights and terrifying curves like 'Thoma' and 'Shuttlecock'. Always amateur and rather upper class, even though it is now international it was, and is, an essentially British creation.

As Prince Philip has said, 'The beginnings of the Cresta had the added twist that the conversion from pastime to sport was made by a collection of invalids. No wonder the Continentals are convinced the British are mad! I can only say that I am all for this sort of madness.'

Italo **BALBO**

Most people in Chicago don't give it a second glance – a 2nd century Roman column on the Lake Front Trail. A relic of the 1933 'A Century of Progress' World's Fair exposition, it's called the 'Balbo Monument'.

Italo Balbo was a Fascist, in fact the youngest of the four *Quadrumvirs* who had organised the Fascist 'March on Rome', propelling Mussolini to power in 1921.

Mussolini appointed Balbo Secretary of State for Air in 1926 and he became a fervent enthusiast of Italian aviation. Among other feats, in 1933 he led a massed flight of 25 flying-boats from Rome to Chicago, so impressive that a 'Balbo' became the American slang word for any large formation of aircraft.

Balbo's visit to the 'Century of Progress' was a smash hit, especially among the many Italians in Chicago. To watch him land on Lake Michigan, thousands of spectators jammed the Chicago shoreline. Balbo was given a parade, appeared on the cover of *Time*, was made an honorary Sioux Indian Chief, and President Roosevelt invited him to lunch, presenting him with the Distinguished Flying Cross. The Balbo monument, a gift from Mussolini, was put in place, and Chicago's Seventh Street was even re-named, and today remains 'Balbo Drive'.

But back in Italy, Balbo's close relationship with Mussolini was fraying. The dictator was not only secretly jealous of his popularity, but there were more serious disagreements. While initially collaborating with German aviators, Balbo firmly objected to the 1938 legislation against Italian Jews, the only Fascist to do so, bravely and publicly. And when Hitler attacked Poland, Balbo advocated an alliance not with Germany but with Italy's old ally, Britain. He warned his colleagues, 'You will all wind up shining the shoes of the Germans'.

'You will wind up shining the shoes of the Germans'

With such views, prescient but inconvenient, Balbo was shifted off to be Governor-General of Libya, but was soon caught up with Italy's war in North Africa against the British.

And on June 28th, 1940, coming in to land at Tobruk, he met his end when his plane was shot down by mistake by his own anti-aircraft gunners.

Italo Balbo could, perhaps, be regarded as a 'good Fascist'. Which is maybe why that monument has never been taken down.

Joseph **BANKS**

One of the world's most important scientists, Sir Joseph Banks, is surprisingly little known, because his influence was so often behind the scenes. Botanists will recognise him as the key visionary behind Kew Gardens and the discovery of new plant uses round the world. Historians might not realise his role in sending off Captain Bligh with breadfruit to feed slaves, leading to the infamous 'Mutiny on the Bounty'. Manchester would probably not attribute its growth into Britain's second biggest city to Banks' advice to send cotton to be grown in the West Indies and America. Nor would the descendants of plantation owners and slaves connect that decision with the South's over-confidence in 'King Cotton', leading to the American Civil War. Australians might question his encouragement to set up a convict colony, but at least they named some places after him.

Joseph Banks was from a rich Lincolnshire family and was educated, bizarrely, at both Eton and Harrow, and both Oxford and Cambridge. Only twenty-one when his father died, he was left a vast fortune, and quickly made his mark as a scientist, becoming a Fellow of the Royal Society at just 23, President at thirty-five – and remaining so for forty years – the longest ever incumbent, with an influence way beyond his first love, botany.

Banks heard of a voyage of discovery to the South Seas under the command of Captain Cook, and persuaded the Royal Society to ask the Admiralty to take him – at his own expense – to study plants and wild life. He sailed in August 1768 on *HMS Endeavour*, as 'a naturalist' with his own party of nine, costing £10,000, half a million today.

With secret orders to search for the fabled Southern continent, *Terra Australis Incognita*, they sailed round New Zealand and discovered New South Wales on the East coast of Australia, where Banks went ashore to study plants, Cook naming the spot 'Botany Bay'.

When they arrived back in England, Cook and Banks were instantly famous. King

George III had invested in the voyage, and Banks became the King's friend and unofficial advisor in setting up the Royal Botanic Garden at Kew. Banks wanted Kew to be a living encyclopaedia, the great exchange house of the Empire, testing plants for their acclimatisation and practical usage in horticulture, medicine and commerce.

Thus it was Banks who sent Captain Bligh to supply breadfruit and Anton Hove to study cotton growing in India, with huge implications for America. He despatched scientists all over the globe. Plants would arrive at Kew and then be re-exported to where they were needed. South America provided rubber for Malaya and *Chinchona succirubra* – the life-saving anti-malaria quinine – for the whole world.

Joseph Banks never sought recognition, but could hardly refuse a knighthood from his appreciative monarch. But so obsessive was his modesty that he begged his relations not to attend his funeral, nor to '*erect any monument in my memory*'. He was duly buried in Heston in an unmarked grave, until, 47 years later the vicar put up a tablet to indicate the final resting place of this remarkable man.

Frederick **BANTING**

Diabetes affects more people than malaria, and as indiscriminately – babies and children, pregnant mothers and adults of all ages, 200 million people in the world. And it used to be a cruel sentence of wasting away to a slow but certain death.

200 million suffer from Diabetes

When the body takes in sugar, it is regulated by part of the pancreas called the 'Islets of Langerhans'. These produce a sugar-loving protein, the hormone insulin. *Diabetes mellitus*, which is incurable, occurs when the body does not produce enough insulin or its cells reject it. The effects can include heart disease, kidney failure and blindness. And if untreated, sufferers will eventually lapse into a coma and die.

Dr Frederick Banting, a courageous man who had won the Military Cross for heroism in 1918, had seen enough juvenile diabetes as a surgeon in the Hospital for

Sick Children in Toronto to know the threat only too well. He knew that scientists had tried to feed patients on extracts of pancreas but had failed. But he then read that while closing off the pancreatic duct had destroyed the secretion of its main product, trypsin, the 'Islets of Langerhans' had remained intact, from which insulin could be extracted.

Frederick Banting (right) with Charles Best, and one of the diabetic dogs.

In 1922, Banting decided to try to isolate insulin in order to give it to diabetes sufferers. For his summer's work he needed an assistant, and two students then tossed a coin to decide who would take the first half of the summer. Charles Best won. That flip of a coin was to make him world-famous.

Banting and Best worked all through that hot summer of 1921 and did indeed succeed in isolating insulin. This was tried on diabetic dogs, and worked. Then, in early 1922, the first human was given insulin. The results were a spectacular success. Volume production could now be started.

Word spread like wildfire across the globe, giving sudden hope to millions, and there was a frenzied rush to obtain supplies. Many patients in a diabetic coma and near death made miraculous recoveries. However, providing insulin was, and still is, not a cure for diabetes. Nor is it pleasant for patients to have to inject themselves several times a day. But at least insulin remains an effective treatment, and diabetes is no longer a debilitating killer in the developed world.

In 1923, Banting was deservedly awarded the Nobel Prize for Medicine, as was, inexplicably, Professor MacLeod, who had merely given over university facilities and had played no scientific or medical role in isolating insulin. Banting was so angry at the unfairness of the decision that he gave half his prize money to Charles Best.

Knighted in 1934, Sir Frederick Banting again stepped forward when the next World War broke out. Tragically, he was killed in an air crash – flying to England to help the airforce with a new flying suit.

We all know people saved by insulin. But how many of them could name their benefactor?

Arjumand **BANU**

At the age of just fourteen, Arjumand Banu was betrothed to Prince Khurram, who was soon to become the Emperor of the Mughal Empire. They had to wait five years, until 1612, before the court astrologers judged the date to be the most hopeful for a happy marriage. And indeed it was. As the Prince avowed, 'I found her appearance and character elect among all the women of the time' – re-naming her Mumtaz Mahal, 'Jewel of the Palace'. And their union was to create what many people consider the most beautiful building in the world – the Taj Mahal.

Prince Khurram became the Emperor Shah Jahan in 1627 and presided over the Golden Age of the Mughals, one of the most prosperous and creative periods of

Indian civilisation. After Khurram's great military successes had ensured political dominance within India, the Mughal Empire became the richest centre for the arts in the world, attracting some of the finest architects, craftsmen, painters and writers – especially from other Muslim countries.

The Empress Mumtaz Mahal bore the Emperor 14 children and, in spite of her frequent pregnancies, accompanied her husband on his military campaigns and was his constant companion and selfless, trusted confidante. They were utterly devoted to each other and had one of the most intense, loving relationships of any royal couple in history.

Thus, when she died giving birth to her 14th child, Shah Jahan was distraught and decided to create a tomb for her unsurpassed in the world.

The Taj Mahal stands by the Jamuna River in Agra. It is an 'elegy in white marble', a stunning architectural beauty with a dream-like quality, especially at dawn and sunset. It took 22 years to build, and was designed by the foremost Islamic architect, Ustad 'Isa, who employed the finest craftsmen from India and beyond. It has a central dome, four smaller ones and four graceful minarets and is decorated with flowers and calligraphy using precious stones like agate and jasper.

Shah Jahan, the greatest of the Mughal emperors, died in 1666 and was himself interred to lie forever next to the body of his beloved Empress in the magnificent Taj Mahal.

A global symbol of devoted love

Now regarded as one of the wonders of the world, the Taj Mahal is also a global symbol of devoted love. So Princess Diana knew exactly what she was doing when she posed 'all alone' in front of this building – announcing to the world that her marriage to Prince Charles was over.

Barney **BARNATO**

It is said that the great 'Colossus of Africa', Cecil Rhodes, once remarked that the only man he feared was 'a cunning little Jew in Kimberley'. And Barney Barnato laughed with pleasure at what he considered was a great compliment. Soon he and Cecil Rhodes would go from rivals to partners in one of the most powerful companies in the world — and all through a deal with social stigma as its catalyst.

Barnet Isaacs had been born in London's East End in 1851 and joined his brother Harry in South Africa when the diamond

rush started in 1873. Harry acted in the theatre, and his brother often called out 'and Barnet, too,' – giving them a new name. The 'Barnato' brothers soon created the Barnato Diamond Company, and by incredible hard work 'Barney Barnato', as he was now called, became a millionaire. Less successful and jealous rivals hinted that he must have done this by trading in illicit diamonds – rumours that took a long time to go away.

The main source of diamonds was Colesberg Kopje, on the top of a 'pipe' of diamond-bearing rock that was soon dug away. Within months, the miners had excavated their little plots deep into the earth. The roadways between the plots collapsed and soon a huge hole in the ground appeared with a vast network of ropes and pulleys taking buckets of ore up to the rim of the mine. The little town, and its big hole swarming with miners, was called Kimberley after Britain's Colonial Secretary, The Earl of Kimberley. 'The Big Hole' eventually went down 1,000 feet and produced over 14 million carats of diamonds from 22 million tons of rock. Still the largest hand-dug hole in the world, at one time it was producing nearly all of the world's diamonds.

Kimberley's 'Big Hole'

Two men were determined to gain control of this vast wealth, Cecil Rhodes of De Beers and Barney Barnato, and it was hard to see who would come out on top. And then something happened which would make a deal possible.

Still standing, and now a hotel, was the Kimberley Club, founded by Rhodes, the absolute social centre of the town with 250 members — all men, many of them millionaires. For years Barney tried to join, but not one member would propose him, because the club was dominated by people who were jealous and suspicious of his success.

When Cecil Rhodes realised that he would have to buy out Barnato and make him a partner, he could offer many things — a huge and profitable shareholding in De Beers; a directorship worth a fortune; a place on the legislature and £5,388,665 — then the largest cheque ever written. But the clincher was Rhodes' offer 'to make a gentleman of you' by proposing Barnato for the Kimberley Club. However, even for Rhodes it took four years for that ambition to be achieved. Thus, the creation of the huge near-monopoly of De Beers Consolidated Mines, the future powerhouse of South Africa, was pulled off by someone wanting social acceptance. Such things happen quite often, but seldom on such a scale.

The story ends with tragedy. In July 1897, Barney Barnato jumped off a liner taking him back to England and was never seen again.

Chuck **BARRIS**

Who hasn't heard of *Blind Date*, the Saturday night hit TV programme that pulled in 18 million viewers for years, hosted by Cilla Black, whose Liverpool accent and catch phrases became part of the language? But who has ever heard of Chuck Barris who started it all?

Blind Date was an exact copy of the American The Dating Game, one of the many shows created by Chuck Barris. Born in New Jersey in 1929, Barris had become a moderately successful music composer. Then, working for ABC in California, he told them that the games being presented to them were much worse than his own ideas. ABC agreed, gave him a chance, and The Dating Game was the first of his many successes over the coming years. The 'flower power' set of The Dating Game reflected that it had been created in 1965 when the 'swinging sixties' had hit their stride. It ran for eleven years and was revived twice.

A trawl through YouTube reveals some fascinating TV moments. In among the many unknown contestants, we are startled to see an already famous Michael Jackson aged 14 asking the girls behind the screen 'What do you do on a date?' Charming, rather goofy bodybuilder Arnold Schwarzenegger's Austrian accent makes him almost incomprehensible. And then there is something much more sinister. Cheryl Bradshaw, a pretty teacher, chooses a very handsome young man with long hair to be her date, Rodney Alcala. 'My best time is night time,' he smirks, and the crowd roars with laughter. But neither Cheryl, the TV host and audience nor the millions of viewers knew that Alcala, with an IQ of 160, had sadistically murdered five girls already, and was on his way to dozens more. Luckily for her, Cheryl thought him 'too creepy' to complete their date. Alcala has now been on Death Row in San Quentin Prison for years.

Not many game shows feature serial killers

Rodney Alcala

Luckily, on both sides of the Atlantic, TV dating games normally create little more danger than the strain of one's toes curling with embarrassment.

Frederic August **BARTHOLDI**

At a dinner in France in 1865 a young sculptor, Frederic August Bartholdi, became inspired. The politician Edouard René de Labaulay was advocating that a monument should be erected in America to celebrate the friendship between the two nations during the American Revolution – with both countries paying for it. The young man volunteered to design it – and it was to be the crowning achievement of his life.

The project was delayed by the 1870 Franco-Prussian war in which Bartholdi served in the cavalry and then as liaison officer to the Italian patriot, Garibaldi. He then visited the United States and personally selected Bedloe's Island, which all ships had to pass when entering New York Harbour. This he decided was to be the site for his huge statue, 'Liberty enlightening the world'. Her face modelled on Bartholdi's mother, the statue was to be a combination of America's symbolic Columbia and Libertas, in flowing robes and bearing a torch for progress, a tablet for law, with broken chains at her feet for freedom.

To cope with the stresses of both wind and heat, Bartholdi enlisted the engineering skill of Alexandre Gustav Eiffel, whose fame was soon to overshadow

Bartholdi's because of his iconic Tower in Paris. Eiffel created a system that anchored the thin copper sheeting flexibly to a steel frame. For its huge size, 151 feet high, the edifice was remarkably light.

The French raised their part of the money – for the statue itself – quite quickly, but it took much longer in the United States to find the funds for the pedestal – until Joseph Pulitzer, of Pulitzer Prize fame, threw his newspaper *The World* into raising donations, 120,000 of them, many coming from the poor giving less than a dollar each.

Eventually the Statue of Liberty was delivered by ship, like a gigantic kit model, in 350 pieces packed in 214 wooden crates. In 1886, it was assembled; thirty-one tons of copper and 125 tons of steel and erected on the 27,000 ton pedestal.

At New York's lavish ceremony of dedication led by President Grover Cleveland, Bartholdi was asked to speak, but modestly declined. It was exactly ten years too late to be the intended 1876 centennial present from the French people, but nobody seemed to mind.

For many immigrants, Bartholdi's masterpiece was their first welcome to the United States. The most famous statue in the world, no less than 200 million people have gone to visit it. But how many of them know the name Bartholdi?

Jean-Dominique **BAUBY**

Jean Dominique Bauby was the highly successful, charismatic editor of the French fashion magazine *ELLE* in Paris, when in December 1995, something terrible and unexpected happened. At only 43, he suffered a massive stroke and after three weeks in a coma, he woke up to find himself completely paralysed.

Bauby was suffering from a rare condition called 'Locked-in Syndrome', in which his brain was functioning perfectly but which left him unable to move nor speak. He could see, hear and understand his circumstances, but the only way he could communicate was by blinking with his left eyelid.

And with that single faculty, Bauby did something truly remarkable. He wrote a book.

Laboriously, the letters of the alphabet were recited to him and Bauby blinked when he heard the letter he wanted. To make the process easier, the letters were arranged in the frequency they appear in the French language, E, S, A, R, I, N, T, U, L and so on. It took nearly two minutes to compose a single word and no less than 200,000 blinks were needed in the ten months required to produce two hundred pages.

The book, an extraordinary memoir of his life and condition, he called *The Diving Bell and the Butterfly*. The diving bell, from the brass helmet on an old-fashioned diving suit, represented his physical restriction, and the butterfly his still lively spirit. The book

is honest, without self-pity and with dark humour.

Tragically, Bauby died of pneumonia just two days after its publication and he probably never knew that not only did the critics give it great acclaim but it that was also an amazing best seller, with 25,000 books bought on the first day, 150,000 in the first week and very soon millions.

What is more, the film version was also a huge success, and not just in France. Newspapers including *The Los Angeles Times*, *Wall Street Journal* and *Washington Post* voted it the best movie of 2007, and among many international awards and nominations it won Golden Globes and a BAFTA.

Many books have been written in difficult circumstances – in prison, in war, by blind and deaf people. But there has surely never been a book written with such feeling and by such a tragically laborious method.

Joseph **BAZALGETTE**

The wealth and power created by the Industrial Revolution in Britain had a dark side. Her population had soared, and, seeking work, half her people lived in cities by 1851 – the first time anywhere in history. Those cities were desperately unhealthy places to be, with many families crowded into just one room and with no system of sanitation or clean water. Charles Dickens, campaigning for improvements, was the first to coin the word 'slum'. Epidemics ravaged the cities – typhus, dysentery, typhoid, and cholera.

Cholera, a killer disease caused by the *Vibrio cholerae* bacterium, was terrifying in its swiftness. In the morning you could be well, and then diarrhoea, vomiting, cramps, headache, delirium and death could follow by nightfall. The medical world vaguely attributed its infectious spread to foul air or 'miasmas'. In fact, Dr John Snow had correctly argued that infected water was the true culprit, but nobody listened to him.

London's drinking water problem had ironically been made much worse by a misguided attempt to improve sanitation. The Metropolitan Commission of Sewers in 1848 ordered that all cesspits be closed, and that house drains, fed by the new invention of the privy, be connected to sewers which emptied straight into the Thames. Already full of industrial waste, dead animals, offal and dung, it immediately became a vast open sewer, and that year a cholera epidemic promptly killed 14,000 Londoners.

Luckily for London, Joseph Bazalgette was, that same year, appointed to the Commission. He was a tiny man, and a brilliant engineer, experienced in land clearance and railway construction. Bazalgette decided that only a huge, properly-designed and closed system could take the dangerous sewage away from the population. But it was not another cholera epidemic in 1854 that enabled him to get his way, but 'The Great Stink' of August 1858. With temperatures in the 90s, the smell of the Thames became so overpowering that the Members of Parliament could scarcely breathe. A bill was rushed through – to construct a vast new sewer scheme and to build up the Embankment to improve the water flow.

Bazalgette set to work building 1,100 miles of underground, brick-lined mains sewers and the same length of street sewers. Backed by pumping stations, the sewage was taken far downstream before being pumped into the Thames estuary. It was still untreated, but at least it was far from the centre of population. London's cholera was at last eliminated.

Joseph Bazalgette was also farsighted. Having made every possible calculation about population growth, he paused to exclaim, 'Well, we are only going to do this once and there is always the unforeseen'. He then doubled the size of his galleries and the diameter of his pipes. Thus, they are still in use today.

Joseph Bazalgette was knighted by a grateful nation in 1874, the year his Embankment opened, where his memorial stands.

Bazalgette in front of some of his drains

? George **BEAUCHAMP**

For musicians, reaching out to a large audience was always a problem. Classical music had made big sound because orchestras were 'big bands' and jazz and swing had plenty of loud, dominant instruments. Then all types of music benefited from the creation of microphones, amplifiers and loudspeakers. But there was one instrument with great flexibility and potential that was still being left behind because it was comparatively quiet – the guitar.

In 1930s America, Hawaiian music was all the rage, but the guitar, its main instrument, did not have the volume to entertain a large audience. George Beauchamp, an enthusiast of Hawaiian music, teamed up with Adolph Rickenbacker to create the first electric guitar. It was a very strange looking cast aluminium lap guitar which had two horseshoe magnets straddling the strings, connected to an amplifier and speaker. Its curious shape, with a circular body and long neck, inevitably attracted the nickname 'The Frying Pan'. However, while it now produced plenty of volume, George Beauchamp discovered that the conventional acoustic properties of the hollow guitar created unwanted 'feedback' caused by sympathetic vibrations. So he rebuilt the neck and body from solid aluminium.

The legendary Les Paul also solved the feedback problem in 1940 with a splendid piece of lateral thinking – actually a piece of wood. Working at home he created 'The Log', quite literally a 4x4 block of wood, with a bridge, a guitar neck and a pick-up

Les Paul shows off his 'Log', sensibly disguised

attached to it. This crude contraption he sensibly disguised with an Epiphone guitar body.

Other guitar makers now made 'solid-body' guitars, notably Leo Fender with his 'Telecaster' in 1946 and the Gibson company of Kalamazoo, who approached Les Paul, as one of the world's most famous guitar players, and they created the 'Les Paul', an all-time record-breaking instrument. Les Paul was no mere instrumentalist, he also pioneered multi-tracking using dozens of acetate disks and as a result he also collaborated with Bing Crosby to develop tape recording, brought over from Germany, which would quickly transform much that could be achieved in the studio.

But it was the more powerful sound produced by the electric guitar pioneered by George Beauchamp that changed popular music forever. Within jazz and swing it now came to the fore, and it transformed Country and Western, taking it from its Irish and Scottish hillbilly roots and making it subtle, beautifully arranged and romantic.

And, of course, its really massive influence was to make Rock 'n' Roll possible. Without the electric guitar, we might never have heard of Bill Haley, Elvis Presley, the Beatles, the Stones and all the rest.

Francis **BEAUFORT**

Francis Beaufort should be remembered for many things – his courageous deeds as a naval officer, his skill as a cartographer, and as Hydrographer to the Admiralty. But if his name is recognised at all, it is probably only for the wind scale that bears his name.

The Beauforts were French Huguenots who settled in Ireland as clergymen. The Reverend Daniel Augustus Beaufort, Francis's father, was a true renaissance man – cleric, savant, agronomist, architect and surveyor (he made an ecclesiastical survey of Ireland in 1792 aided by his son). Francis joined the Honourable East India Company aged 14, but was shipwrecked off Sumatra when his ship struck the very rock the captain was sent to identify. He transferred to the Royal Navy and towards the end of his illustrious career was awarded the Navy Medal with three bars, one for each major campaign.

Beaufort had long been aware of the problems of recording weather conditions, and in particular quantifying the force of the wind. He therefore adopted a shorthand for his own use in his ship's logs by adapting an existing land scale (designed for windmills) for use at sea. He used the amount of sail needed by a frigate in a chase – full sail for no wind, Force 0, up through various breezes to a gale, Force 10, then to Force 12 and 'bare

Beaufort Wind Scale	
Force 0	Calm
Force 1	Light Air
Force 2	Light Breeze
Force 3	Gentle Breeze
Force 4	Moderate Breeze
Force 5	Fresh Breeze
Force 6	Strong Breeze
Force 7	Near Gale
Force 8	Gale
Force 9	Strong Gale
Force 10	Storm
Force 11	Violent Storm
Force 12	Hurricane

poles' in a hurricane. After his death, his scale (in the age of steam, modified to record the state of the sea) was adopted internationally and given his name in his honour.

He was appointed Hydrographer of the Admiralty in 1829. During his 25 years in the post he was responsible for issuing a prodigious number of charts around the world. So reliable were they that 'as safe as an Admiralty chart' became an everyday expression.

One of his surveying captains, Robert Fitzroy, asked him to find him a naturalist to accompany him in HMS *Beagle* to South America. Beaufort came up with the young Charles Darwin, the voyage leading to Darwin's 'Theory of Evolution'.

Beaufort retired as a Rear Admiral and was made a Knight Commander of the British Empire. Over two centuries later the Beaufort Scale has never been surpassed, and is still used today throughout the maritime world.

Ernest **BEAUX**

Marilyn Monroe once famously replied to a journalist asking what she wore in bed, 'Why, Chanel No. 5, of course!' If the perfume was already iconic, it was to become even more so, confirmed as the most famous and seductive in the world.

The fragrance was actually created by Ernest Beaux, who had been introduced to Coco Chanel by her lover, the Grand Duke Dmitri Pavlovich. Ernest Beaux was born in Russia, because his French grandfather had been in Napoleon's doomed *Grande Armée* and was captured outside Moscow in 1812. When freed, he stayed there. Ironically, Ernest Beaux's first great success as a parfumier to the Russian Court was his men's eau de cologne, *Le Bouquet de Napoleon*, commemorating the 1912 centenary of the battle of Borodino.

After serving in the French army throughout World War I, Beaux stayed in France and resumed his career as a parfumier, and in 1920 presented his samples to the new fashion star, Coco Chanel. Out of a batch of little bottles labelled 1-5, she chose number five, commenting, 'I present my dress collections on the fifth of May, the fifth month of the year. So we will let this sampler, number five, keep the name it has already. It will bring good luck. Later she added 'That was what I was waiting for. A perfume like nothing else. A woman's perfume, with the scent of a woman'.

However, it may equally have been chosen because the number 5 had a long resonance with Coco. She was brought up in a convent orphanage founded by the

Cistercians who especially valued the number 5, and the surrounding gardens were full of *Cistus*, the five-petalled rockrose from which the Cistercians derived their name. She had always regarded the number as significant.

'Chanel No. 5' was launched by Coco on May 5th, 1921, and has been a spectacular success ever since. Helped by Marilyn Monroe's unpaid endorsement, the advertising slogan was soon to be 'Every woman alive wants Chanel No. 5'.

Alphonse **BERTILLON**

Mankind has always searched for some certain way to tell one individual from another, apart from simply using our eyes. Two main systems emerged – fingerprinting, and anthropometry, or measuring the body.

Interestingly, fingerprinting is much older, first used in ancient Babylon on clay tablets for business deals, as were thumbprints in 2nd century BC in China. In British India, a modern practical use for fingerprinting first emerged. Sir William Herschel, Chief Magistrate in Jungipoor, used fingerprints in 1858 on contracts. The locals believed that personal contact made the contract more binding than if they simply signed it. Thus, the first wide-scale use of fingerprints was based on superstitious beliefs rather than scientific evidence.

A Scotsman, Dr Henry Faulds, sent his own studies to Charles Darwin, who, feeling too old to do them justice, passed them to his cousin Sir Francis Galton in 1880. Twelve years later Galton published his book *Fingerprints*, complete with a classification system, calculating the odds against two individuals having the same fingerprints as 1 in 64 billion. Galton's work inspired Juan Vucetich in Argentina, who in 1892 perfected an excellent fingerprinting system, soon adopted in all of South America.

However, from the obscurity of a back office in Paris, a rival system had emerged. The theory of a police clerk, Alphonse Bertillon, was that key measurements of the body do not change after the age of twenty. From this he set up an elaborate system of 'anthropometry', involving eleven precise measurements: height, reach of both arms, trunk height, width and length of the head, length and width of the right ear, length of the left foot, length of the left middle finger, length of the left little finger and length of the left forearm.

These were noted on cards with photographs, skin and hair colour and other details. *Bertillonage* seemed a great step forward. It was adopted not only in France but also swept Europe, reaching the United States in 1887. In vain did Galton and advocates of fingerprinting express their doubts about the statistical odds. Anthropometrics relied upon the recorder being perfectly exact in his measurements, not tired or inattentive, nor the suspects being drunk, ill, or uncooperative. The system was slow, the equipment cumbersome and expensive, and it depended on a massive filing system. Above all, it did not connect a suspect with a weapon or a crime scene – unlike fingerprints.

Nevertheless, Alphonse Bertillon was heaped with praise and honours. Then something happened which vindicated all the doubters. In 1903, prisoner Will West (left) was delivered to Leavenworth Prison, Kansas. He was duly processed using the Bertillon System and denied having been there before. The records clerk did not believe him, and in triumph, retrieved a Bertillon card. The trouble was that it belonged to another prisoner of the same name, William West (far left), who had

been in the prison for two years. Their fingerprints were then checked and, of course, were completely different.

The 'West' incident wrecked everything for Bertillon, as the disturbing news swept the police forces of the world. However, instead of acknowledging the superiority of fingerprinting, he obstinately clung to his system, even snubbing Vucetich rudely when he came to Paris. It did no good. Fingerprinting triumphed.

Bertillon, plucked from obscurity by his flawed 'method', died in 1914, bitter – and once more obscure.

Bobby **BEVAN**

In 1923, young 'Bobby' Bevan, the son of two famous artists, joined the London advertising agency, S.H. Benson. Almost his first task was to find out why an Irish stout called Guinness sold so well without owning lots of pubs, as most beer companies did. He discovered the answer to this strange conundrum – quite simply people thought it was good for their health. The dramatic result was the iconic 'Guinness is Good for You' advertising, beginning one of the world's great advertising-led success stories and propelling Guinness into one of the most famous brands in the world.

In 1752, Arthur Guinness, aged 17, was bequeathed £100 by his godfather, the Archbishop of Cashel, and with it the young Arthur started a brewery in Leixlip, outside Dublin. Seven years later he moved into the city, to a four-acre site at St James's Gate, and signed one of the longest leases in history, 9,000 years, for the princely sum of £45 a year. Initially, he brewed dark 'porter' beer, well-known in England. But soon a unique blend of roasted barley, hops, brewers' yeast and isinglass finings (made from fish air bladders), gave Guinness the distinctive taste we still know today. In 1799, Arthur Guinness resolved to focus on this one brand, and expanded the brewery to produce it.

One of the key, unusual features of a company based in Ireland was its desire to export. The first few barrels of Guinness were sent in 1769 to England, where its popularity grew amongst all classes, and where it was enjoyed in the lowliest pub right up to 10, Downing Street, where Prime Minister Benjamin Disraeli developed a special taste for it. 'Black Velvet', Guinness with champagne, was then invented in 1861, somewhat strangely honouring the death of Prince Albert, Queen Victoria's beloved husband.

But it was the 1920's advertising that made Guinness into a true phenomenon. There is, in fact, some truth in the health claims that Bobby Bevan unearthed and publicized, because the anti-oxidants, similar to those in fruit and vegetables, slow down cholesterol deposits. The first advertisements, written by Bevan and the novelist Dorothy Sayers, and illustrated by John Gilroy, certainly implied health advantages which could not be claimed today – 'Guinness for Strength', 'Guinness makes you strong',

'My Goodness, My Guinness' and 'Guinness is good for you'. Illustrations were witty, with cartoon animals including the toucan, that became ever associated with the brand. Dorothy Sayers even used Bobby Bevan as the inspiration for Mr Ingleby in her thriller *Murder Must Advertise*.

S.H. Benson kept the Guinness account, under Bobby Bevan's supervision, until the 1950s. It then became one of the most prized accounts in British advertising, with agencies pitching their top teams to the creative challenge, and with Guinness advertising winning award after award. In fact, 'Surfer', in 2000, featuring white horses in the sea, was voted in a *Sunday Times* and Channel 4 poll to be the best British TV commercial of all time.

And *The Guardian* explained the care taken to protect the brand. *'They've spent years now building a brand that's in complete opposition to cheap lagers, session drinking and crowds of young men boozing in bars. They've worked very hard to help Guinness drinkers picture themselves as twinkly-eyed, Byronic bar-room intellectuals, sitting quietly with a pint and dreaming of poetry and impossibly lovely redheads running barefoot across the peat. You have a pint or two of Guinness with a slim volume of Yeats, not eight mates and a 19 pint bender which ends in tattoos, A&E and herpes from a hen party'*.

Guinness is now enjoyed all over the world and Guinness pubs can be found in the most unlikely places. And drinking Guinness is an essential part of the great St Patrick's Day Parades in New York and Chicago, let alone those in Ireland.

Guinness enabled the company to become one of Britain's largest, acquiring the Distillers Company in 1986, famous for many brands, and Grand Metropolitan in 1997, to form Diageo with sales of billions.

It's amazing what a drop of the 'Black Stuff' can do.

Agnes Gonxhe **BOJAXHIU**

Later in life, Agnes Bojaxhiu explained her various roots. 'By blood, I am Albanian. By citizenship, an Indian. By faith I am a Catholic nun. As to my calling, I belong to the world. As to my heart, I belong entirely to the Heart of Jesus.' By then the world knew Agnes as 'Mother Teresa' and she was famous and revered all over the world. Winner of the 1979 Nobel Peace Prize, with many polls rating her as the world's 'most admired woman', with scarcely anyone knowing her real name.

Agnes Bojaxhiu was born in August 1910 in Skopje, Albania. As a child she was fascinated by the stories of missionaries in India and decided to devote herself to religion and missionary work. After a stint with the Sisters of Loreto at Rathfarnham in Ireland, where she learned English, in 1929 she arrived in India and began to teach in Calcutta while becoming a nun under the name 'Teresa'. After twenty years of teaching, she was exposed to two shattering events – the Bengal famine of 1943 and the Hindu/Muslim violence erupting around India's independence in 1946.

That year in September, travelling by train to her annual retreat in Darjeeling, she received 'a call' to leave the convent and to help the poor while living among them.

By 1948, dressed in a simple white sari with a blue border, she was in Calcutta's slums tending the destitute and starving – '*the poorest among the poor*'.

Two years later the Vatican gave her permission to start the 'Missionaries of Charity' with her mission 'to care for the hungry, the naked, the homeless, the crippled, the blind, the lepers – all who feel unwanted, uncared for and shunned by society'. The charity started with just 13 nuns and by the time Teresa died in 1997 had over 4,000 of them running orphanages, hospices and charity centres all over the world.

In 1979, this remarkable figure was awarded the Nobel Peace Prize 'for work undertaken in the struggle to overcome poverty and distress, which also constitutes a threat to peace'. This was but one of many awards for her work and she had become a symbol, an icon, and constantly voted 'the most admired woman'. By now she was known all over the world as 'Mother Teresa'.

However, the picture is far from perfect, and Mother Teresa was criticised for some of her beliefs. When she created her first 'Home for the Dying' she said, 'a beautiful death is for people who have lived like animals to die like angels – loved and wanted'. Yet patients would often die in agony because Mother Teresa refused them painkillers. 'The most beautiful gift for a person is that he can participate in the suffering of Christ' is a philosophy that most of us might not welcome as we enter a hospice. She has also been criticised by distinguished journals like *The Lancet* for the haphazard and inadequate approach to medicine in her medical centre, orphanages and hospices.

Nevertheless, the overall influence of Mother Teresa is of a great and inspirational woman. Indeed, in 2003, she was beatified and became the 'Blessed Teresa of Calcutta'.

A sainthood? That remains to be seen.

Norman **BORLAUG**

Norman Borlaug was one of the greatest life-savers of all time. Yet this remarkable man, creator of the 'Green Revolution', credited for preventing one billion deaths through starvation, is still a remarkably little-known name. In 1970 he was awarded the Nobel Peace Prize for increasing the world's food supply, especially in Mexico, India and Pakistan.

Borlaug was born in Iowa in 1914, and experienced the horrors of the 'Dust Bowl'. At university he became fascinated by plants and their diseases. In 1944 he went to Mexico and, backed by the Rockefeller Foundation, developed a new kind of wheat with a stout, short stalk. This high-yield, disease-resistant, low pesticide 'dwarf wheat' underpinned the 'Green Revolution' which saw Mexico increase its output of wheat by six times. The world now relies on such 'dwarf wheats'.

With populations rocketing, Borlaug decided that the only solution was high yield crops, sustained by inorganic fertilizers and irrigation. By 1963, in spite of huge U.S. food shipments, India and Pakistan faced famine. Borlaug imported 35 truckloads of seeds to plant the non-traditional crop of wheat, only for war to break out between the two countries. Some of Borlaug's planting had to be done under shellfire, but yields jumped by 70%. Paul Ehrlich wrote in *The Population Bomb* in 1968 that '*India cannot possibly feed 200 million people by 1980*'. Borlaug proved him hopelessly wrong. By 1974 India had 600 million people, yet was self-sufficient, as was Pakistan.

> **'India cannot possibly feed 200 million people by 1980'**

When he was presented with his Nobel Peace Prize in 1970, Borlaug stressed that the 'Population Monster' had not gone away and he turned his attention to Africa. Suddenly he was blocked by a green movement, which equated providing more food with encouraging population growth, and he became enraged at the environmental lobbyists. But with the encouragement of former President Jimmy Carter, himself a farmer, soon many countries in Africa also saw their yields leap. They certainly needed to, because Uganda, for instance, will soon have the same population as Russia.

Before he died, at last recognised as a great man, Norman Borlaug realised the need for a radical next step. Population growth was critical since there was no more arable land, water tables were falling, climate change was causing droughts, and fertilizer and fuel for tractors were getting too expensive.

Genetic manipulation of organisms (GMO) was the next way to increase food production. He also felt that GMOs were not inherently dangerous, but were vital. Indeed, if GM had been around in 1845, the potato blight, *Phytophora infestans*, might not have starved a million people to death in Ireland, nor would *Phylloxera* have wiped out Europe's vines.

There has been strong opposition to GM, especially in Europe. 'Genetically modified' seems to evince 'creepy' connotations ('Frankenstein Food'). However, there are forty different GM plant varieties now being grown in 29 countries by 16.7 million farmers on 395 million acres – the size of Europe.

The most significant recent move is by China which is trialling GM rice, a crop that feeds half the world, and GM maize to feed its 500 million pigs and 14 billion chickens and ducks. With China embracing GM for fibre (cotton), feed (maize) and food (rice), the rest of Asia will surely follow.

Bill Gates, who has donated millions to help agricultural research and GM, told the audience at the 2009 World Food Prize Symposium, 'We have the tools. We know what needs to be done. We can be the generation that sees Dr Borlaug's dream fulfilled – a world free of hunger'.

The **BOSWELL SISTERS**

Generations brought up on 'The Supremes' or 'The Spice Girls' may be surprised to hear that it was 'The Andrews Sisters' who were the best-selling female group in popular music history, with even more Top Ten hits than Elvis Presley or The Beatles.

However, their popularity would not have been possible without another gifted and pioneering sister trio, whom very few people can remember – 'The Boswell Sisters'.

Born in New Orleans between 1905 and 1911, Connee, 'Vet' (Helvetica) and Martha Boswell hit the big time when they reached New York in 1930. A close-harmony group, their records are regarded as milestones of vocal jazz. Remarkably, Connee always sang from a seat or wheelchair because of either polio or a childhood accident.

She produced superb re-workings of the melodies and rhythms of popular music, and this was backed by the top jazz and swing bands, like Glenn Miller, Benny Goodman and the Dorsey Brothers. At a time when the notation and arrangements on sheet music were regarded as sacrosanct by the powerful music publishers and record companies, The Boswell Sisters were among the very few performers who were allowed to make changes, rearrange melodies, slow down or speed up the tempo and change keys in mid-song. Their influence was huge on musicians and singers, especially Ella Fitzgerald, who patterned her singing on Connee particularly.

But the Boswells' most famous imitators were 'The Andrews Sisters'– Laverne, Maxine and Patty – who came to national attention with their Decca Number One hit *Bei Mir Bist Du Schön ('To me you are beautiful')*, originally a Yiddish song.

This was followed by hit after hit. The Andrews Sisters could even *choose* whom they were going to sing with – Benny Goodman, Glenn Miller, Buddy Rich, The Dorseys, Gene Krupa, Paul Whiteman, Nelson Riddle, Xavier Cugat and many others. What is more, they were so versatile that time after time they paired with many other artistes and singers — no less than 47 times with Bing Crosby. They sold something approaching a staggering 100 million records.

Not bad for another three sisters most people can't even remember.

Edward **BOWES**

Aficionados of talent shows like Simon Cowell's *Pop Idol, The X Factor* and *Britain's Got Talent* might think, if they are old enough, that it all started with Britain's *Opportunity Knocks*, a 1940s radio show that transferred to TV and ran for ages. But dig a little deeper, and the rather unlikely name of Major Bowes springs out.

Edward Bowes was born in San Francisco in 1874 and became a successful real estate dealer until the 1906 earthquake ruined him. In New York he became a well-known musician and Broadway stage producer until he took over the Capitol Theater,

which he ran with the military efficiency befitting his former rank and title – which he insisted that everyone used.

Having hosted a number of small amateur nights, Bowes decided in 1934 to create a special show for New York's WHN radio station – *The Major Bowes Original Amateur Hour*. It was an instant success, with 10,000 hopefuls a week applying to be on the show, whittled down to just 20. Bowes, like Simon Cowell, became one of the richest men in show-business and became far better known than most of the amateur talent – except for a skinny Frank Sinatra, who but for the Major, might have gone on singing small time in Hoboken, New Jersey for ever.

Edward Bowes was, in private, a kindly and avuncular figure who frequently took his worried candidates out to dinner to calm their nerves. He also featured more aspiring black performers than other American shows. But he was soon to become famous for his abrupt termination of poor performers, first with an impatient 'All right, all right', and then with the banging of a gong – brutally cutting off the act to loud laughter from the live audience. He even had a burly bodyguard standing by 'ready to grab the poor boob before he can say anything vile!'

Simon Cowell's version is his signature phrase on *American Idol*, 'I don't want to be rude, but...' followed by biting appraisals of the hopeful contestants. However, Cowell is a charismatic figure and probably more attractive than Major Bowes could ever be. So it is unlikely that in the future there will be the equivalent of comedian Alan King on the *Johnny Carson Show* banging on the floor and shouting 'Can you hear me down there, Major Bowes?'– suggesting that the show host was now in Hell for his cruel treatment of young performers.

But then, who knows where Simon Cowell will end up?

Charles **BOYCOTT**

The word boycott is common enough, with everything from Olympic boycotts and boycotts of products to Civil Rights bus boycotts and election and political boycotts. The word means to shun, to ostracize, to ignore. And it all started in Ireland.

In 1880, just 10,000 people or .02% of the population owned the land of Ireland. Worse, the 750 richest landlords owned half the country and many of them were absentee landlords, their tenants often being treated harshly. Typical of these was the Earl of Erne who owned 40,000 acres. He employed agents to manage his properties, and at Lough Mask, County Mayo, 1,500 acres were managed by Captain Charles Boycott, a retired army officer.

Land rights had become a boiling issue in Ireland, and tenant farmers were fighting for the 'three Fs' – fair rent, fixity of tenure and free sale. Michael Davitt founded the Irish National Land League and asked the great Irish politician Charles Stewart Parnell to be its leader. It was Parnell who in September 1880 told a meeting in Ennis to stop 'talking of killing landlords or agents', but rather to shun them in every way.

That very month Lord Erne told Captain Boycott not to allow a 25% rent reduction due to a poor harvest, but to evict eleven protesting tenants. The locals, heeding Parnell's advice, shunned Boycott. His servants and farm workers left; the postman, blacksmith and laundry and all the shops refused to serve him or even talk to him. He was besieged, writing to *The Times* bemoaning his fate.

Eventually, to get in the harvest, four English newspapers raised the 'Boycott Relief Fund'. Fifty imported Ulstermen arrived in Lough Mask, protected by 1,000 troops and police, in a move eventually costing £10,000 to harvest just £500 worth of crops.

That November, Charles Boycott left for the station in an army ambulance (right) because no local would drive him. In Dublin, his hotel asked him to move out in case they were 'boycotted'. Indeed, the actions and words 'to boycott' spread like wildfire throughout Ireland and boycotting did bring in the land reforms demanded. By 1888 the word had also entered the *Oxford English Dictionary*, and was soon to spread to many other languages.

When Boycott visited America, his notoriety was so great that he decided to call himself 'Charles Cunningham', He died peacefully in Suffolk in 1897 holding no grudges against Ireland. But this rather unimportant man had managed to give the world quite an important word.

Henderson William **BRAND**

Our whole world is full of brands and brand names, and brand identity and protection is a vast global business, with fierce competition from major players. Untold millions are spent on such brands as Prada, Nike, Gucci and Guerlain, and crucially protecting customer 'brand loyalty'.

There are regular surveys as to which brands are the most valuable, with Coca-Cola, Google, IBM, Microsoft, General Electric, Apple, Intel and McDonalds jockeying for position.

But there is only one brand that was actually created by someone called Brand, and it was way back in 1824. Henderson William Brand was the Head Chef to Britain's King George IV. One day he produced a steak sauce for his monarch, and the King was said to have sat back and exclaimed, 'A1'. The chef went on to create Brand & Co, and began to produce the 'A1' sauce commercially.

'A1' Steak Sauce was a great success. For many years in Britain, for instance, the whole chain of popular Lyons Corner Houses displayed it on every table, and it was introduced to the United States in 1895, where it took off.

There, it was first owned by G.F. Heublein, then taken over by R.J. Reynolds, after that by Nabisco and now Kraft. The brand continues to be a market leader, supported by some amusing advertising, with the slogan, 'Yeah, it's that important.'

One company, on the other hand, has been bright enough to focus on the name BRAND, typically in the Far East. For many years, Cerebos Pacific in Singapore has had 'BRAND chicken broth' as a leading product. They claim that William Brand gave such a broth to George IV when he was feeling ill, and their museum displays (left) one of the original tins of *'Brand & Co's Essence of Chicken by appointment to the late King George IV'*.

It is comforting that a chef has had his most memorable product maintained for 160 years, and that his own name has not been entirely lost.

? Heinz **BRANDT**

At the 1936 Berlin Olympics, Adolf Hitler was delighted with the performance of young Lieutenant Heinz Brandt as his horse 'Alchemy' sailed over the jumps to win Germany a coveted Gold Medal. Little could the Führer have imagined that this otherwise unknown officer would one day save his life – by chance, by mistake, and with terrible consequences.

Eight years later, Heinz Brandt, now a Colonel, was on the staff at Hitler's Headquarters in Rastenburg, East Germany. On July 20th, 1944, Count Claus von Stauffenberg, a handsome, religious aristocrat, arrived at the 'Wolf's Lair' planning to kill Hitler. Dynamic and daring, Stauffenberg also had to lead the revolt and win over the fainthearted in one last conspiracy to get rid of Hitler and the Nazis before it was too late. By now Germany was in real trouble. The Allies were advancing from their Normandy beachhead and the Russians were only 60 miles from German soil. In deep despair, hundreds of army officers were now part of *Operation Valkyrie*, a plan to take over Berlin, Paris and Brussels, arrest the SS and Gestapo and make peace with the Allies. This was their third attempt to kill Hitler with a bomb. Indeed, Brandt himself, in 1943, had actually smuggled a bomb disguised as brandy bottles on to the Fuhrer's plane. Failing to explode, it remained undetected.

Arriving at Rastenburg, von Stauffenberg was given bad news. With the hot weather, the Führer's briefing would be held in a wooden hut with open windows – not nearly as deadly in an explosion as a concrete bunker. It was also to be held early so Hitler could welcome his fellow dictator, the recently rescued Mussolini. So they had to move quickly. Von Stauffenberg and his adjutant went to 'freshen up' and carefully assemble and prime the two bombs they had brought. However, they were interrupted and told they were late for the briefing, so decided that one bomb must suffice. The Colonel hurried to the conference, knowing that acid was eating away at a ten-minute fuse. He placed his briefcase under the wooden table only a yard from Hitler's feet, and awaited a pre-arranged 'urgent telephone call' which gave him the excuse to leave the room and head for Berlin.

Stauffenberg (left) with Hitler

Then Heinz Brandt, one of those bit-part characters who can alter history, did exactly that. Becoming irritated by the briefcase at his feet, he reached down and lifted it to the other side of the table support. Thus, when the bomb exploded, Hitler was saved from most of the blast by the thick oak support, and able to stagger out, blackened, shaken but alive, and soon showing Mussolini the wrecked room. 'Duce! I have just had the most enormous good fortune!' Brandt had not. His leg was blown off and he was rushed to hospital.

Stauffenberg was convinced he had killed Hitler, but after a three hour flight was appalled to find that no action had been started in Berlin by his more cautious colleagues. Gradually the plot unravelled. Stauffenberg and his comrades were arrested and shot – his last words, 'Long live sacred Germany!' 5,000 people, not just officers, but also civil servants, professionals and clerics were executed, while the war dragged on, killing millions.

Colonel Brandt, who had saved Hitler's life by mistake, died in hospital. At first, he was promoted by a grateful Führer to General to increase the pension for his family, until fellow patients recalled him crying out in delirium, 'How callous of Stauffenberg to place the bomb at my feet, when I was one of the conspirators!'

It is hard not to feel sympathy for his point of view.

Brodir of **MAN**

The man who was to change Irish history, Prince Brodir of Man, was a fearsome figure – tall, with his hair so long he tucked it into his sword belt, and wearing a suit of chain mail 'that no steel could bite'. In 1014 he received an offer he couldn't refuse – from Sitrygg, the Viking King of Dublin. Brodir and his brother Ospak were to come to his aid against Brian Boru, the High King of Ireland. Brodir's reward would be the throne of Ireland and marriage to Sytrigg's still beautiful mother Gormlaith. One little problem. Sytrigg had made the same secret offer to Sigurd, Viking King of the Orkneys. No matter. Brodir sailed for Dublin from the Isle of Man with 1,000 men, while Ospak, disgusted, went off to join the 'good King' Brian.

The marauding Vikings arrived in Ireland in the 8th century. Their fortified villages had become towns and Ireland's future cities – Cork, Wexford (*Waesfjord*), Limerick, Waterford (*Vaderfjord*) and *Dubhlinn*. Many had settled down, inter-married with the Irish and had become Christians. However, this did not stop tensions and warfare within Ireland.

Brian was the son of the King of Thomond. Their tribe, the Dalcassians, straddled the River Shannon, with Brian dubbed 'Brian Boroimhe' (Brian of the tributes), because of the tolls he levied on the river crossings. Their rivals were the Vikings in Limerick, and the Dalcassians both fought them and traded with them. In 976, Mahon, Brian's elder brother was lured to a 'reconciliation meeting' and murdered. Brian, aged 35, now King of Thomond, took his revenge, personally killing the Viking King, Ivar. For twenty years, Brian, intelligent and educated, built up his power base, and often in partnership with the Vikings.

In 1002, his rival, King Malachy of Meath, bowed to the inevitable and allowed Brian to take his title of '*Ard Rí*', or High King – no mere honorary title, because Brian knew how vulnerable a small island with splintered interests could be. He continued his conquests throughout Ireland, rebuilding monasteries and roads, and improving the country. But things started to unravel. Máel Mórda, ruler of Leinster, with Sitrygg, revolted. Brian besieged them in Dublin, but had to retreat due to the winter weather. Now Brian's rather enthusiastic love life intervened. Many women had played a role in his life, including four wives. His divorced third wife Gormlaith added extra complications, because she was Máel Mórda's sister and Sitrygg's mother and, moreover, had been married first to the King of Dublin, then to Malachy and finally to Brian. Now this beautiful and dangerous woman became Brian's nemesis, treacherously sending for Brodir and the other Vikings.

Brian returned in the spring. Now quite an old man, he had lost none of his determination. Not all the Irish would join Brian. Some would fight for him, some against. Some, like Malachy, on the pretext of a slight, would stand aside. Vikings like Ospak would fight on both sides.

At dawn on Good Friday, 23rd April 1014, the two armies began their massive battle to the north of the city, at Clontarf. The sea was full of Viking ships, but Brian noted the state of the tide. Because of the holy day, he directed the battle while not participating.

Vicious hand-to-hand fighting raged all day, with most of the leaders on both sides falling. The foreign Vikings finally broke and tried to make it to their ships. Most failed. The incoming tide meant that they were now half a mile out to sea.

Irish victory turned to tragedy. Brodir, with a small group, found Brian Boru praying in his tent and felled him with his axe. But the dying King, aged 73, struck back and killed Brodir, and their bodies were found together.

Brodir's vengeful axe was to have an unforeseen but lasting influence on Ireland. Although the power of the Vikings was broken, Brian's death and those of most of his family removed the vital unifying force needed to resist foreign invasion. While the Irish squabbled, over the sea in England, William the Conqueror had won the Battle of Hastings. Soon the forceful, efficient Normans were to arrive in Ireland, which would then be ruled by outsiders for another 800 years.

'The Death of Brian Boru' by Thomas Ryan RHA

Sam **BROWNE**

What item of clothing have Prince Charles, William, Harry, Hitler, Mussolini, George Patton, Douglas MacArthur, John Pershing, David Niven, Michael Collins, the US Marines, the 'Mounties' and the New Jersey Police all worn?

A leather belt with a diagonal strap, called a 'Sam Browne'. But who was Sam Browne?

At the height of the Indian Mutiny in 1857, young Captain Sam Browne of the 2nd Punjab Irregular Cavalry, a regiment that he had created, charged a cannon and its crew with great bravery, for which he was awarded the Victoria Cross. But he was slashed with two sword cuts, one of which severed his left arm.

He continued to serve in the army, but found, without a left arm, he could not hold the scabbard to draw or return his sword. As a result, he devised a diagonal cross-belt that supported the sword's weight and also held it in place perfectly. Other officers began to copy it and before long it was standard in the British Army, soon to be taken up by Imperial forces when they saw it during the Boer War. The 'Sam Browne' then gradually became generally popular with any forces who had also to carry heavy revolvers, with its use spreading all over the world.

After a long and distinguished military career, General Sir Samuel Browne died in retirement in 1901, and his original belt is still to be seen at the Royal Military Academy at Sandhurst.

William **BRYDON**

Until a few years ago, most people did not even know where Afghanistan was (almost certainly, quite a few still don't). But this large, rugged, inhospitable and trouble-torn place was in the news a long time before George W. Bush invaded it as part of his 'War on Terror' – to get rid of the Taliban and their friends in Al-Qaeda.

There are many worrying similarities between the Afghanistan of today and that of 1842 – but let us pray not too many. The British, or rather the British East India Company, had in 1839 invaded Afghanistan to block Russian ambition. After a brisk and competent campaign, the British had replaced the ruler Dost Mohammed, who was exiled to India, with an unpopular puppet. They had then settled down to a complacent Victorian life in Kabul, complete with tea parties, hunting and cricket. Unfortunately, the British Government at home, going through a bout of 'austerity', then decided to cut the subsidies paid to the tribes.

Without such bribery, the Afghans saw few attractive reasons to remain under British rule and began guerrilla warfare. State Secretary William Macnaghten blandly reported this as '*the usual state of Afghan society*'. In command of the much weakened British and Indian garrison was the aged and ailing Major-General William Elphinstone, a veteran of Waterloo, but now described as 'the most incompetent soldier who ever became a General'.

In November 1841, the son of Dost Mohammed, Akbar Khan, raised a general revolt and murdered a senior official, Sir Alexander Burns, who mistakenly thought that he commanded Afghan respect. Elphinstone's force of 4,500, of whom 640 were Europeans, weakly abandoned the town of Kabul. An over-confident Macnaghten now went to negotiate an orderly retreat of the British forces and civilians over tea, but was killed as he dismounted – with his body dragged ignominiously through the streets.

To the horror of his officers, Elphinstone then signed a capitulation, and the Afghans promised him a safe passage across the snowy passes. Leaving behind their sick and wounded, who were promptly butchered, a column of 16,000 men, women and children, set off with little food or ammunition across the frozen hills heading for Jalalabad 90 miles away. At once they were attacked by about 30,000 tribesmen. After only a few dreadful miles, thousands had died or been killed, the women had surrendered as hostages, many to die, as did the pathetic Elphinstone. On 12th January, a tiny remnant of the 44th Regiment of Foot made a last brave stand at Gandamak.

The next day sentries on the walls of Jalalabad were watching anxiously for the expected returning army. Suddenly, they saw a lone survivor on a dying horse. He was Assistant Surgeon William Brydon, who had survived a sword slash to the head only because he had stuck a thick magazine into his hat to ward off the cold. Asked about the army, he said, 'I *am* the army' (15 years later, poor Brydon also survived the horrific seige of Lucknow during the Indian Mutiny).

The appalling disaster led to an 'Army of Retribution' retaking and levelling Kabul and the eventual demise of Akbar Khan. However, ever since, Afghanistan has been an international problem. Russia's failed intervention in the 1970s caused the break-up of the Soviet Union; the Afghan poppy fields have become the world's drug larder and Al-Qaeda chose this wild place from whence to launch its terror.

Let us hope that Lady Butler's symbolism of Dr. Brydon in her tragic painting *The Remnants of an Army* does not bode badly for the years to come.

'The Remnants of an Army', by Elizabeth Butler © Tate London 2013

Bob **BURNS**

At the height of the euro crises in 2011, David Cameron was urging Angela Merkel to use a 'big bazooka' to solve the problem. The bazooka he was presumably referring to was the quite small recoilless anti-tank weapon. Ironically, in 1943 the Germans had copied it and produced a more effective 88mm version called the *Panzerschreck*. But in Eurozone rhetoric, asking the German Chancellor to use a '*Big Panzerschreck*' might be politically incorrect or strange. Even more strange was the origin of the word 'bazooka'.

Born in Arkansas, Bob Burns was a popular American musician and entertainer. As a teenager, one night early in his career practising with his band in a plumbing shop, he picked up a length of gas pipe and blew into it, creating an unusual sound. He then attached a widened old whiskey funnel and a slide, creating a sort of crude trombone. He called it his 'bazooka' after the Dutch *bazuin* for trumpet.

In World War I, he became well-known playing it in the Marine Corps jazz band and he registered the name in 1920.

Then in the 30s he used his strange instrument to back up his folksy radio performance as 'The Arkansas Philosopher' telling tales of his 'Uncle Fud' and 'Aunt

Doody', and regularly featured on the Paul Whiteman and Rudy Vallee radio programmes. He became really famous in 1935 on Bing Crosby's *Kraft Music Hall*. So it is only natural that when in 1942 the US Army developed the M-1 anti-tank rocket fired from a tube widened at the ends, they called it the 'bazooka'.

While the anti-tank weapon went from strength to strength, the musical instrument did not seem to attract too much of a following. As Bob Burns said in a 1946 TV programme, musing over his iconic instrument, 'The other bazooka kills you instantly. This one sort of just worries you to death!'

Pope **CALLIXTUS II**

Have you ever wondered why the Catholic religion has unmarried priests?

The first answer might be that by avoiding physical love, priests were somehow more free to concentrate on the deity. But when you think about it, most of Jesus's disciples were married – as were many early Popes, many of them succeeded in office by their sons. St Patrick, Ireland's patron Saint, was the son of a deacon. Priests continued to marry and St Ulrich of Augsburg sensibly commented 'When celibacy is imposed, priests will commit sins far worse than fornication.' Events have proved him only too right.

There were, however, strong ascetic pressures building up. In the eleventh century, Peter Damian, a fanatical advisor to several Popes, called the wives of clerics, 'harlots, prostitutes, unclean spirits, demigoddesses, sirens, witches.' His pupil, Pope Gregory VII, declared that priests, 'must escape the clutches of their wives'. Riots occurred when Pope Urban II, his successor, ordered the wives of priests 'to be rounded up and sold into slavery.'

However, it was a much more mundane issue that eventually brought in Catholic celibacy – property. In the early twelfth century, Pope Callixtus II faced a serious financial threat. Much valuable church property was being bought and sold by the wives and relatives of priests, so in his Lateran Council of 1123 he declared clerical marriages invalid. This was a momentous decision with results lasting to the present day.

Change was actually very slow, with many priests still married four centuries later.

In Britain, the muddled attitude resulted in the tragic reign of 'Bloody Mary'. Many of the 287 people she burned at the stake in 1555 were priests who had married during the more relaxed reign of her father Henry VIII. Children were hidden away and wives had to pose as servants.

Today, the most direct result of Callixtus's decision is the wave of sexual scandals now wracking the Catholic Church all over the world, a crisis exacerbated by the problem that in many countries the church runs the educational system – giving access to and power over young children. In Ireland, for instance, ugly revelations about the church mean it will perhaps never regain its uniquely respected and powerful position in society.

Seldom can a decision over a temporary financial crisis have had such profound and long-term results.

Chester **CARLSON**

Copying documents used to be tricky. Typewriter carbon paper was dirty and any mistakes on each copy had to be corrected, as did the stencil in a mimeograph machine. No wonder secretaries were trained to make very few mistakes.

Chester Carlson had been inspired by great inventors like Thomas Edison, and was determined to invent something useful himself. As a patent lawyer, he had often suffered from the need to prepare multiple copies of patent applications, taking hours. He eventually hit on 'photo conductivity', whereby when light and shadow strike an electrically charged plate, the dark parts can attract a magnetic powder, while the light part repels it. If the powder could then be fused or melted on to the page, it could then form a copy of the original document.

The method took him many years to perfect, and he had enormous trouble obtaining financial help for the research. Then the Haloid Corporation licenced his 'xerography' or 'dry writing', and the company became Haloid Xerox in 1958. At first they worried that nobody could readily pronounce the curiously spelled 'Xerox', but once people got the hang of saying 'Zerox', they never forgot the name.

In 1959, the iconic, push-button, plain paper Xerox 914 appeared, and using clever advertising, it swept the market. To demonstrate its ease of use, advertising agency Papert, Koenig & Lois showed a little girl making copies. However, the TV networks then complained that it was not believable, so the child was replaced by a chimpanzee. There were no more arguments, because, as George Lois commented, 'The chimp was a better actor'.

Xerox now had a ground-breaking product, a memorable name, and great advertising. What it needed next was overseas distribution, and it struck lucky with The Rank Organisation, a British company which, with underused film distribution offices all over the world, provided a ready-made sales network.

As 'making a Xerox' became a standard phrase in all offices, Chester Carlson and his backers became rich, and the Xerox Corporation became a Fortune 500 company. It even created the Xerox Alto, the first true personal computer – albeit rather too expensive. Xerox then showed everybody what it was doing, which was rather over-generous to say the least. One visitor, young Steve Jobs of Apple, said 'They just had no idea what they had', while quickly copying Xerox's WIMP (Windows, Icons, Mouse and Pulldown menus).

Chester Carlson's real impact was five decades ago, with the removal of time-wasting, dirty, infuriating carbon copy production in the office. Not surprisingly, some people now want to call that 'Cc' computer field 'Courtesy Copy', not 'Carbon Copy'.

Joseph **CARPUE**

'The Sarkozy Effect' is not a French political movement. Nor is the removal of 'Gordon Browns' and 'Mandles' a British one. Again, the elimination of 'Simon Cowells' is not a reaction by viewers fed up with *The X Factor*. Rather, these are all slang terms used in contemporary plastic surgery.

Derived from the Greek *plastikos*, to shape, plastic surgery has been around for a long time – from 2,000 BC, in India and Egypt. The Romans knew how to do it technically, but their religion frowned on dissection, thus it was Arab translations of the ancient Indian work that first filtered into Europe.

Joseph Constantine Carpue, an English surgeon, was about 30 when he read in 1794 about 'Rhinoplasty' being practised in India and decided to travel there. In 1816, he published his '*Account of Two Successful Operations for restoring a lost nose from the Integument of the Forehead*'. This practice of grafting of skin from the forehead became known as 'Carpue's Operation'. Other European surgeons followed Carpue's lead, as well as several in the United States.

However, progress was inhibited by the fact that any surgery on healthy tissue is horribly painful, and that infection could also kill the patient. Only in the direst straits would patients ever elect to submit to such an ordeal.

However, anaesthetics and antibiotics arrived and plastic surgery duly found its vital place in medicine. Such 'reconstructive surgery' helped those disfigured by war or condemned to misery by the ugliness of a childhood defect or ravaging disease.

But this new science then unleashed the far more controversial 'cosmetic surgery' – just in time for the pressures of 'celebrity' and high definition television. Now, not just film stars and models, but ordinary people could, and indeed felt they needed to, slow the ageing process and look prettier and sexier – 'facelifts', 'nose jobs', 'tummy tucks', 'boob jobs', 'thigh jobs', 'eyelid surgery' – even 'a Brazilian butt-lift'! Each year, there are now 11 million operations in the United States alone, a 50% increase since 2000, and popular women's magazines devote pages to speculating who has done what to which parts of themselves.

Nor is this phenomenon confined to women. Especially in recession, men want to reduce their 'moobs'(man boobs) and 'mandles'(Man love handles) and use 'Boytox' to look their dynamic best at their next job interview.

One wonders what Joseph Carpue and all those other pioneers would think of the rather frivolous, selfish and self-regarding purposes to which their skills are increasingly turned.

Michael Jackson, a distressing example of things going wrong

❓ Jean and Alastair **CARRUTHERS**

What do Madonna, Cher, Celine Dion, Victoria Beckham, Hilary Clinton, Harrison Ford, Kylie and Dannii Minogue, Cliff Richard, Catherine Zeta-Jones, Fergie, Simon Cowell and Gordon Ramsay have in common? They all *appear* to have benefited from the smoothing and rejuvenating facial effects of BOTOX.

Seldom has a substance so medically and cosmetically beneficial had such dangerous origins. In 1817, German physician Justinus Kerner described *botulinum toxin* as 'sausage poison' or 'fatty poison', because it caused poisoning from improperly kept or prepared meat. A hundred years of refinement confirmed that, in tiny quantities, the refined toxin could be used for therapeutic purposes, by reducing muscle activity.

By 1980, Dr Alan Scott, a San Francisco opthalmologist successfully used 'botulinum toxin type A' to cure patients of *strabismus*, in which the eyes are crossed or not properly aligned. He teamed up with Allergan Inc, an innovative Californian company first famous for its anti-histamine drops. Since then BOTOX has become generally used for all kinds of medical disorders, from excessive blinking and sweating to migraine.

But to most people, BOTOX is not about these serious medical uses, but about the world of glamour. And that is all down to a husband and wife doctor team in Vancouver – British dermatologist Alastair Carruthers and Jean, a leading Canadian opthalmologist. They noticed that while they were using BOTOX injections to cure eye muscle disorders, the 'frown lines' of their patients would soften, including those of their own receptionist. They, and Allergan, conducted clinical trials into this phenomenon, and in 2002, obtained FDA approval for cosmetic use.

Seldom has a product swept the world so quickly. Faced by high-definition TV, few stars dare leave anything to chance. Nor can the critical world of fashion and beauty. However, in a media dominated age where youth and looks are so important, a fear of looking older has also engulfed many ordinary people, with the result that millions of women, and indeed men, have turned to BOTOX to rejuvenate their looks. There are no less than five million such treatments in the United States each year, and in Europe it is becoming equally popular.

Jean Carruthers never patented BOTOX for cosmetic use, but later said, 'I missed out on a fortune, but we have had the most enriching experience using it on patients over the years. It changed so many lives, including my own.'

George **CAYLEY**

Normally, 18th century British aristocrats, if they worked at all, went into the army, church or politics. Sir George Cayley, 6th Baronet, was one of the exceptions who devoted themselves to science and inventions. The Wright brothers carefully studied his work before they flew at Kitty Hawk, and many have dubbed Cayley 'the father of aerodynamics'.

Cayley was born in Yorkshire in 1773 and inherited the mansion and estates of Brompton Hall. A brilliant polymath, he loved engineering and worked on a huge range of inventions reminiscent of Leonardo da Vinci – electricity, ballistics, optics, railway signals, lifeboats, caterpillar tracks and the wire wheels we use on bicycles.

But it is aviation for which Sir George Cayley should be remembered. Remarkably, drawings in his early schoolbooks show him on the way to creating his cambered airfoil to create lift. And crucially, he was to work out the key forces that would govern flight – thrust, lift, drag and gravity, and their inter-relationship. Built in the 1840s, his model gliders looked like modern aircraft – monoplanes with tailplanes at the rear with a vertical fin.

In 1853, a full-scale glider flew across Brompton Vale, but this time it had a pilot – the first manned flight by a heavier-than-air machine. It was not Sir George. The family claim it was the coachman, who when the glider crashed, declared, 'I am paid to drive, not bloody fly', and promptly resigned.

Replicas of Cayley's glider have flown again, first at Brompton in 1973, again by Sir Richard Branson in 2003, and then in Kansas to welcome Steve Fossett landing the Virgin Atlantic GlobalFlyer after his flight round the world.

So one of the shortest flights was celebrated with the longest, 150 years later.

William **CHALONER**

Isaac Newton was one of the giants of the Scientific Revolution. While few of us might be able to explain his Calculus Theorem or recite his three 'Laws of Motion', most of us remember the story of him watching an apple falling from a tree and realizing the concept of gravity.

Exhausted from his scientific work and needing an income, Newton became Warden of the Royal Mint in 1696, helping to overhaul the whole currency system, implementing the 'Great Recoinage'. In the process, he became the nemesis of the biggest and most outrageous forger in British history – William Chaloner.

Chaloner was a natural criminal and 'Honour among thieves' was certainly not his motto. He 'snitched' and cheated on his friends and collaborators, even sending several to the gallows, while saving and enriching himself; as unpleasant a friend or foe as one can imagine.

The son of a Birmingham weaver, William Chaloner first came to notice churning out 'Birmingham Groats', forgeries of genuine silver coins. Throughout Britain, the currency was in chaos. Thousands of people were 'clipping' slivers from real gold and silver coins, melting the clippings with lead or brass, and stamping out false coins in backstreet presses, making them look older and then passing them off through a crooked network of shopkeepers and tavern owners. Over a tenth of the coins in circulation were, amazingly, false – so 'coining' was a serious crime, endangering the whole money system. As 'High Treason' against the Crown it was often punished by hanging.

Chaloner arrived in London in 1680 and after a brief stint cruelly selling quack medicines to desperately ill people, again began to counterfeit coins but now on a grand scale, with a team of a goldsmith, a master engraver and husband and wife 'fences', who passed off the coins through the criminal underworld. He became rich, buying a large house in affluent Knightsbridge, with 'the appearance and airs of a gentleman'. But he was coming to the attention of Isaac Newton.

Sir Isaac Newton

The famous scientist had been making strenuous efforts to tackle the counterfeiting crisis. The coins had already been 'grained' with raised edges and engraved with *'Ducus et Tutanem'*, still on £1 coins. He also tackled the quality, the weight and fineness of coins, and also cleverly gleaned information from criminals in the clipping and coining game. He now had a special grudge against Chaloner who, over-confident, had issued pamphlets accusing the Royal Mint of corruption and proposing himself, through Parliament, to be appointed to sort things out – an offer sensibly declined.

Meanwhile, the monstrous Chaloner had been making handsome rewards by pretending to uncover Jacobite plots, getting yet another of his collaborators executed. Targeting the new Bank of England, he forged its £100 notes, denouncing his partner (duly hanged) and then collected a reward while pocketing his counterfeiting profits.

With a lottery scam, he denounced a colleague to achieve his own ends. And out in the woods of peaceful Egham, his secret machines were steadily churning out forged coins.

However, Isaac Newton had carefully gathered evidence, and in March 1699 Chaloner found himself in Newgate Prison, this time unable to lie, denounce or bribe his way out. He duly went to trial charged with forging French and English coins. Many witnesses remembered all too well Chaloner's repeated self-serving treachery to his partners and colleagues. Having feigned madness unsuccessfully, he was sentenced to hang, and wrote letters – in turn ingratiating and insulting – to Newton.

Newton understandably did not deign to answer, and Chaloner went to the gallows.

Anthony **CLEAVER**

Today we take for granted the convenience of the 'hole-in-the-wall' cash machine, and most people would assume that, as with so many innovations, it was created by Americans. The reality is surprising.

Late one Friday in December 1969, Anthony Cleaver, a young British systems engineer at IBM in Chiswick in London, was told that he was now to look after some of IBM's banking customers. Within days he found himself with Lloyds Bank, who had a problem. Most customers were then paid weekly, and at Friday lunchtimes they flooded into branches to raise money for the weekend. The result was often chaotic, with long queues and delays and the need for extra cashiers. Could IBM and Tony Cleaver come up with an automated solution?

He put together a team and looked at options. De La Rue, best known for bank note printing, had produced a dispensing machine. But you had to pay £100 in advance for a card with which you could withdraw £10 a time. Most people didn't have £100 (now about £1,300) ready to advance up front, so the system was hardly very practical.

Tony Cleaver and his team worked out that a successful 'automatic teller machine' would need to: a) identify the customers and check if they had the money to withdraw, b) give out money in varying amounts, and c) have a mechanism that could quickly count and dispense the cash.

Identifying the customer had been made easier because Lloyds was installing a complete IBM branch network linked to Head Office. The software was more of a problem and might have to be specially written.

For a new machine, Cleaver had to submit a 'Request Price quotation' to IBM in America, which was something of a struggle. Luckily, at that moment a British colleague, John Fairclough, was transferred to IBM in the US. Friendly with Cleaver, he knew what was needed and he then began to work on a prototype. IBM had just produced a ticketing system for San Francisco's Bay Area Rapid Transit, using tickets with strips of magnetic stripe encoding tape. That, they thought, might suit the cards for the new cash machine.

To check that the prototype could handle the weight, size and paper of British notes, they had to ask the Bank of England for permission to ship out £10,000 in new and used notes to America to feed into the machine – this at a time when the British were only allowed to take abroad £25 a year!

With the prototype working, Cleaver was summoned to IBM's New York Head Office which had done a worldwide 'forecast survey' among banks, and of 1,600 requests, 1,500 were from Cleaver's customer, Lloyds. Top management could not understand the market for a network cash dispensing system because all American banks then had quite small branch networks. (The Glass-Steagall Act had forbidden banking across state boundaries, which is why 80% of travellers' cheques were used *within* America,

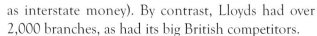

as interstate money). By contrast, Lloyds had over 2,000 branches, as had its big British competitors.

At last, the IBM Board approved the project for roll-out, and in May 1971 Lloyds ordered the first 500 machines – on condition that Tony Cleaver stayed on to complete the programme. He did, then persuading Lloyds to do something even more radical – placing machines not just inside, but outside the branches, so-called 'through the wall' machines'. Lloyds were initially sceptical that customers would want cash outside banking hours. But soon 'Cashpoints', as they were called, could be seen in every high street.

Tony Cleaver went on to be Chairman and Chief Executive of IBM UK – as well as filling many other distinguished posts, and was duly knighted in 1992 for services to British exports.

Now, of course, every bank in the world has ATMs. Citibank, in its advertising, boasts having 26,000 of them, also claiming to have ' *pioneered round the clock banking with our first ATM machine in 1977*'. Not quite. Lloyds beat them to it by about five years.

Eddie **COCHEMS**

For a rugby fan, the origins of American football are there to see, even if obscured by its complex moves. However, there is one obvious difference, and a spectacular one – the forward pass. With the quarterback protected by his 'pocket' of defensive players, he will throw the ball, accurately spinning like a rifle bullet, huge distances to a 'receiver' running at full tilt, hopefully to score a touchdown.

The change to the rules allowing such forward passes arose from a serious crisis. American College Football had become incredibly dangerous. In the 1905 season, 18 young men had been killed and 159 seriously injured, a toll that threatened the abolition of the sport. But President Theodore Roosevelt personally intervened, and new rules were created – the most important allowing the forward pass.

While many coaches then began to work on the forward pass, it was Eddie Cochems of St Louis University who really grasped its possibilities and then perfected the technique. An excellent former player, *'wonderfully built, handsome and affable'*,

he once ran with the ball 98 yards for a touchdown. But while he appreciated such a running game, he could also see what could be done with the new pass, and took his team off to a Jesuit sanctuary, specifically to perfect what he called 'the projectile pass' or 'air attack.' In the first 1906 game, his star quarterback Brad Robinson threw the first legal forward pass ever for a touchdown and the team never looked back, undefeated with 11 straight victories.

Even with these successes, the new pass was surprisingly slow to take off. Knute Rockne, coach at Notre Dame at South Bend, Indiana, had certainly taken note, but commented, 'One would have thought that so effective a play would have been instantly copied and become the vogue.'

In 1913, he and his friend Gus Dorais practised the plays round the forward pass on a beach. The results of their planning were spectacular. The 'Fighting Irish' of Notre Dame, with a barrage of passes, beat the favoured Army cadets of West Point 35-13. In 1917, Rockne became a legend as head coach, and for the next 13 years Notre Dame dominated, with a winning percentage record that lasts to this day.

The Super Bowl, the final match in the American Football season, watched by 110 million Americans, has been called 'the greatest show on earth.' For glitz, it does make the Cup Final and the Six Nations rugby look like village cricket. And the Eddie Cochem's forward pass is one good reason for all that glamour and success.

Pierre de **COUBERTIN**

At the impressionable age of eight, young Baron Pierre de Coubertin was very distressed by France's unexpected and decisive defeat by the Prussians in 1870. He became convinced that only better physical education would give France the strength to resist her enemies in the future.

In his youth, de Coubertin had been much influenced by English novels for boys, which stressed the importance of physical education and sportsmanship. In 1883, this prompted him to visit the renowned headmaster of Rugby, Dr Thomas Arnold, and then other British public schools, becoming ever more convinced of the motto *Mens sana in corpore sanu* (a sound mind in a sound body). His book, *L'Education d'Angleterre*, stressed that organised sport created moral and social strength. De Coubertin also visited Yale University 'to acquaint himself with the management of athletics in American universities'.

Sadly, his efforts to improve sport in French schools largely failed, but they were certainly to lead to something even bigger. He had always been fascinated by the ancient Olympic Games, held every four years between the Greek city states with running events, a pentathlon, boxing, wrestling, equestrian events and chariot races – a tradition lasting a thousand years until 426 AD.

In England, Dr William Penny Brookes formed a National Olympic Association, even running national 'Olympic Games' at London's Crystal Palace in 1866. Brookes and de Coubertin wrote to each other, and in 1890 the Frenchman visited Brookes. Meanwhile, the Greeks themselves had been working on the idea of reviving the Games. Evangelis Zappas, a rich philanthropist, paid for the refurbishment of the ancient Panathenaic Stadium.

Building on the work of Brookes and Zappas, Pierre de Coubertin created the first International Olympic Committee, which met in 1894, deciding to hold the first modern Olympic Games two years later in the stadium that Zappas had rebuilt. After the success of these Games, the Greeks wanted to hold them perpetually in Athens, but the IOC farsightedly decided that it would be better if they rotated between countries.

Except during the two World Wars, the Games have been held every four years ever since, joined by the Winter Olympics in 1924 and, for disabled athletes, the Paralympics in 1948.

In spite of political problems, boycotts, drug scandals and even terrorism, the Games have proved a stunning success as a tool to promote friendly international rivalry and understanding – with 10,000 athletes from 200 countries watched by four billion people.

For all this we can thank Pierre de Coubertin and his quest for schoolboy fitness.

Nathaniel **COURTHOPE**

Many people know the early history of New York and how the Dutch arrived there. Perhaps more intriguing is how it became British, and why New Yorkers owe their name to a forgotten hero and to some violent events the other side of the world.

In a legendary bargain, in 1626 the Dutch purchased Manahatta ('hilly island') from the Menates Indian tribe for 24 dollars worth of trinkets, naming it 'New Amsterdam.' The remaining Indians, the Lenapes, introduced the new settlers to maple, sugar, tobacco, maize and corn. At what is now the Battery, the Dutch built a fort which could overlook both the Hudson and East Rivers and pushed the settlement up a wide Indian trail, *De Heerewegh*, or 'Broadway', protecting themselves by a wall at 'Wall Street'.

But Manhattan was always going to be dominated by events back in the Old World. The Protestant Dutch were escaping from the oppression of the Catholic Spanish and French. The English victory over the Spanish Armada in 1588 made it possible to challenge Spain everywhere, including the New World. Above all, the riches of the East meant that Europe was sending explorers to find a short sea route to the east; the fabled 'North-West Passage'. Verrazano tried to reach Cathay, Jacques Cartier reached as far as present-day Montreal. Henry Hudson also failed, but his report to the Dutch of the area's abundance of valuable furs led to their own arrival.

Peter Stuyvesant did a good job of building up the Dutch colony, but suddenly lost everything when in 1664 four British naval ships arrived in the name of Charles II – and then renamed the island New York after his brother, the Duke of York. Stuyvesant was not to realise that, bizarrely, the English attack was the direct result of bitter struggles over the nutmeg spice, four decades earlier and ten thousand miles away.

Today, it is hard for us to grasp the huge economic and political importance of spices in the past, equivalent to gold and now oil. Two thousand years before Christ, the spice trade from the East was already fully developed. In 950 BC, the Queen of Sheba visited King Solomon. And why? To ensure that his fleet did not bypass her kingdom (now Yemen), ruining its wealth on the spice route. Egypt, Rome, Venice, Genoa and Constantinople were crucially dependent on spices, as were Portugal and Spain later on. Soon the English and Dutch entered the market and were competing and fighting, especially over the 'Spice Islands' of Molucca and Banda, and it was nutmeg that provoked the New Amsterdam confrontation and one of the strangest twists of fortune in history.

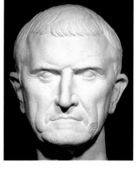
Myristica fragrans (Nutmeg)

On the other side of the world from North America, the tiny, two square mile island of Run – covered in precious sweet-smelling nutmeg trees – was ceded in 1616 by the Bandanese islanders to Nathaniel Courthope, a British merchant navy officer from Kent, representing the British East India Company. As the only spice island not under their control, Run was then besieged by the furious Dutch. Cut off, Courthope, with 39 men and the Bandanese, bravely led its stout defence for three long years until he was trapped and killed. His followers, and many other British traders, were then horribly tortured by the Dutch at the 'Massacre of Amboyna'. This stupid, brutal atrocity created fierce hatred and a desire for revenge. And that was why the British decided to capture Manhattan.

Both sides met at Breda in 1667 to end an exhausting war. After weeks of argument, the Dutch were offered the choice of the two islands. They decided to give up Manhattan for what they considered to be the much more valuable island of Run.

Run today is a sleepy, unremarkable little island. New York has, of course, become became a little more important.

Marcus Licinius **CRASSUS**

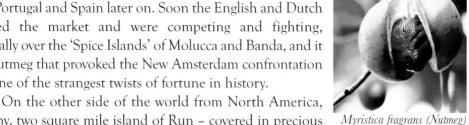

Compared with other Romans he is not a familiar figure, but Marcus Licinius Crassus was certainly a very unattractive one.

Born into a life of power and wealth, his wealthy father dubbed *Dives* (rich), young Crassus determined to build up his wealth, first by 'proscribing' some of his fallen enemies and acquiring their wealth, then through silver mines and slave owning. His huge property portfolio was augmented by his ownership of Rome's fire service and his unpleasant habit of turning up with his fire crews and negotiating slowly while houses were burning, with the owners forced to sell at knock-down prices.

The richest man in Rome, Crassus too was now nicknamed 'Dives', using his great wealth to finance an impoverished Julius Caesar. However, his political career was blighted by his rivalry with Pompey the Great, with fatal consequences.

The Spartacus slave revolt gave Crassus a chance for glory, as he personally financed, equipped and led an army. This did not go smoothly. He punished a retreating Legion by unpopular 'decimation' (killing one in ten). Eventually he won, and brutally crucified 6,000 surrendered slaves all along the Appian Way into Rome. Even then Pompey was partly credited with the victory, fuelling Crassus's hatred. Mediation through Julius Caesar led to the three of them ruling Rome as a secret and uncomfortable 'Triumvirate'.

Serving as a Consul with Pompey, Crassus was rewarded with Syria as 'his' province – more wealth, but not enough. He wanted final military glory, enough to rival Pompey or Julius Caesar. Once more at his own expense, he decided to invade the Kingdom of Parthia, akin to a politician today, rich from the City of London or Wall Street, for no good reason of state, invading France!

It was a very foolish decision, soon compounded by others. Learning nothing of Parthian equipment and tactics, he trusted that 35,000 Roman legionaries and 8,000 cavalry would be more than a match for anything. At Carrhae he seemed vindicated when faced by a mere 10,000 cavalry.

But the Parthians used fearsome composite bows with arrows capable of penetrating Roman chain mail armour. Their 'cataphracti', heavily armoured horsemen, ambushed his own cavalry and eliminated them. The Roman infantry were swamped by barrages of arrows fired backwards by Parthian cavalry – the famous 'Parthian shot'. The Romans formed protective 'testudos', but the cataphracti smashed into them, and when they tried to charge, the horse archers rained arrows on them. Crassus's son, Publius, was killed, and his head, on a pike, did little for morale.

Eventually, weakened by heat and thirst, the surviving Romans forced Crassus to

go and parley with the Parthians. He was seized and killed – some say by having molten gold poured down his throat – 'finally to sate his thirst for wealth'.

With 20,000 dead, 4,000 wounded and 10,000 captured, Crassus had created a terrible Roman defeat. What's more, the death of this unpleasant man removed the crucial 'balance of power' between Pompey and Caesar, and led to civil war between them, the loss of the Republic and the creation of the mighty Roman Empire.

Gabriele **D'ANNUNZIO**

Gaetano D'Annunzio was born in Pescara in 1863, soon earning the nickname 'Gabriele' because of his angelic looks. In time he would earn another and much more significant, nickname – 'The John the Baptist of Italian Fascism'.

We could know D'Annunzio for his literary prowess. His first book of poetry was published at 16, and his prolific output would consist of poetry, novels, plays (one written for the actress Sarah Bernhardt), and musicals. His work was marked by originality, power and decadence – the Vatican banned his plays. Meanwhile, his private life was punctuated by tempestuous love affairs, over-spending and debt.

In 1914, he made speeches in Rome urging Italy to join the Triple Entente, and in that World War he distinguished himself as a fighter pilot, losing an eye. After the war, he was outraged that, at the Versailles Conference, Italy was not treated as a world power by her erstwhile allies and that territory promised by the British was reduced by half. He was even angrier that Fiume, with its majority of Italians, was to be handed to the new state of Yugoslavia. And now he did something really dramatic.

With a force of 2,000 veterans, he invaded Fiume, forcing the withdrawal of American, British and French occupation forces and begging the Italian government to back him and annexe the place. This they refused to do, blockading Fiume and, under pressure from the League of Nations, eventually bombarding the city, forcing its surrender and transfer to Yugoslavia. During that year of ruling Fiume, D'Annunzio adopted the rituals and trappings of Fascism that we now associate with Mussolini, calling himself 'Duce' (leader), speaking passionately from balconies, adopting the Roman salute and with his men parading in black shirts.

A year after the failure of Fiume, D'Annunzio was nearly murdered for his popularity, and crippled after 'falling' out of a hotel window. Mussolini ensured his withdrawal from politics by bribing him, saying, 'When you have a rotten tooth you can either pull it out or fill it with gold. I have chosen the latter with D'Annunzio'.

Having adopted all D'Annunzio's pioneering

Mussolini ignored D'Annunzio's advice

Fascist elements of dictatorship, Mussolini foolishly resisted D'Annunzio's advice not to form an alliance with Hitler, rejecting his entreaties in 1937 on a railway platform to pull out before it was too late.

A year later D'Annunzio died of a stroke. He was given a state funeral by Mussolini, who later admitted how much he bitterly regretted ignoring that advice.

Gustav **DALÉN**

In Britain at least, there has rarely been a brand that inspires as much love and loyalty as the AGA cooker. So symbolic is the AGA of a certain type of upper middle class rural lifestyle that the novels of Joanna Trollope and others writing about this echelon of society have even been labelled 'Aga Sagas'.

However, the famous cooker was almost an afterthought in the career of its Swedish inventor, Gustaf Dalén. A brilliant engineer, Dalén had worked on improving gases for lighthouses, including acetylene, and a storage system called Agamassen, or Aga for short. Lighthouses all over the world were soon using the Dalén light and later the 'Dalén Flasher', a flashing light equipping both lighthouses and buoys.

In 1912, this ingenious inventor was rewarded for this work with the Nobel Prize for Physics, but by now something dreadful

Gustaf Dalén

had happened. He had been blinded by a gas explosion; indeed, his brother had to collect his prize.

Undaunted, Gustaf Dalén continued as Managing Director of Svenska Actiebolaget Gasaccumulator or AGA, producing dozens of new products and over 100 patents.

Forced to stay at home, he realized how laborious cooking seemed to be for his wife. Despite his blindness, he decided to design a completely new type of cooker, with two lidded hobs for boiling and simmering, and ovens operating at different heats, excellent for baking. The result was a cooker that not only worked differently from any other, but also looked quite different; solid, comforting, reassuring – instantly evoking 'the heart of the home'.

A stroke of luck for AGA was that a young man of 24 called David Ogilvy started his illustrious career by selling expensive AGAs in Scotland – at the height of the Depression. He was brilliantly successful and was duly asked to write a sales bible, 'The Theory and Practice of Selling the AGA Cooker'. *Fortune* magazine called this *'the best sales manual ever written'* (and Ogilvy went on to became one of the world's greatest advertising writers).

As a result of such innovative thinking, the AGA gradually established itself as an iconic item in British country houses, a reputation that it has never lost to this day, with owners like Madonna, Sting, Colin Firth and Camilla Parker Bowles all extolling their AGAs and their pivotal role in their lives. Sharon Stone went so far as to declare that it was the first thing she 'would save in a fire'. Quite how, with the cooker's immense weight, is another matter.

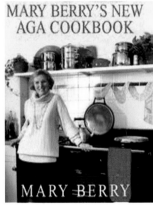

Mary Berry has created a speciality in cooking on the AGA. She wrote the cookbook given away with each AGA. has had 14,000 AGA owners attending her cooking workshops and has written 70 books, many covering cooking on an AGA. She has no doubt of its position in the family, 'Apart from my cooking, it dries clothes and I even use it to germinate seeds for my garden. Our home revolves around the kitchen and the AGA certainly earns its keep. No other cooker outlives its owner. AGAs are here for eternity.'

Hopefully, she's right, although AGA's strong brand position as a rural, middle-class essential has recently been dented by both recession and the spiralling cost of fuel, exacerbated by the way they used to remain on all the time. However, AGA has now created an electronic 'Intelligent Management System' to solve this problem.

And with so many owners saying, 'I could not live without my AGA', the brand will surely survive – and thrive.

Vernon **DALHART**

Train Number 97 – the 'Fast Mail' from Washington to Atlanta – was running late on September 27th, 1903, unusual because the United States Post Office fined the Southern Railway for every minute the mail was late. Driver Steve Broady then took over the train, soon to be immortalised in a famous song.

> *Well they gave him his orders in Monroe, Virginia*
> *Sayin' 'Steve you're way behind time.*
> *This is not 38, this is old 97*
> *You must put her into Spencer on time'.*

Unfortunately, Steve tried to obey orders and went fast, too fast. Approaching Stillhouse Trestle near Danville:

> *He was going down the grade makin' 90 miles an hour*
> *His whistle broke into a scream.*
> *He was found in the wreck with his hand on the throttle*
> *Scalded to death by the steam.*

Probably going closer to fifty mph, Steve Broady sadly met his end along with ten others, with seven injured. The nearly new locomotive was recovered and repaired, working on for another 32 years. Not, therefore, a huge railway accident, but the song made it the most famous ever. 'The Wreck of the Old 97', probably written by the dead fireman's cousin, was made a hit in 1924 by Vernon Dalhart, a singer whose career had started with an audition by the recording inventor Thomas Edison, who may have been the one who sensibly advised him to change his name from Marion Slaughter. Dalhart, now a largely forgotten singer, was so prolific, also singing under pseudonyms, that he is thought to be the most recorded artist in history.

Vernon Dalhart's 'The Wreck of the Old 97' was the first Country-style song to sell a million records, alerting the record companies to the potential of Country music, and eventually selling seven million – extraordinary for the 1920s.

This classic has since been recorded by dozens of artists including Johnny Cash, Woody Guthrie, Pete Seeger, Boxcar Willie and Britain's Lonnie Donegan. Some of us may find it a bit of a relief from the bulk of Country songs, which now seem all to be about 'lurve' for girls like 'Ruby' and 'Jolene'.

Jean **DANJOU**

Each year, on 30th April, the men of the French Foreign Legion are paraded, and the story of Camerone is read out. Then the wooden hand of Captain Danjou is solemnly carried out on to the parade ground and the Legionnaires march past in salute.

The French Foreign Legion was formed in 1831 by King Louis Philippe. Its purpose – to use volunteers like failed recent revolutionaries, footloose foreign soldiers, those on the run for petty crimes, perhaps lovesick or just bored. From such unlikely material, the Legion became one of the world's elite fighting units, with a unique 'Code of Honour'. Always led by the finest French officers, it often found itself in some desperate situations. One of them was in Mexico.

In 1863, France was using 40,000 troops in an ill-fated attempt to impose the Austrian Archduke Maximilian on to Mexico, ruled by Benito Juarez. On 29th April, the 1st Battalion of the Legion was ordered to send a company to escort a vital convoy carrying pay and munitions to the troops besieging the town of Puebla. But all the 3rd Company's own officers were on their sick beds. So Captain Jean Danjou, the Battalion's Quartermaster, volunteered to lead them. A top graduate of the Saint-Cyr military academy, and a seasoned Legion veteran of many wars, he had lost his hand ten years before in battle and wore a wooden replica. Together with the Pay Officer – Lieutenant Vilain, and Second Lieutenant Maudet, Danjou led 62 Legionnaires out on to the dangerous road to Puebla.

After passing a ruined little hamlet called Camerón, they were suddenly attacked by 800 of Colonel Milan's Juarist Mexican cavalry, followed up by 1,200 infantry.

The Legionnaires conducted a fighting retreat back to Camerón. But they had lost eighteen men, as well as the pack mules with their rations, precious water and ammunition. Danjou's men desperately fortified Camerón's crumbling hacienda. All morning they beat off assault after brave Mexican assault, refusing Milan's demands for surrender. 'We have munitions, we will not surrender,' Danjou calmly replied. He also swore to fight to the death and made his men, one by one, swear the same.

But with 2,000 Mexican rifles firing at them, casualties mounted. At noon, Captain Danjou was shot in the chest, two Legionnaires vainly protecting his body until he died. Vilain stoutly continued the defence, refusing fresh Mexican demands to surrender. His men were reeling from hunger, and especially thirst in the intense heat. Vilain was killed at 2pm.

By evening, only Maudet, a Corporal and four Legionnaires were still standing, and with only one bullet left per man. So Maudet drew his sword and ordered them to fix bayonets. They charged the mass of amazed Mexicans. Maudet and two men were quickly shot down, but the last three were pinned down and spared. Even then they refused to surrender, unless in accordance with their Code of Honour, 'we can care for our injured men and retain our rifles.'

'Nothing can be refused to men like you', agreed the Mexican officer, with extreme chivalry considering he had 300 men dead and the same number wounded.

The Emperor, Napoleon III, ordered that 'Camerone' be embroidered on to the Legion's colours, and that the names of Danjou, Vilain and Maudet be engraved in gold in the Invalides in Paris. At Camerón itself, a monument was erected in 1892 and Mexican troops salute it to this day.

And every year the Legion still carries out that strange ceremony of saluting the wooden hand of Jean Danjou.

? Humphry **DAVY**

There are many people whom, quite correctly, are well-known for one thing: for example, Guinness for brewing, Kalashnikov for his rifle, Ferrari for cars, Wrigley for chewing gum, Rothschild for banking, Plimsoll and Maginot for their 'lines' and Halley for his comet.

And then there are those whom we vaguely remember for one action or invention, but who deserve to be recognised for so much more. Humphry Davy is just such a man.

Davy was born in Penzance in Cornwall in 1778, the son of a wood carver. and was lucky enough to have a mentor – Robert Tonkin – an eminent surgeon who had adopted his mother. Recognising how precociously bright Humphry was, Tonkin persuaded the boy's father to send him to a grammar school where he thrived in science and, curiously, in poetry. At 16 he was apprenticed to a surgeon and became a chemist, constantly experimenting. 'He is incorrigible. He will blow us all up,' worried his friends.

After pioneering work on Galvanic corrosion in ships, Davy, aged 21, became an assistant at the Pneumatic Institution in Bristol, where he experimented with nitrous oxide gas. He once breathed in 16 quarts in seven minutes and 'became completely intoxicated'. Because it made him laugh, he called it 'laughing gas' and said it was 'highly pleasurable, thrilling'.

Sadly, the young man did not pursue 'laughing gas' as a potential anaesthetic. It took until 1842 for American doctors to rediscover it, calling it 'the Yankee Dodge', as a way to avoid the horrible pain of surgery – later progressing to ether.

However, Davy's research paper on the gas attracted the attention of Joseph Banks, the great scientist and founder of Kew Gardens, and in 1801 he moved to the new Royal Institution in London. There his lectures became huge hits,

A career of great scientific achievement

with spectacular demonstrations, some of them with 'laughing gas'. Handsome, young and charismatic, Davy's audiences were often filled with adoring female admirers.

But these glamorous and almost frivolous events masked a serious career of great scientific achievement. Using electrolysis to split up compounds, Davy discovered new metals like sodium and potassium, worked on chlorine and gave it its name, discovered calcium, magnesium, boron and barium, showed iodine to be an element, and in 1812 achieved the remarkable double of being given a science medal by Napoleon and being knighted by George 111. He also claimed that his 'greatest discovery' was Michael

Faraday, his assistant, whose work on electricity would make him more famous than Davy.

In 1815, after a devastating gas explosion in a Yorkshire coalmine, Davy perfected his safety lamp using wire gauze to isolate the lamp's flame from 'fire damp' or methane. 'The Davy Lamp' was soon adopted all over the world, and is the main reason why people remember his name. Four years later he was made a Baronet, the highest honour ever given to a scientist at that time, as well as becoming President of the Royal Society, then the world's greatest scientific institution.

It is a somewhat sad for Humphry Davy to be known for just his lamp, but perhaps better than not being remembered at all.

Reginald **DENNY**

Just as 'IEDs', or Improvised Explosive Devices, have entered our tragic lexicon of warfare, today we hear a lot about drones, or 'Unmanned Aerial Vehicles' – small pilotless, radio-controlled aircraft capable of flying for hours above hostile territory. They can 'see' through cloud and darkness and, now armed with missiles, they can attack what they see. Many Al-Queda or Taliban fighters, confident that they are safe in the wilds of Afghanistan, have been killed with no warning by some American pressing buttons at a console thousands of miles away.

Curiously, drones have a very unlikely origin – an English actor called Reginald Denny. The son of an actor and singer, Reginald Denny was born in Richmond in England in 1891 and started acting professionally aged 16. He was also, unusually, a national boxing champion and an opera singer. Volunteering in 1917 for Britain's new Royal Flying Corps, he developed a lasting interest in aviation that would run parallel with his acting career. Seeking his fortune in America, Denny appeared in his friend John Barrymore's Broadway hit of *Richard III* before starting a long and distinguished career in Hollywood. He acted first in silent films and then in the talkies, often as a comedy Englishman alongside the likes of Katharine Hepburn, Greta Garbo, Danny Kaye, Laurence Olivier and Jane Fonda. His very last role was in the 1966 version of *Batman*.

But his love of aeroplanes had never gone away, and with an interest in radio-controlled model aircraft, in 1934 he opened his 'Reginald Denny Model Shop' on Hollywood Boulevard in Los Angeles. Believing that a cheap radio-controlled aircraft

would be very useful for training anti-aircraft gunners, he bought a design from Walter Richter, then improved it and showed it to the US Army, who ordered, as an experiment, 53 Dennyplanes complete with their Dennymite engines. But after Pearl Harbor, this increased to thousands, built for the army, navy and airforce in a huge new plant in Los Angeles – a plant, incidentally, where a photographer spotted a pretty girl working, Norma Jean Baker, his photographs propelling her into being 'Marilyn Monroe'.

Nearly 15,000 drones were built during World War II, curiously the same number as famed P–51 Mustangs. A few years later the Denny company was bought by Northrop, which now provides some of those deadly un-manned aircraft droning above the badlands of Afghanistan.

Boxer, singer, actor, pilot and drone visionary – an extraordinary combination, yet a man so extraordinarily little known.

Henri **DESGRANGE**

Only one person has ever created a sport and then gone on to dominate it for three decades. But Henri Desgrange, with the Tour de France, not only created bicycle stage racing but also an event that is one of the biggest and most gruelling in the world.

Desgrange was born in Paris in 1865, one of twin brothers. His first claim to fame was as a brilliant track cyclist who set twelve world records, later graduating to running cycling velodromes.

When Captain Alfred Dreyfus was falsely accused of spying, *L'affaire Dreyfus* bitterly split French opinion – even within the sport of cycling and its magazine, *Le Vélo*. Many advertisers in *Le Vélo* broke away to form a new magazine, *l'Auto*, and chose Henri Desgrange as its Editor.

Desgrange knew he must win the circulation war and decided to capitalise on the growing popularity of long-distance road cycle races. In a crisis meeting, his young assistant Géo Lèfvre suddenly blurted out the dramatic idea of a cycle race around the country. Desgrange stared at him.' If I understand you right, petit Géo, what you are proposing is a Tour de France.'

In January 1903, *L'Auto* duly announced 'a cycle race to cover 2,428 km in (six) stages between 31st May and 5th July'. But with just a week to go before the closing date for entries, only fifteen riders had taken up the challenge. Conditions were obviously considered too harsh and its stages too long. Desgrange reduced the entry fee and offered an incentive for the first fifty finishers. Eventually, on 1st July, 60 riders began the race which was to last

Bradley Wiggins won the 2012 Tour (Josh Hallet)

until 19th July. Some were established French cycling stars, competing with Swiss, Belgian and German riders.

The Tour was a roaring success. Thousands of spectators turned out to greet the riders, and sales of *L'Auto* soared. From then on Desgrange ran the Tour in autocratic, despotic fashion. 'He rejected advice, certain of his authority and decisions, powerful in a world where his word had the force of law' wrote one journalist. He was quite capable of heavily penalising star riders or even ejecting whole teams (perhaps comparable with Bernie Ecclestone and modern Formula One).

When over fifty and already silver-haired, Desgrange volunteered to fight in World War I and won the *Croix de Guerre*, returning in 1919 to build up his beloved Tour. During his last one, in 1936, he was suffering from prostate cancer and was propped up in a car full of cushions to reduce the pain. He died in 1940, his country once again ruined by war.

The distances covered and speeds maintained by the Tour de France riders mark them out as athletes of the highest calibre. Indeed, some have compared the race with running a marathon every day for a month. The modern Tour, although varying in route, always includes several mountain stages, taking the riders up the steep, winding roads of the French Alps, where freezing fog and snow, even in July, add to the misery of the gradient and altitude, and with the descent faster than most motoring speed limits.

The Tour de France is the biggest live spectator event in the world, averaging 750,000 enthusiasts lining the route a day, and millions more glued to daily live TV coverage in many countries. It is second only to the Olympics as a television sport.

And if you watch the Tour, try to spot the tiny 'HD' on the yellow jersey worn by the race leader, immortalizing its charismatic creator.

Maria **DICKIN**

There is something peculiarly British about a genteel young woman devoting her life to the care of neglected and suffering animals. Moreover there is definitely a touch of British quirkiness in creating a medal for the bravery of animals in warfare.

Maria Dickin came from a slightly eccentric background, born in 1870 the eldest of eight children and the daughter of a minister in the Free Church, a somewhat spiritual faith and one that did not provide enough income for such a large family. So, against the conventions of the time, Maria decided to work, and then created a voice training studio near Harley Street where her clients included some of Britain's greatest singers.

When she married Arnold Dickin, a chartered accountant, she gave up work to devote herself to being an amusing and helpful social support for her ambitious husband. However, she became restless in this role, and a visit to London's East End during World War I was to change everything.

Whitechapel – notorious for the 'Jack the Ripper' murders of a few years before – was unpleasant enough for human beings, with its severe poverty, thousands of prostitutes and rampant crime. But there were scores of other forgotten victims. For the animals, it was equally terrible or even worse. It was not just the mangy, crippled dogs and cats that Maria saw scavenging in the gutters, but goats and rabbits ill-kept in back yards and the working horses and donkeys, crippled by overloading and often lame. Maria was horrified, as she later wrote in her book called *The Cry of the Animal*: '*The suffering and misery of these poor, uncared-for creatures in our overcrowded area was a revelation to me. I had no idea it existed, and it made me indescribably miserable'.* She decided to open a clinic where the poor could bring their sick animals and have them treated for free. She started in a Whitechapel basement, but soon had to move her 'People's Dispensary for Sick Animals' to larger premises before also creating mobile horse-drawn P.D.S.A. clinics across the country.

As we see with so many beneficial medical breakthroughs, the 'establishment' initially scorned her charity, seeing it as a threat. But in 1937 she responded tartly to the Royal College of Veterinary Surgeons *'If you are so concerned about proper treatment for the sick animals of the poor, open your own dispensaries'.*

A few years later, Maria Dickin initiated something even more remarkable. She created a medal, sometimes called 'the animals' Victoria Cross' – for animals 'that have displayed conspicuous gallantry or devotion to duty while serving with any branch of the Armed Forces or Civil Defence Units'. The Dickin Medal was first introduced in

1943 and then awarded to 32 carrier pigeons, 18 dogs, three horses and the wounded 'Simon', the cat on the frigate HMS *Amethyst* on the Yangtse River in 1949, who continued his rat catching under fire from the Communist Chinese.

It has since been awarded to three dogs helping in the World Trade Center during the 9/11 disaster, and most recently the 63rd Dickin Medal was awarded to 'Treo', a black Labrador which had sniffed out innumerable bombs and 'Improvised Explosive Devices' in Afghanistan, saving many lives.

Medal winner Treo

Carl **DJERASSI**

It is almost impossible now to imagine the agony that millions of unmarried women went through wondering if they were pregnant. The prospect of a 'back street' abortion, or the opprobrium of society and parents that was heaped on unmarried mothers was never far away. Even if partners had been 'careful', there were mistakes. Fear of pregnancy and public shame was instilled in daughters, overshadowing sexual relationships. Many women underwent the tragedies of forced adoptions, or doomed 'shotgun marriages', or the struggles of bringing up children alone – cruelly called 'bastards' by an unforgiving public.

There was no simple, ideal or foolproof solution for family planning, or for truly spontaneous carefree sex.

It is hard to think of any other individual who has had such a profound influence on women's lives as Carl Djerassi, the inventor of the contraceptive pill, but whose name is still so remarkably little known.

Carl was born in Vienna of Jewish parents who escaped from the Nazis in Austria. In 1939, he and his mother managed to reach the United States with just $20. Enterprisingly, young Carl wrote from school to the President's wife, Eleanor Roosevelt, and received 'veiled advice' about a choice of college. Graduating with an organic chemistry degree, in 1949 he joined a company called Syntex in Mexico. It was there that his team developed 'the Pill'.

$150,000 from the American birth control pioneer, Margaret Sanger, funded Djerassi's invention, *Progestin Norethindrone*. This mimics how natural hormones work in a woman's body, tricking it into thinking it is already pregnant and stopping the release of new eggs. Djerassi himself was amazed by where the research had led, 'Not in our wildest dreams did we imagine it'.

'The pill' swept the world, and in Britain, Health Minister Enoch Powell stood up in the House of Commons in 1961 to announce that the National Health Service would prescribe it – in time for, and no doubt promoting, the 'swinging sixties'.

Carl Djerassi received the National Medal for Science from President Richard Nixon. He has since been honoured as a scientist all over the world, with innumerable prizes and doctorates.

However, two unforeseen problems emerged. The first is the pill's oestrogen, excreted through urine and which cannot be filtered out of our drinking water. So men are receiving this very female hormone daily in ever-increasing quantities. Many scientists think that male fertility is falling as a result. So planned infertility in women may be accompanied by *unplanned* infertility in men.

Then Djerassi himself recognised that there is another downside to his invention. When combined with changing social conditions worldwide, it is leading to plunging birth rate levels. In the spring of 2009, now aged 85, he described the demographic decline in Europe as a 'horror scenario' and a 'catastrophe'. even castigating young Austrians who fail to procreate as 'committing national suicide'.

Does it matter? Very much. Developed areas like Europe and parts of Asia could see their populations *halve* in 65 years, with ageing populations, shrinking cities, pension crises, health care problems and weakened economies.

It must be a shame for Carl Djerassi to have created something so vastly helpful to so many, but with long-term results so unpredictable.

? Douglas **DOUGLAS-HAMILTON**

On May 11th 1941, Prime Minister Winston Churchill was at Ditchley in Sussex, restlessly alternating between watching a Marx Brothers film and going outside to stare at the heavy bombing of London. Suddenly the telephone rang. The caller was a personal friend, the Duke of Hamilton, who had almost incredible news of 'cabinet importance'. It was to be one of the strangest incidents of the war – and even in history.

From an ancient noble Scottish family, Douglas Douglas-Hamilton was born in 1903, and educated at Eton and Oxford. A keen sportsman all his life, he was Amateur Middleweight Boxing Champion of Scotland and rowed at Oxford, and for ten years – until he succeeded as the 14th Duke of Hamilton in 1940 – was a Member of Parliament.

A flying enthusiast, he was the chief pilot in a famous 1933 flight above Everest which demonstrated the need for pressurised cockpits. Flying himself to the 1936 Berlin Olympics as part of a Parliamentary group, he was at the same receptions as the Nazi leaders.

Hamilton's report to Churchill was extraordinary. Hitler's close confidant and Deputy Führer, Rudolf Hess, had flown alone 900 miles from Augsburg to Scotland in a Messerschmitt 110, shut off its two engines, rolled the aircraft to avoid hitting its tail and parachuted into the darkness. Amazingly, he had landed just ten miles from the house of the Duke, whom he demanded to see in hospital.

It turned out that Hess, having never even actually met the Duke during the Olympics, had embarked on a quixotic quest for peace between Britain and Germany – partly to please and regain influence with his beloved Führer.

The planning and execution of the flight was brilliant, but its purpose was an appalling miscalculation. Ridiculously naive, Hess assumed that the Duke of Hamilton was some kind of leader of an 'opposition party'. As 'Lord Steward', he 'presumably dined with the King every night and could persuade him to make peace in spite of Churchill's war-mongering clique.' In fact, the Duke was one of four brothers, uniquely all Squadron Leaders, gallantly serving in the RAF. Indeed, it was the Duke's radar team at RAF Turnhouse that had detected and puzzled over the mysterious lone 'Hostile Raid 42J'.

Hess did not even seem to know the names of any 'opposition leaders', nor realise that after two years under attack, Britons were united in their hatred of Hitler's Nazis. To the

'The Fall of the Deputy Führer' by Charles Thompson GAvA: ASAA

Duke and to other questioners, Hess insisted he was 'on a mission of humanity', that 'Hitler admired Britain, and only wanted a free hand in Europe in exchange for Britain's free hand in its Empire', and that 'Germany was bound to win the war anyway.' He did not reveal his strongest motive, which was, with the imminent attack on Russia, to avoid a two-front war. His captors merely felt he was half mad. Hess must have been shocked and amazed when he did not meet the King, nor the 'opposition party', and was quietly locked up by Churchill in The Tower of London for the duration of the war.

For his part, a furious Hitler ordered his old friend to be shot if he ever returned, and went back to planning his treacherous attack on the Soviet Union in a few weeks time. Indeed, the greatest consequence of the bizarre Hess adventure was that Stalin became so suspicious that he ignored Churchill's helpful warnings – gleaned from ULTRA code-breaking – that he was to be attacked, thus aiding the success of the German invasion.

The Duke of Hamilton went on to be a distinguished figure in Scottish business and cultural life. Hess was less fortunate. Condemned as a war criminal, he ended up as the last prisoner in Spandau, where he died in 1987, aged 92, apparently having hanged himself.

? Alfred **DOUGLAS**

It is always foolhardy to become involved in a family feud whose nature we do not fully grasp. However, that is precisely what Oscar Wilde allowed himself to do, because of his love for 'Bosie', Lord Alfred Douglas.

Wilde was born in Dublin, but brought his Irish wit to flower in England, where he became famous as a fop and a flamboyant aesthete. The Prince of Wales even asked for an introduction, because 'Not to know Mr Wilde is not to be known in society'. He was, indeed, one of the first to be 'famous for being famous'. However, he was about to make his mark as a writer, with *The Picture of Dorian Gray*. Although married with children, he was already a homosexual. Lord Alfred Douglas, the third son of the Marquess of Queensberry, had sulky, almost feminine good looks. Gay since his schooldays at Winchester, he was notorious at Oxford.

Alfred Douglas

In June 1891 a friend introduced them, and Oscar invited 'Bosie', as Alfred was known, to his club. They briefly became lovers, but Bosie preferred boys of his own age; 'All for youth and beauty and softness'. Wilde was 37, no longer slim but highly intellectually attractive. 'Much as I was in the long run crazy about Wilde, I never liked that part of the business and he soon cut it out altogether.'

However platonic their own relationship had become, the pair indulged with other (usually working class) men and rent-boys, enjoying the danger of 'feasting with panthers'. Bosie was a talented poet, and it was he who so eloquently described the then illegal homosexuality; 'I am the love that dare not speak its name'.

The Queensberry family had more than its fair share of lunacy, suicides and alleged curses. Bosie's father, the 8th Marquess (after whom the boxing rules are named) had a vicious and mutually hate-filled relationship with Bosie, who had come down from Oxford with no degree and had no job, living off money from his mother. Queensberry blamed Bosie's idleness on the romantic, platonic and very public affair with Wilde, and wrote manic letters to his son about *'shooting Wilde on sight'*. Bosie, also a master of vicious invective, responded by telegram, 'WHAT A FUNNY LITTLE MAN YOU ARE.' Queensberry then threatened 'to make a public scandal in a way you little dream of.' Sadly, for all concerned, he was to be as good as his word. But the spoiled, unstable Bosie took dark delight in continually provoking his father, and acted with no thought for Wilde's safety or reputation.

Wilde was in financial straits when he tried to leave Piccadilly's Avondale Hotel and take his luggage on 28th February 1895, partly due to Douglas's extravagances It was also very upsetting, because Bosie had also left in a huff with a another young boy, and had written him a cruel letter. Worse was to come. Wilde now went to the sanctuary of his club, the Albemarle, to find a card that had been waiting for ten days. This was from Queensberry and was addressed to *'Oscar Wilde, posing somdomite'* (sic). Furious, frustrated, hounded – as he saw it – as much by Bosie's aggressive attitude as by Queensberry's implacable rage, Wilde made a fatal slip. He saw no way out but to have Queensberry arrested for libel.

Bosie was delighted. Here was his chance to disgrace in court his loathed and loathsome father. Wilde and his friends had their misgivings, well-founded because in court everything Wilde had driven so hard to hide came to light. Queensberry had been resourceful, and the jokes in court stopped as Wilde's true sexual nature was aired from the mouths of rent-boys and hotel maids. His libel suit collapsed, and within hours the

findings were sent to the Director of Public Prosecutions. Foolishly, Wilde did not leave the country as Bosie had done, and a criminal trial condemned Wilde to two years of imprisonment. His spirit was broken, and his muse crippled.

On his release, the two friends were reconciled in Paris. But Oscar, now poor, did not have long to live. 'I am dying beyond my means!' 'My wallpaper and I are fighting a duel to the death. One or other of us has got to go',

Oscar Wilde, by Michael Grimsdale

Wilde died in 1900, but Bosie lived on for another 45 years, mainly well-known for being in court. In 1923, Winston Churchill sued him for claiming he had killed Lord Kitchener as part of a Jewish plot! Douglas was jailed for six months. But he will always be labelled and reviled as the one who ruined a fabulous, brilliant, but self-destructive genius.

Edwin **DRAKE**

For Edwin Drake, for Titusville and for Pennsylvania it was a very good thing that the US mail service was slow.

Before 1859, the oil industry was neither glamorous nor powerful. Although people had realized oil's growing importance for both lighting and machine lubrication, and oil refineries were already in operation, nobody had yet found a way to harvest it in large quantities. Whale oil was dwindling along with the whales themselves. The only other way to obtain oil was to find a place where it seeped out of the ground and 'skim' it off, using a wool cloth to absorb the oil and then wringing it out – hardly a method to produce large yields.

However, a new idea was mooted at the Pennsylvania Rock Oil Company. Could oil perhaps be extracted in larger quantities by drilling, as had been achieved for salt and water for centuries? There were plenty of sceptics. One banker, when asked to lend money, scoffed 'Pumping oil out of the earth as you pump water? Nonsense!'

But the company was not to be deterred. It hired a former railroad conductor, Edwin L. Drake, to travel to Titusville in Pennsylvania and make a historic attempt to drill for oil.

Everything went rather slowly. 'Colonel' Drake (a title he had made up to impress the locals) spent a year searching for funding and for assembling his equipment, including a steam engine to power a rig. However, his early attempts came to nothing, as each hole he drilled soon collapsed. 'Crazy Drake', as he was now called by jeering onlookers, then employed William 'Uncle Billy' Smith in an admirable piece of lateral thinking – a man used to drilling salt wells, who suggested containing the drill inside a metal pipe to stop the well collapsing – the very basis of modern oil drilling.

Encouraging as this innovation was, The Pennsylvania Rock Oil Company was losing heart. As unease grew, it was decided that the company should cut its losses. The directors duly sent a letter to Drake ordering him to abandon the project. Had the postal system been quicker, Drake would never have broken his way into the history books – because, whilst the letter was en route to the site, he was finally to meet with spectacular success.

On August 27th, at a depth of 69 feet, the drill suddenly broke through into an underground cavern, and it became apparent that the prospectors had finally struck oil. Thus, by the time the letter arrived, its contents were irrelevant. Now Titusville's population boomed from 250 to 10,000.

Well-known names also flocked to the area, like the future steel magnate Andrew Carnegie, the rock bit inventor Howard Hughes Sr. and John D. Rockefeller, who was soon – by rather dubious methods – to dominate refining and, with Standard Oil, the entire oil industry.

Drake (right) with his rig

All were to make fortunes from the industry that Drake had launched – but sadly not Drake. Unlike Howard Hughes, he failed to patent his technique and lost all his money, to be eventually propped up by charity donations from Pennsylvania, the state he had made rich.

Henry **DUNANT**

The old man had been in the little Swiss resort of Heiden for three decades, forgotten by the world until the press rediscovered him.

Henry Dunant was born in Geneva in 1828, into a devoutly Calvinist family. While his father was a businessman, both parents were actively involved with social work and this influenced their son, who would always be a mixture of businessman and philanthropist. When these roles competed for his attention, his social conscience usually won. This would prove good for the world and bad for him.

By 1856, with funding from Geneva, Dunant had created a corn-growing and trading company in France's colony of Algeria. Struggling to get water rights for irrigation, he resolved to appeal directly for support to the Emperor, Napoleon III. Napoleon, however, was busy fighting a war with Austria. Dunant arrived on the very day of the brutal Battle of Solferino, finding thousands of wounded soldiers left to die.

So horrified was Henry Dunant by what he saw, that he quickly organised local women to come out and care for the wounded from both sides – even paying for medical supplies himself. Some of the wounded were brought in under white flags with a red cross traced in their own blood.

Back in Geneva, he then wrote and produced *A Memory of Solferino* and sent the book to Europe's political and military leaders. The book ended with two radical ideas that would have immense results – to create a voluntary, neutral, international organisation to care for wounded soldiers, and to enshrine in law rules of behaviour towards the wounded and other helpless victims of war.

Dunant's ideas were received favourably by Gustave Moynier, of the Geneva Society of Public Welfare. With three other prominent medical and military figures, they created in 1863 'The International Committee for relief of the wounded'. They then held a conference, inviting several countries including military powers like France, Prussia, the Russian Empire and Great Britain.

Thus was born the Red Cross, and one year later, it was followed by the Geneva Convention. However, disaster overtook Dunant, who had quarrelled over policy with Gustave Moynier, and because of devoting his energy to creating the Red Cross, had neglected his agricultural business in Algeria. This had collapsed, forcing Dunant into bankruptcy, with many others in Geneva losing money. He was now forced to flee his home city for ever, losing his position with the Red Cross. He wandered Europe, obscure and broke.'*I dined on a crust of bread, blackened my coat with ink, whitened my collar with chalk and slept on the street*'.

He eventually hid himself away in Heiden, but over 30 years later, with the Red Cross now spread across the globe, the press found him and strenuously reminded the world of his heroic efforts. As a result in 1901, at the age of 73, he was awarded the first Nobel Prize for Peace.

The Red Cross has proved to be one of the great influences for good in the world, and one of the most recognisable and memorable symbols of all time. But how many people recognise the name of Henry Dunant, a man who luckily wanted to approach the Emperor about some water rights?

Jean-Baptiste **EBLÉ**

In the summer of 1812, Napoleon made his greatest mistake. He attacked Russia, with 530,000 men of twenty nations, 30,000 wagons and 170,000 horses. He crossed the River Niemen on pontoon bridges built by General Jean-Baptiste Eblé, who was soon, quite literally, to save Napoleon's skin, by disobeying an order.

Eblé was an austere and resourceful officer who had fought for his Emperor, from Austerlitz to Spain. Now in charge of the pontoon bridge train, he had welded his *pontonniers* into an elite force with specialised equipment, including mobile wagon-mounted forges.

Unusually, Napoleon's supply system was creaking from the start, with his normal ruthless foraging useless in the impoverished countryside. Thousands of troops and horses succumbed to the heat. None of his usual decisive victories came, and the Battle of Borodino lost him thousands of men and officers, including 35 Generals. He captured a deserted Moscow, furious that he had nobody to negotiate with, and the city then burned down.

With the dreaded Russian winter approaching in late October, Napoleon reluctantly decided to retreat, but his initial decision to leave nothing behind meant that progress was fatally slow, with the horses failing as snow began falling.

To appreciate the feats of Eblé and his men, consider the weakened state into which the *Grande Armée*, now only 105,000 strong, rapidly descended in that terrible retreat. Hunger, illness and the extreme cold, -20°F, took a steady toll on even the finest officers and men. Napoleon, too late, ordered all the wagons to be destroyed – including Eblé's pontoons. Eblé begged at least to retain his workshop wagons, but Napoleon, who was burning his own papers as an example, refused. Eblé then quietly disobeyed his Emperor – an inspired decision, because suddenly came the fearful news that the only bridge across the raging ice-filled Berezina River had been destroyed.

The army seemed trapped by the huge Russian armies closing in. But a reasonably shallow spot just to the north was found and Eblé and his 400 men set to work, tearing down a village for its timber. Now the saved wagons with their tools, mobile forges and precious charcoal came into their own. The feverish construction was the easy part, because now the trestles had to be manhandled into the freezing water, with chunks of floating ice hitting the struggling men. However, within hours, the first bridge for infantry and cavalry was ready and Napoleon's troops rushed across to block the Russians. Three hours later, the artillery and wagon bridge was

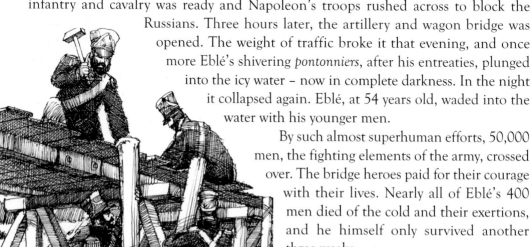

opened. The weight of traffic broke it that evening, and once more Eblé's shivering *pontonniers*, after his entreaties, plunged into the icy water – now in complete darkness. In the night it collapsed again. Eblé, at 54 years old, waded into the water with his younger men.

By such almost superhuman efforts, 50,000 men, the fighting elements of the army, crossed over. The bridge heroes paid for their courage with their lives. Nearly all of Eblé's 400 men died of the cold and their exertions, and he himself only survived another three weeks.

Napoleon had many more famous officers, but perhaps none to whom he owed so much.

Theodor **EICKE**

Concentration camps are the most hideous and enduring symbols of the Nazi era, a roll-call of sinister names: Belsen, Treblinka, Sobibor, Buchenwald, Mauthausen, Ravensbrück - and the greatest killing machine of all time, Auschwitz. Many were smaller and unknown. But one, Dachau, was the first and prototype model for all the other horror camps.

On 27th February 1933, the mysterious 'Reichstag Fire', which was blamed on the Communists, was the perfect excuse the Nazis needed to snatch dictatorial powers and turn brutally on their enemies. Only three weeks later, Heinrich Himmler gave orders for the first *Konzentrationslager* to be created at Dachau, near Munich. Thousands of political opponents – Communists, social democrats, trade unionists, conservatives and liberals arrived at a disused munitions factory. Initially they were guarded by police, but the SS quickly gained control, and that very day, 11th April, the first four murders took place. Amazingly, the Munich judiciary started to take legal action against the Kommandant, whom, equally amazingly, Himmler was forced to move.

But his replacement was to be a more evil figure, Theodor Eicke – the youngest of 11 children, a school drop-out, who hated Jews, Communists and the Weimar government – perfect Nazi material. This largely unknown man converted arbitrary terror into a *terror system*, under which many infractions were punished by automatic and brutal death. He designed every day to be filled with methodical and sadistic cruelty.

In June, Hitler decided to get rid of his now-inconvenient rival, Ernst Röhm, head of the three million Brownshirts of the *Sturmabteilung*, in the 'Night of the Long Knives'. It was not Hitler, but the faithful Eicke, who finished off his old comrade. In gratitude, Hitler and Himmler made Eicke the Chief of Staff for all concentration camps, and he promptly brought to bear all the techniques that he had created at Dachau.

By 1942, Hitler was confident enough to proclaim in a newspaper 'Der Jude wird ausgerottet' – 'the Jew will be exterminated.' He was referring to the secret Wannsee Conference, with its plans for the methodical killing of the 11 million Jews in Europe. Now the pace quickened. Auschwitz was soon killing 60,000 a day. And Jews from the Warsaw ghetto, promised 'resettlement', walked calmly off daily trains and out of the pretty, entirely false railway station at Treblinka to join the million corpses in the field behind.

The bestial Nazi attitudes had come from the top. From the beginning, Adolf Hitler gloried in it: 'Cruelty is impressive. Cruelty and brutal strength'. In Theodor Eicke, Hitler had found his man to create this instrument of terror – a man virtually unknown to history, who died fighting with the Waffen SS in Russia. But Eicke had set in train a colossal brutality machine, with over a hundred major concentration camps among nearly 10,000 other locations, employing half a million men and women. It killed over six million innocent people and scarred the lives of millions more.

Only in the extraordinary era of the Nazis could such an unlikely figure have had such a devastating and appalling impact.

Alicia **ESTEVE**

Of all the shocking and extraordinary stories to emerge from the tragic 9/11 attacks, one of the most bizarre was that of Tania Head. She had become the face of the survivors of the Twin Towers, and it was she who in 2005, at the World Trade Center Visitor Site, greeted New York's Mayor Michael Bloomberg, former Mayor Rudy Giuliani and the former state Governor, George Pataki.

It was Gerry Bogacz, a founder of the World Trade Center Survivors' Network, who first heard about a survivor called Tania Head and invited her by email to join.

Tania's story was that she was on the 78th floor of the South Tower when United Airlines 175 hit. She appeared to be one of the 19 survivors from above the point of impact, her arm being damaged in her struggle to escape. She said that her fiancé, Dave, with whom she had just become engaged on a trip to Hawaii, had perished in the North Tower, that a dying man had given her his wedding ring to give to his wife, and that her blazing clothes were put out by Welles Crowther, the 'Red Bandanna Man' hero, who later died when the building collapsed.

Soon Tania was dynamic President of the Survivors' Network, and its spokesperson. 'I was there at the Towers. I'm a survivor. I'm going to tell you about that'. Eventually the media attention given to this plump, blonde and confident woman prompted the *New York Times* to do a major Tania feature. However, she seemed suddenly reluctant to meet the *Times* reporter, backing out of three meetings. When the media become suspicious, they usually find something – and in Tania's case they did.

It took only a little probing to discover that Tania had no job at Merrill Lynch, nor had she attended, as she claimed, Harvard and Stanford Universities. 'Dave's' family had never heard of his alleged fiancée, nor recalled any trip to Hawaii. Then, even more of a shock was the discovery that 'Tania' was not American but Spanish, in fact called Alicia

Fame? Tania with Rudy Giuliani

Esteve, the daughter of a Barcelona shipping magnate who had just been indicted for fraud. She had actually been at Barcelona's ESADA Business School studying when the 9/11 attacks occurred 3,000 miles away. Her Spanish friends revealed that she had damaged her arm in a car accident and that 'she loved everything about America' and, above all, 'wanted to be famous'.

After these revelations in September 2007, 'Tania' was kicked out of the Survivors' Network, with many of those whom she had befriended devastated. And then she disappeared.

From any angle, this is an extraordinary story. It might have been just slightly more 'normal' and comprehensible if this fantasist had been a real New Yorker, propelled into fantasy by being grief-stricken about what she had witnessed at the Towers. But for a Spanish girl to arrive three years later, to create a complete New York persona, to cook up a detailed story of her miraculous survival, to take very public control of the Survivors' Network and to get away with it for nearly five years is truly remarkable.

If she had been a spy, we might have applauded such ingenuity and nerve. But most now despise her for trampling on the feelings of the genuine victims of the 9/11 tragedy.

Philo **FARNSWORTH**

In 1932 came an historic meeting between the two men who 'invented' television, a Scot and an American. First John Logie Baird demonstrated his mechanical system to Philo Farnsworth, explaining its 'superiority'. Then Farnsworth showed his system. After a few minutes, Baird advanced slowly, 'as if hypnotized'. He stood for some time, then turned without a word and left.

The British, and the Scots would always claim that Baird was the true 'inventor' of television, following in the footsteps of great Scottish innovators like Watt, MacIntosh, McAdam, Simpson, Lister, Fleming, Bell and Watson-Watt. But, with television, perhaps both Baird and Farnsworth deserve equal credit.

The lesser known of the two was Philo Farnsworth, born in a Utah log cabin in 1906 to Mormon parents. When they moved to Idaho, the boy found the farm had electricity, and rebuilt an abandoned electric motor, attaching it to his mother's manual washing machine. He also found – and devoured – a hoard of technology magazines. At High School he produced sketches and prototypes of electron tubes; indeed one of his blackboard diagrams would one day be used in his television patent case against the mighty Radio Corporation of America.

Two San Francisco philanthropists backed the young man to move to Los Angeles and work on his idea for electronic television. This was different from Baird's approach, whereby a device mechanically scanned an image through a spinning 'Nipkow' disc with holes cut into it, then projected a tiny reproduction. Farnsworth wanted to produce a vacuum tube that would reproduce images *electronically*, by shooting a beam of electrons, line by line, against a light-sensitive screen – inspired by the back and forth motion of ploughing a field. In fact, this is now the basis for all televisions. He patented his invention in 1927, and demonstrated it to the press the next year.

Philo T. Farnsworth   20c

In 1930, on his way to RCA, engineer Vladimir Zworykim visited Farnsworth and later copied his system. This would lead to years of patent litigation with RCA, which Farnsworth eventually won. And it was over in London, when raising funds to fight RCA, that he had that meeting with Baird, who then realised that he was in a technological dead-end.

John Logie Baird, born in Dunbartonshire in 1888 and educated at the University of Glasgow, followed a German scientist who had transmitted half-tone still pictures over long distances between 1902 and 1907, and Paul Nipkow who had created the scanning disc and a television system before Baird was even born.

Starting with moving silhouette images in March 1925, by October Baird transmitted a moving picture of a ventriloquist's dummy and then an office worker, William Taytin, the very first person to be televised. Seeking publicity he visited the *Daily Express*, but the News Editor missed a real scoop, because he was terrified – telling his assistant, 'For God's sake, go down and get rid of a lunatic who says he's got a machine for seeing by wireless. Watch him – he may have a razor!'

Three months later Baird did rather better with *The Times* and the Royal Institution

Baird with early camera

and the next year he transmitted between London and Glasgow. Then, in 1928, he transmitted from London to New York and started the first television programme for the BBC. Both men were prolific as inventors, whether of television systems or beyond – Baird demonstrated the first colour TV in 1928, then stereoscope 3D television. In 1943, he proposed a 1,000 line system, comparable with today's High Definition TV, and then went on to create a thermal undersock, fibre-optics, radio direction finding and infra-red night vision.

Farnsworth, in addition to the video camera tube used in all television cameras until recently and one hundred other television parts, created a fuser to create nuclear fusion, and also worked on radar, infra-red night lights, the electronic microscope, the baby incubator and the astronomical telescope, holding no less than 300 US and foreign patents.

Sadly, Philo Farnsworth was cheated out of making real money from his key television role. *'My contribution was to take out the moving parts and make the thing entirely electronic –the concept that I had when I was just a freshman at High School at age 14'.*

But when Neil Armstrong landed on the moon, his image beamed back by Farnsworth's 'image dissector', Farnsworth was able to turn to his wife and say, 'This has made it all worthwhile'.

? Rebecca **FARNWORTH**

Katie Price, once famous for 'being Jordan', is a glamorous former Page 3 girl who has incredibly amassed a £50 million fortune by turning herself into a 'celebrity'. And one of the ways that she has achieved this extraordinary feat is by apparently writing a number of books. Except, in common with so many other celebrity 'authors', they have actually been written by a 'ghost writer'. In the case of Katie's novels, this was Rebecca Farnworth, who has now written her own successful books.

Katie Price, aka 'Jordan'

The supermodel, Naomi Campbell, eventually came clean about her novel *Swan*, written by the talented writer Caroline Upcher, who after a distinguished career in publishing has written 14 of her own books, some under the name Hope McIntyre. A ghost writer ghost writing for herself?

Naomi Campbell eventually admitted, 'I just did not have time to sit down and write a book', also reportedly quipping, 'Write it? I haven't even read it'. US President Ronald Reagan, with typical wit, commented more stylishly about *An American Life*, his autobiography, actually written by Robert Lindsey, 'I hear it's a terrific book. One of these days I'm going to read it myself'.

It is not only for books that ghost writers are routinely used, but for political speeches, academic and medical papers, pop songs – even religious tomes.

Most ghost writers know they will earn plenty of money by remaining strictly anonymous. There are certainly enough of them, or how else would certain celebrities, and especially footballers – some of whom in real life do not appear to be able to string two complicated words together – produce often quite passable memoirs?

Harry **FERGUSON**

If you visit any farm, from Texas to Suffolk, from India to the Ukraine, from China to Chile, you will see tractors. They often look much the same – small wheels at the front, a diesel engine, large wheels at the rear and a cluster of bars and tubes attached to some implement. Most tractor drivers will never have heard of Harry Ferguson, but without him, they might not be there.

Harry Ferguson could have been famous for many things – his own tractors, his pioneer flying, his revolutionary four-wheel-drive racing car. But his importance can be attributed to something much more basic – his 'three point hitch'. Mention this and most of us not involved in agriculture would look blank, but you can find this device on nearly every one of the millions of tractors in the world – one of the greatest and most enduring advances in the world's search for food.

Ferguson was born on a farm in County Down, Northern Ireland in 1884. With an early interest in all things mechanical, he set up a company with his brother repairing cars and bicycles, took time off to race motorcycles and became fascinated by the new craze of aviation. Indeed, he was the first pilot to fly in Ireland, and moreover, in a monoplane he had designed and built himself.

However, with his company selling American tractors, he detected a flaw in the way they worked, simply towing ploughs just as horses had done for thousand of years. He decided that any implement should be rigidly attached to the tractor with three links, soon to be called the '3 point linkage' in Britain or the '3 point hitch' in America. The two lower arms could be raised, lowered or tilted by the tractor's hydraulic system. A growing number of complex implements could be attached to the tractor, some mechanically operated by drive from the engine. These could include ploughs, seed drills, hoes, mowers, tillers, muck-spreaders, harrows, rakes, wood-chippers, water pumps, hole borers and many more. The

3 point hitch was nothing short of a revolution in how tractors could be used.
In 1939, Henry Ford made a 'handshake agreement' (left) to use the 3 point hitch on all Ford tractors, and when Ford's grandson suddenly ended this deal, Ferguson sued

for $250 million and went off to create his own tractor range that soon captured 80% of the British market, eventually selling out to Massey Harris.

But Harry Ferguson's real claim to fame should be his 3 point hitch, and today there is hardly a tractor that does not use it anywhere in the world.

Carl **FISHER**

Racing motor cars was always going to be a dangerous sport, especially on open roads. One of the first races, the 1903 Paris-Madrid race, was stopped after eight deaths and even brought in 20 mph speed limits on Europe's roads.

The answer was to build closed circuits, and the first was in England in 1907, created by a rich landowner. In spite of its high speeds and two spectacular long bankings, Brooklands was the home of wealthy, often aristocratic, amateur drivers. Its snobbish slogan, 'The right crowd and no crowding' was even printed on the programmes.

But in Detroit, the home of America's car industry, Carl Fisher had other ideas.

As the maker of Prest-O-Lite carbide headlights, he and three motor industry friends bought 320 acres near the city of Indianapolis and built a 2.5 mile rectangular track. After a disastrous 1909 race on its dangerous surface, Fisher resurfaced the track with three million bricks, which is why it is still called 'The Brickyard'.

American racing fervour created plenty of competition, from county fair dirt tracks to the 'Boards', steeply banked wooden tracks similar to bicycle racing velodromes. However, Carl Fisher then made two inspired decisions. He opted for just one race a year, of over 500 miles, and then created the richest purse in the world. The result: the world's most important single motor race. An 'Indy 500' winner could earn more in a day than the fabled Babe Ruth in a whole baseball season.

At first European cars dominated the Indy 500, but gradually American specialist expertise took over with engine designers like Miller, Duesenberg and Offenhauser.

By the end of the 1950s, design had stagnated. In 1960, all the big, long, front-engined 'roadsters' were powered by identical 4-cylinder Offenhauser engines, as they had been ever since 1949. Speeds hardly changed from year to year and Indy had become a technical backwater.

Suddenly, in 1961 Jack Brabham arrived with a small mid-engined 'funny car' from England. Indy veterans laughed, and Indy champion driver A.J. Foyt described it as 'a bunch of tubes held together with chicken wire', boasting loudly that he would never drive one.

All that changed pretty quickly when Britain's Jim Clark and Graham

Brabham changed the race forever

> **'A bunch of tubes held together with chicken wire'**

Hill started winning races. Now Indy cars look identical to Grand Prix cars, and indeed, many are built in England.

A hundred years after Carl Fisher had planned it, his Indy 500 is a very American event, and is still the biggest and richest motor race in the world.

Robert **FITZROY**

Tune into the BBC Weather Forecast and you hear a long list – 'Rockall', 'Irish Sea', 'Dogger', 'Dover' – all areas or places. But one is named after a person, because 'Fitzroy' replaced 'Finisterre' a few years ago, in recognition of the troubled life of the man who created the Weather Forecast.

Robert Fitzroy was born in 1805 into a very aristocratic family. His great grandfather was Charles II, his father Lord Charles Fitzroy and his mother the daughter of the Marquess of Londonderry. More significant, his favourite uncle was Lord Castlereagh, Britain's renowned Foreign Secretary. And this is where suicide enters the scene. Castlereagh

Suicide enters the scene

suffered from depression, and despite the efforts of his friends George IV and the Duke of Wellington to hide all sharp objects, had stabbed himself to death in 1822.

Robert Fitzroy entered the Royal Navy aged 13. After excellent progress, he was appointed temporary Captain of the brig HMS *Beagle* – because her Captain had shot himself through depression. When *Beagle* was chosen for a long voyage of discovery, Fitzroy, through his mentor Francis Beaufort, Hydrographer to the Admiralty, got himself re-appointed as Captain and spent his own money readying the ship. But he was worried. He knew that he himself had a precarious mental balance.

Fitzroy already had an official naturalist for the voyage, Robert McCormack, the ship's surgeon. But what he did not have was a mealtime companion of his 'own class'. At the prospect of being condemned, by Navy tradition, to dine alone for five long years, he worried that melancholy would bring him down as it had his beloved uncle. So, through Beaufort, he asked his friend John Henslow, a Cambridge botanist, to come on the voyage. Henslow declined, but suggested his promising, aristocratic twenty-one year old biology student, Charles Darwin.

Thus Charles Darwin went on the voyage that was to make him famous, initially not as a scientist but merely as someone to keep Fitzroy content at mealtimes. But once they reached the isolated Galápagos Archipelago in 1836, the creatures he discovered there astonished him. They were unique and diverse. Many of the animals and plants looked similar to those he had seen in South America, but they were certainly not exactly the same. Many species on the islands – the giant tortoises, marine iguanas, cacti and finches – were all unique to Galápagos. Darwin believed that this diversity had the potential to 'undermine the stability of species'.

During the voyage Fitzroy did display some extraordinary outbursts of temper, bordering on insanity as Darwin recalled, and earning the crew's nickname 'Hot Coffee'. But generally the two got on well.

On their return in 1837, Darwin analysed everything he had found and secretly formulated his 'Theory of Evolution' But because he anticipated real opposition, particularly to the idea that man was descended from monkeys, he retired quietly to the country, hiding his discoveries. Now married to the very pious Emma Wedgwood, daughter of the great potter, informing her that the world was not created in six days would certainly ensure trouble.

Meanwhile, Fitzroy (right) had become a Member of Parliament and the first Governor of New Zealand. But it was his last appointment that enabled him to make his second mark on history. Under the influence of Beaufort, he was made head of a new department to study the weather, soon to become the Meteorological Office. There he created a new type of barometer, placed in every port. He devised new charts to predict the weather, and soon had fifteen shore stations linked by the new telegraph to his office. By 1860 *The Times* was publishing daily 'weather forecasts'.

And it was in that year that Darwin at last published his *Origin of Species*. Fitzroy had become much more religious since their voyage together. He was now dismayed, once holding a huge bible up in public, imploring people to ignore his old friend's new and dangerous theory. Five years later, just as he had always feared, he committed suicide.

However, but for Fitzroy's melancholic tendency, Darwin would never have gone on that famous voyage and we might never have heard of either of them.

Howard **FLOREY** & Boris **CHAIN**

Today we take antibiotics largely for granted. They have made our lives infinitely less dangerous and much of the expansion of our whole giant pharmaceutical industry stems from one discovery, the 'wonder drug', penicillin. It is a sobering thought that many of us might not even be here but for penicillin, because our parents or grandparents could have died from something as trivial as a cut finger.

And most of us know the name of the man who discovered penicillin – because of a legendary event. Professor Alexander Fleming was later to say, 'When I woke up just after dawn on 28th September, 1928, I certainly didn't plan to revolutionise all medicine by discovering the world's first antibiotic, or bacteria killer. But I suppose that was exactly what I did'.

Fleming, a brilliant but somewhat untidy scientist, returned from holiday to discover that one of his petri dishes containing *Staphylococci* had been left open and was contaminated by a blue-grey mould, *Penicillium notatum*, and that it had destroyed the closest bacteria. He experimented with his 'mould juice', eventually calling it 'Penicillin'. However, while finding that it could affect the bacteria causing scarlet fever, pneumonia, meningitis, diphtheria and gonorrhoea, Fleming realised that cultivating penicillin would be very difficult, and felt it might not last long enough in the human body to work. Thus he gave up on it and moved on to other projects. Later, when famous, he was modest about 'the Fleming Myth' and praised the two men who were to transform his laboratory curiosity into a practical drug.

Fleming gave up on Penicillin

These two worked at Oxford University – Howard Florey and Boris Chain. Raised in Adelaide, Florey was later described by his Prime Minister as 'the most important man born in Australia'. Boris Chain (right) was one of those Germans who fortuitously escaped Hitler's anti-Jewish persecution and would join England's war effort. With war looming, Florey and Chain managed to isolate penicillin and produce it in small quantities, at first using a bizarre array of culture vessels,  including baths and milk churns, soon succeeding in protecting mice against dreaded *Streptococci*. Treating a policeman scratched by a thorn rose, after great improvement to his huge abscesses and swollen face, they ran out of the precious penicillin and he relapsed and died. Sadly, with tiny quantities to work with, only children could be treated.

To protect against the impending masses of war wounds, penicillin would have to be produced in huge quantities. The overstretched British chemical companies could play a part, but they would have to turn to the still-peaceful United States. Florey arrived in October 1941 for inconclusive meetings with the drug companies Merck, Squibb, Lilly and Pfizer. But his second meetings in December were galvanized by the Japanese attack on Pearl Harbor eight days before. Now there was urgency, but it was not going to be easy. As one American put it, 'the mould is as temperamental as an opera singer, the extraction is murder, the purification invites disaster and the assay is unsatisfactory'.

However, moulds discovered on a rotting cantaloupe melon doubled the yield, then corn steep liquid improved this by nearly twenty times. By 1943, 21 billion units of penicillin were mass-produced, jumping to 1,663 billion the next year – just in time for D-Day. By 1945, when Fleming, Florey and Chain were awarded the Nobel Prize for their penicillin efforts, there was at last enough for civilian use.

Penicillin, along with its derivatives, has proved to be the most important drug ever created, estimated to have saved 80 million lives so far. While we all owe an immense debt to that chance discovery by Fleming, it was the dedicated work by the far less well-known Florey and Chain that really made it possible.

Howard Florey, honoured on an Australian banknote

? Tommy **FLOWERS**

Because of strict security, it took decades for the secrets about the fabulous successes of Britain's code-breaking at Bletchley Park to leak out. Now many people know about Alan Turing and the way that his ' bombes' had beaten the Germans 'Enigma' machines, providing vital information to the Allies' military leaders.

The Germans had been over-confident about Enigma, with its odds of being broken at 158 million, million to one. However, for communication at the highest level between Hitler and 30 key centres, they had created the *Lorenz SZ 40/42*, with 12 rotors instead of Enigma's three. Much harder to break, it would, however, give a real insight into Hitler's intentions. At Bletchley, a young mathematical genius, Bill Tutte, began to make progress, aided in August 1941 by a lazy Lorenz operator in Athens, who sent the same long message twice to Vienna without changing his rotor settings. Gradually and laboriously messages were revealed, with the greatest coup being to warn the Russians of the crucial German attack at Kursk. But obviously some faster method of beating Lorenz was required.

The solution came from a General Post Office engineer called Tommy Flowers. A quiet, hesitant man born in London's East End, Flowers first helped to build 'Heath Robinson', an electro-mechanical machine designed to speed up Lorenz decoding. But Flowers said he could do better and build something that could read 5,000 characters a second. For this he proposed to use 1,800 valves, or vacuum tubes, which caused scepticism at Bletchley, but Flowers pointed out that the Post Office routinely used thousands of them, and if left on permanently, they were reliable. Thus was born

'Colossus', the world's first semi-programmable computer, which Flowers partly paid for himself. His team at Dollis Hill built the first 'Colossus' in eleven months and it arrived at Bletchley Park in January 1944. The second 'Colossus' (right), with 2,400 valves began working there on June 1st 1944 just in time to reveal to Eisenhower that Hitler had been fooled that the Normandy invasion was just a feint. It was the first of many such crucial successes.

Ten 'Colossi' were built and two survived the closedown of Bletchley Park and the destruction of its evidence. These two formed the backbone of the Cold War code-breaking efforts of the new centre at GCHQ in Cheltenham – right up to 1960.

In 1946, the Americans proudly announced the creation of ENIAC, 'the world's first semi-programmable computer'. Neither Flowers, nor any other veteran of Bletchley Park, were allowed by the Official Secrets Act to disabuse them.

At about the same time, Flowers, who had never even been fully reimbursed for his own investment, asked the Bank of England for a loan to develop a 'Colossus-type' computer, but was turned down because the bank did not think such a machine would work! Flowers, ironically, could not, of course, reveal that he had already built several.

Tommy Flowers died in 1998, and for a while was lost to history. Only recently, have people begun to realise that it was he, not Alan Turing, who was the 'father of modern computing'.

William **FOX**

Most of us are familiar enough with the name of 20th Century Fox and the searchlights that have preceded so many of our favourite films. We may also know that Fox Broadcasting is today one of the most successful parts of Rupert Murdoch's media empire. But who on earth was Fox? Sadly, the owner of that name,

William Fox, was condemned to obscurity by film industry chicanery and real bad luck.

William Fox was born Vilmos Fried in Hungary in 1879, arriving in America as a baby, he was called after his mother's family, Fuchs. Like so many in the early film community in Hollywood, Fox had no experience in film-making but used his success in textiles to purchase his first cinema.

In 1925 he obtained the rights to the successful sound-on-film system and his Fox Film Corporation became a major force in Hollywood. Then in 1927, Fox was offered the opportunity to buy into Metro-Goldwyn-Mayer. However, Louis B. Mayer, who was not actually a shareholder in MGM, was desperate to block the move, and used his political connections to cite anti-trust laws. In normal circumstances Fox could have successfully fought the move in the courts, but fate intervened. Fox was badly hurt in a car crash. By the time he recovered, his world had been overwhelmed by the 'Wall Street crash', which wiped out his fortune. Far from taking over MGM, he struggled for years to fight off bankruptcy. Eventually he lost control of his company and even went to jail briefly for trying to bribe a judge.

Poor Fox was forced to watch from the sidelines as Fox Film Corporation was merged with Twentieth Century Pictures to become 20th Century Fox. Three decades after his death in 1952, the company that bears his name was merged into Rupert Murdoch's empire and continues as Fox Broadcasting and the Fox Network which competes successfully with CBS, ABC and NBC, and is well-known for everything from *The Simpsons* to *American Idol*.

William Fox died in 1952 in New York. Sadly, but typically, nobody from Hollywood attended his funeral.

? Rosalind **FRANKLIN**

It seems that Rosalind Franklin was not the easiest of people to deal with. And her abrasiveness would ensure that this great scientist would be largely written out of the public's awareness of one of the world's greatest discoveries – DNA – with its enormous implications for genetics and biochemistry.

Born in 1920 into a prosperous London Jewish family, Rosalind attended St. Paul's, then one of the few girls' schools that taught physics and chemistry. Her banker father was rather against higher education for women, but eventually she graduated from Cambridge and then went to Paris to become an expert in X-ray diffraction techniques.

It was this expertise that took her to King's College, London where John Randall wanted her to take over the diffraction work on DNA or *Deoxyribonucleic Acid*. Unfortunately Randall had neglected to inform the incumbent scientist, Maurice Wilkins, of her role, who returned to his laboratory and assumed Dr. Franklin was a new junior technician. Having started on the wrong foot, things did not improve. Perhaps propelled by the incredibly male chauvinist attitude at King's, Franklin tended to stare hard at people, speaking fast, and was impatient and confrontational. Wilkins, by contrast, was very shy, slow-speaking and could not look anyone in the eye. In spite of their differences Franklin continued to work on DNA, and with her cutting edge photography was close to publishing a paper describing its double-helix structure.

However there were others working on DNA, notably Francis Crick and James Watson at Cambridge. James Watson was, at 23, twelve years younger than Francis Crick when he arrived at Cambridge. Born in Chicago of Scottish and Irish parents, he was a controversial figure – sometimes amusing, sometimes offensive or politically incorrect. Calling Franklin 'Rosie' was not going to help.

Francis Crick's studies had been interrupted by World War II, during which he developed torpedoes. Both men were fascinated by DNA, and both were worried that the American scientist, Linus Pauling, might discover DNA's structure first. Luckily for them, Pauling, regarded as politically suspect, was not permitted to leave America and therefore could not see the British research that might have given him crucial insight.

One day Watson came to London and met Rosalind Franklin to talk about keeping ahead of Pauling. She gave him a typically hard time. Watson backed off and stumbled across Wilkins, who had heard the argument. Wilkins, exasperated by his colleague, showed Watson, without her permission, a key Franklin photograph – the legendary No. 51. '*Our dark lady is leaving us this week*', Wilkins wrote to Watson on March 7th, 1953. The way was clear for the Cambridge pair to complete their work, and on April 25th they published in *Nature* magazine, the double-helix of DNA. Franklin's article appeared, but merely in support.

Rosalind Franklin moved on to Birkbeck College to work on other projects. But two years later she was diagnosed with cancer and died in April 1958.

In 1962, Watson, Crick and Wilkins were awarded the 'Nobel Prize in Physiology or Medicine' for their DNA work. The unfortunate Rosalind Franklin sadly could not be honoured because Nobel prizes cannot be given posthumously.

Perhaps if this '*dark lady*', way before her time, had been a little more temperate in her human relationships, we might have known more about her and her vital role in one of the great steps forward in science. How tragic that such able females were often denied their place in history.

Josef **FRANTISEK**

In the long history of warfare, few heroes have volunteered to fight for more than their own country. Josef Frantisek did – for four nations, one after the other. Josef, the son of a carpenter, grew up near Prostejov in Czechoslovakia, perilously close to a menacing Nazi Germany. Aged 20, he joined the Czech Air Force as a pilot. His ill-disciplined approach, including lateness and drunken fights, nearly saw him kicked out, but because in the air he was exceptional, his superiors made him a fighter pilot.

Stationed near Prague in 1938, with Hitler threatening to invade, the Czechs waited to fight the Luftwaffe, but the spineless betrayal by France and Britain at Munich first gave away half their country, and a year later Germany occupied the rest. Frantisek did not wait for internment, but flew north and joined the Polish Air Force just in time for the German invasion on 1st September, 1939. After three weeks of desperate fighting, the last six aircraft, three piloted by Czechs, flew to Romania. Interned, they escaped, Frantisek deciding to head for France.

There he joined his third airforce, *L'Armée de l'Air*, volunteering to fly once again with his friends, the Poles. Like them, he had little reason to love the Germans, who once again in May 1940 invaded with the usual swarms of screaming dive-bombers and fighters. Frantisek is credited with shooting down 11 of them, receiving the *Croix de Guerre* for his actions.

With France overwhelmed, Frantisek took ship to Falmouth and by August was with 303 Squadron, a Polish unit based at Northolt. He arrived just in time to play his own legendary role in the 'Battle of Britain'.

Now the Luftwaffe pilots met their match – modern Spitfires and Hurricanes in a radar-controlled, integrated defence system. On September 2nd, the Hurricanes of 303 Squadron were scrambled three times and Frantisek shot down a Messerschmitt Bf 109 fighter, repeating the exploit the next day. Three days later it was a bomber and a fighter, just five minutes apart. And it was the same again three days after that.

In desperate fighting against experienced enemies, several of his Polish friends died. One day Frantisek – with wings, fuel tank, engine and radiator full of holes – landed in a cloud of smoke in a cabbage field in Kent. Like any other commuter, he calmly caught the train from Brighton to London to go back to work.

His score mounting, it became obvious that his ill-disciplined approach was successful, sometimes leaving the squadron to hunt down German planes heading for home, with tired crews, low on fuel and ammunition. His Squadron Leader cleverly declared Frantisek a 'squadron guest' and, as a spare pilot, he was free to continue his lone wolf '*metoda Frantiszka*'.

His best day was September 11th, with two fighters and a bomber. The Poles and their Czech guest brought a murderous determination to the 'Battle'. Air Marshal Dowding had, cautiously, released them late, but 303 Squadron, with 126 'kills', was the most successful

Courtesy of Tony Cowland

squadron in the Battle. Frantisek was the highest scoring pilot of any nationality during that September, with 17 confirmed victories and one probable.

But just after the Battle, after a routine patrol on October 9th, Josef Frantisek was found dead in a field, his neck broken, near his crashed Hurricane. It may have been extreme fatigue or perhaps, once again, lack of discipline – maybe flying an aerobatic stunt to impress a girlfriend.

Nevertheless he was certainly a hero for any of the four countries that he served.

Alan **FREED**

Curiously, the first use of the phrase 'rock 'n' roll' was by railroad crews in the early 1900s, complaining about the unpleasant swaying motion of large articulated steam engines. And in the 1934 film *Merry-Go-Round*, the Boswell sisters had sung a nautical number called 'Rock and Roll.' However, by the 1940s, the term was much more widely used by the African-American community as slang for sex.

The musical use of the term 'Rock'n' Roll' in the 1950s can be put down to one man, the disc jockey Alan Freed – born in Pennsylvania in 1922 to a Welsh mother and a Lithuanian father. When the family moved to Ohio, Alan showed an early enthusiasm for music, forming a school band called 'The Sultans of Swing', in which he played the trombone. However, his ambition to become a professional bandleader was wrecked by an ear infection, although his interest in radio landed him several jobs in small radio stations in Akron, Ohio.

When Freed moved to Cleveland, and to its WXEL-TV station, a new idea emerged. His friend Leo Mintz, the owner of a record store, pointed out that lots of white teenagers were buying 'Rhythm & Blues', normally regarded as 'race music' for African-American audiences. He persuaded Freed to try Rhythm & Blues on his station, who went on air on July 11th 1951, calling himself 'Moondog'. The show was an instant success and forced the other stations catering to white audiences to follow suit.

One of the key reasons for his success was Alan Freed's clever name change for the music. A black vocal group, 'The Dominoes' had just topped the 'R & B' chart with *Sixty Minute Man*. Its highly suggestive lyrics included the words 'Rock 'n' Roll' – with their usual meaning. This gave Freed an idea. To describe 'Rhythm & Blues' he now substituted 'Rock'n' Roll Party'. The irony of its usual connotation in the black community seemed to be lost on his white teenage audience. In 1952, he staged a 'Moondog Coronation Ball' in Cleveland. It had top black performers and was a sell-out, with a two thirds white audience.

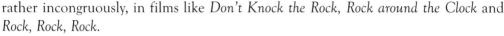

Freed then moved his show to New York's WINS radio station, where it went straight to Number One. He also staged reviews at the Brooklyn Paramount Theatre and even appeared, rather incongruously, in films like *Don't Knock the Rock*, *Rock around the Clock* and *Rock, Rock, Rock*.

Freed's career went downhill in the late 1950s. His ABC national television show was abruptly cancelled in 1957 when ABC's affiliate stations in the South violently objected to the black star Frankie Lyman actually dancing with a white girl!

A year later, his Boston Arena Rock 'n' Roll show developed into a riot for which he was blamed. Then, among dozens in the business, he was the only one found guilty of accepting favours for playing records and was indicted for tax evasion. Under the strain, he drank more and more and eventually died a broken man, aged just 43.

But in his brief career, Alan Freed had transformed a very American form of music into a worldwide phenomenon. He had even made its name half respectable.

Claudius **GALEN**

When William Harvey in 1628 published his breakthrough revelation that the heart is a pump, he was rewarded by vicious criticism from his fellow physicians. Why? He was questioning the ancient teachings of the great Claudius Galen, dead for fourteen hundred years.

'Galen of Pergamon' was admittedly a giant of a man – a physician, surgeon and philosopher and polymath who contributed a huge amount to the knowledge of anatomy, physiology, pharmacology and neurology in the ancient world.

Born in 129 AD into a wealthy family, in the cultural city of Pergamon, Galen travelled widely, studying medicine and philosophy before becoming the physician to a prestigious gladiator school, giving him plenty of practice in surgery and healing. He was later the physician to three Roman Emperors – Marcus Aurelius, Commodus and Septimus Severus.

In spite of his vast amount of dissections and excellent experimental work, Galen unfortunately supported Hippocrates' theory that the body is ruled by the four 'humours': blood, phlegm, yellow bile and black bile. Too much of each was considered to make people either too sanguine, phlegmatic, choleric or melancholic. After two thousand years of faithful adherence to this belief by the medical profession (and widespread public acceptance, not least by Shakespeare), this, of course, was proved to be a complete medical 'dead end'.

Galen was splendidly over-confident. 'Never have I gone astray whether in treatment or prognosis, as have so many other physicians of great repute'. Unfortunately, in the case of the heart he had indeed gone astray, postulating that the liver continuously made large amounts of blood and the body then absorbed them, and that the heart existed to heat the body and the lungs to cool the heart.

Harvey looked at such long-accepted theories with scepticism. Highly respected as the Court physician to King James I and his son Charles I, he experimented for twelve years. Having deduced that the function of the heart was to pump blood, his own calculations showed that it would pump a fifth of a ton daily, impossible for the body to produce and then consume. In 1628 he published *De Motu Cordis et Sanguinis*, correctly explaining that the blood worked in a closed system.

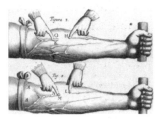

In spite of his standing, Harvey was pilloried for questioning the great Galen. Some doctors were so stubbornly illogical as to vow that they would 'rather err with Galen than proclaim the truth with Harvey'. The controversy raged for twenty years. With the realisation that the body only contains eight pints of blood, the practice of lancing, bleeding, and applying leeches 'to let out bad blood' should have stopped. But we find that even 55 years later Charles II was being bled on his deathbed several times, which no doubt hastened his demise, one of the last victims of Galen's muddled thinking.

Marcel-Bruno **GENSOUL**

Britain in 1940 had her back to the wall. Her pilots were battling the Luftwaffe, many of her ships had been sunk off Norway and then Dunkirk, invasion was expected in days and France had capitulated. A vital part of France's fleet, the fourth largest in the world, was moored at Mers-el-Kebir, in French Algeria. Winston Churchill knew that it was crucial that this fleet should not fall into the hands of the Germans. If it had, Britain might have lost control of the Mediterranean, the Middle East oilfields and perhaps even the war.

'Force H' arrived off Mers-el-Kebir, commanded by a reluctant Vice-Admiral Sir James Somerville, with one aircraft carrier, two battleships, one battlecruiser, two cruisers and eleven destroyers. Somerville had been ordered to deliver a carefully worded ultimatum to the commander of the French Fleet, Admiral Marcel-Bruno Gensoul. It was to be firm, but very friendly and polite, and offer four options:

–*Sail your ships to British harbours and join the fight alongside Britain.*

–*Sail to a British port, from which the crews can be repatriated.*

–*Sail to the West Indies, with the ships entrusted to the neutral United States for the duration of the war.*

–*Scuttle your ships.*

If none of these were adopted, Somerville would be forced to open fire.

Somerville sent Captain Cedric 'Hooky' Holland, commanding the aircraft-carrier *Ark Royal*, in to negotiate with Admiral Gensoul, because Holland was very pro-French, and spoke the language excellently – having been Naval Attaché in Paris.

However, things were to go very wrong. First, the French were not as keen on their former ally as the British thought they were. Dunkirk, for them, was a cowardly retreat and a betrayal. There was, sadly, an atmosphere of touchy mistrust.

Then Gensoul, with fatal Gallic pride, huffily refused to negotiate with someone junior to him, sending his deputy to meet Captain Holland. Eventually, he relented and Holland boarded his flagship, the *Dunkerque*. There, in the stifling heat of the battened-down ship, they negotiated for two hours. But, unknown to Holland, Gensoul had made a terrible and fateful error. Inexplicably, even though it was close to one of the options the French had been considering, the most attractive option c), allowing the French to sail to the United States, was never sent to Gensoul's rather anti-British Marine Minister, Admiral Darlan. Years later, Gensoul was to admit, '*I still cannot explain why I did not do it, or why my officers did not draw it to my attention. I think it was the obsession that haunted me that I was being offered two alternatives, either to sink my ships or see them sunk by the British*'.

Whatever the reasons, it had the effect of Darlan ordering French ships to rally to Gensoul – a signal immediately intercepted by the British. Churchill became impatient. Captain Holland saluted, with tears in his eyes, as he left the *Dunkerque*, because he 'could not believe this was happening'.

At 5:15 pm, Somerville was forced to give a 15 minutes ultimatum; 'Accept, or I must sink your ships'. At 5:54 pm, the *Hood*, *Valiant* and *Resolution* opened fire with

huge 15-inch shells. In ten minutes, several of the French ships were sunk in the harbour, with 1,300 Frenchmen dead. The battle cruiser *Strasbourg* and four destroyers escaped to France (above) where, ironically, in 1942, the Germans tried to seize them, and the Vichy government kept its promise and scuttled them.

This one-sided and murderous battle between two former allies horrified all but the Germans. Somerville wrote to his wife: '*And so that filthy job is over at last. An absolutely bloody business.*' Captain Holland asked to be relieved of command of *Ark Royal*, ending his naval ambitions.

The Free French leader, General Charles de Gaulle, in his broadcast to the French people, called the action 'deplorable and detestable', but he added that it was better the ships be sunk rather than join the enemy. The most positive influence was actually on American opinion. The startling ruthlessness of the decision against a former ally and friend convinced Roosevelt and his government of Churchill's and Britain's absolute determination, and strengthened their desire to help. The short-term tragedy caused by that missing clause helped the Allies in the long-term to win the war.

? Carter **GLASS**

During the banking and financial crises of the last few years, we have heard a lot of pundits say that traditional commercial banking and the riskier investment banking should be separated and that 'we should bring back something like Glass-Steagall'.

Carter Glass was born in Virginia in 1858 and made his name as a reporter, eventually owning the Lynchburg News. However, although a Democrat, his actions and views were not exactly democratic. Questioned about his 1902 proposed poll tax on voters, he fired back 'Discrimination? Why that is exactly what we propose. To remove every negro voter that can be gotten rid of legally'.

Luckily for his reputation, we now know of two, rather more honourable, acts which bear his name. The first was the 1923 Glass-Owen Act when he was Secretary of the Treasury and which created the Federal Reserve System, America's central bank. Twenty years later came the Glass-Steagall Act, which as a Senator he sponsored with Alabama Representative, Henry Steagall.

The 1929 'Wall Street Crash' and the great Depression that followed had devastated the American banking system and over 5,000 banks had gone bust. There were many beneficial reforms in the Glass-Steagall Act, but the one we now remember is the mandatory separation of the traditional, deposit-taking, High Street commercial banking from the riskier aspects of stockbroking and investment banking.

The system that evolved worked well for decades but was repealed by the Clinton administration in 1999. The bankers were delighted. Now they could all participate in the enormous bonuses and huge salaries enjoyed by the investment side of the business. Investment banks exploded in size and enormous numbers of extraordinary and opaque financial products emerged, many of which the traditional bankers could neither control – or even understand. The public was amazed to find that their banks, both in America and in the rest of the world, were threatened by exposure to something called 'sub prime mortgages' in America, which had somehow been bundled up and sold on to other banks all over the world as valuable investment products. This was only exposed when the US housing market collapsed, and the mortgages, far from being assets, became worthless. To rescue the depositors' savings on both sides of the Atlantic, we watched as once respectable institutions were effectively nationalised, merged or disappeared. In 2008, the banking crisis and the stock market crisis infected each other, pulling down the world's entire economy.

The banks are no longer conservative icons of respect. Greedy 'fast buck' attitudes have proved toxic to reputations, while the rest of us suffer from the results of their avarice.

Joseph **GLIDDEN**

On the American Great Plains in the 1860s there was a huge problem. After the Civil War, the population was expanding and hungry, but the days of the great free-ranging cattle herds being rounded-up and driven a thousand miles up the trails to the railroads were over. Ranches had to be permanent and the cattle somehow had to be contained.

In Europe, there were stonewalls or wooden fences, but on the prairie there were no stones and few trees. Smooth wire was tried, but the thick-skinned longhorn cattle simply knocked the fences aside. Several people now simultaneously came up with the idea of placing barbs in the wire. One was Joseph Glidden, an Illinois farmer who had seen a wooden rail with nails protruding from it, displayed at a county fair. This inspired him to experiment.

Back home in his kitchen, he used a coffee grinder as a mechanism to twist the barbs, spacing them along a two-strand wire. This was a simple enough idea, so hundreds of patents for barbed wire were soon filed by other people. Indeed, it took almost two decades for Glidden to be legally declared 'The Winner'.

But whatever fights occurred in the courts, they were as nothing compared with the conflicts over the wire itself. Religious groups noted the pain suffered by the cows on their first encounters with the barbs, calling barbed wire 'The Devil's Rope'. The

Native Americans also hated the invention, watching as the wire protected the hated 'Iron Horse's' railroad tracks that were invading their land.

But the real fighting occurred between those who wanted to enclose and those who wanted the cattle to continue to roam. Lethal 'Fence Wars' broke out, of which the most famous was the 'Lincoln County Cattle War' in Texas, which launched the murderous career of a teenage William Bonney – 'Billy the Kid'.

The rapid commercial success of the wire was inspired by a brilliant young salesman, John 'Bet a Million' Gates, who allegedly had earned his name by betting on which raindrop would slide down a railway car window fastest. He now won a bet from a group of sceptical Texas ranchers that even the most maddened longhorn would not break through a wire corral. Like Joseph Glidden, thanks to barbed wire, Gates would become one of the richest men in America. Soon barbed wire, along with the rifle, the six-shooter, the telegraph and the railroad, had 'won the West'.

Other countries quickly adopted the invention, and in 1885 the longest barbed wire fence was erected across 2,400 miles of Australia – the 'Dingo Fence'.

Unfortunately, barbed wire was used not just for the beneficial restraint of animals. In the Boer War, the British strung hundreds of miles of it between regular concrete block houses to divide up the veldt and stop the free movement of the Boers, using more such wire to imprison the Boer women and children in the very first 'concentration camps'. The barbed wire fences at Auschwitz still stand in tragic testimony as to where that led.

It was the British, too, who in 1888 officially noted that barbed wire offered protection from attack by infantry, and especially, cavalry. Ten years later, Theodore Roosevelt was the very first American commander to deploy it, to protect the flanks of his 'Rough Riders' against the Spanish in Cuba.

Russian barbed wire, now combined with machine-guns, killed 60,000 Japanese in their *successful* assault on Port Arthur in 1905. Evidently not enough strategists noticed, because a decade later it was barbed wire, now in huge concertina rolls, that solidified the horrors of trench warfare in the First World War. Before any attack, 'cutting the wire' soon became the first essential objective of artillery fire. It was often unsuccessful. On just the first day of the battle of the Somme, 19,000 British troops were killed and 38,000 wounded, victims of that same deadly combination of barbed wire and machine-guns.

The obvious weapon to crush and negate the wire was the tank, which the Germans first called, in 42 letters, *Schutzengrabenvernichtungspanzerkraftwagen*, or 'Firing Trench Destroying Armoured Motor Vehicle'. What they really meant was 'wire destroying'. Sadly, tanks came too late for the millions of men of all nations who died, helplessly shot to pieces on the dreaded wire.

For some, Joseph Glidden's invention had been a blessing. For others, it was a curse – truly 'The Devil's Rope'.

Thomas **GLOVER**

In Japan's Nagasaki there is a house visited by two million tourists a year. Looking out over the sea, it is the 'Glover House', the first western-style house to be built in Japan and a monument to a Scotsman who had a remarkable influence on that nation's destiny.

Thomas Blake Glover was born in Aberdeenshire in 1838, one of eight children, and the son of a coastguard officer. After working in Nagasaki for the trading giant Jardine Matheson, itself founded by two Scotsmen, he left to found, at just 23, his own Glover Trading Company. His first (and illegal) success was the sale of ships, guns and gunpowder to the Samurai clans who were trying to topple the ruling Tokugawa Shogunate. Luckily for Glover, with his help, the clans succeeded and became the powers in the Meiji Restoration.

What then occurred was extraordinary, because in an era of anti-western fervour in Japan, the 'Scottish Samurai' as he was soon dubbed, played a huge role in Japan's rapid development from a feudal state to a thriving western style economy. At a time when it was forbidden to leave Japan, he smuggled out bright young executives to be trained in London, developed the first coal mine and first dry dock, brought in the first steam locomotive and delivered the first modern armoured warships — built in Aberdeen. Almost single-handedly, he was paving the way, 30 years later, for Japan's victory over the Russians and her accession as a great world power.

Glover's more modern legacy stems from his founding of the giant Mitsubishi conglomerate, first famous for shipbuilding (and perhaps infamous for the Zero fighter) and now for cars and a myriad of other products. Another market leader that he created was Kirin beer, and on the labels a mystical creature sports a moustache like Glover's. Each year, to this day. there is a ceremony on his birthday at the foreign cemetery at Nagasaki and a can of Kirin Beer is placed upon his gravestone.

Never in history has a foreigner arrived and transformed a nation in such a way, and it is little surprise the Japanese gave him 'The Order of the Rising Sun'. Nobody had helped it to rise as high.

Manuel de **GODOY**

Lust has played its role in shaping the destinies of many nations, but seldom as disastrously as with Queen Maria Luisa of Spain, wife of Carlos IV, an amiable, weak king who preferred hunting to either ruling or controlling his wife. By all reports she was not particularly attractive, with a beaky nose, pinched mouth and beady eyes. However, this did not seem to stop her from bedding a procession of nobility, politicians and even lusty soldiers.

Eventually in 1788, her eyes lit on a new member of her Royal Bodyguard, Manuel de Godoy, the 17 year-old son of an impoverished aristocrat, a well-built, handsome and rather vacuous youth, sixteen years her junior. Within a year, this unlikely object of her affections was made a Colonel, aged just 18, and loaded with grand titles. Two years later, almost incredibly, he was promoted to General by her very obviously compliant husband, the King.

His frequent promotions and favours plainly showed the huge influence he had over the royal couple, and it was never very difficult to work out why. Prime Minister Floridablanca went as far as to accuse him of having an affair with the Queen. But the next year he fell from office, as did his successor Aranda. Now the besotted Queen did something truly silly and dangerous. She not only persuaded her foolish husband to make Godoy a Duke, but also Prime Minister. This was a post he was to hold for sixteen years. For Spain, those years proved nothing short of a catastrophe.

Completely out of his depth, Godoy managed to become embroiled, with little success, in the French Revolution; then to cede, in 1800, Spain's precious Louisiana Territory to the French (and thence to the United States); to wreck Spain's economy by declaring war on England, thus cutting Spain off from its rich South American colonies; to have his fleet destroyed at Trafalgar in 1805 and his country invaded by Napoleon in 1808. Such was the string of catastrophies that Godoy managed to reduce Spain from one of the richest world powers to an 'also ran'.

The Spanish people were so understandably disgusted that they rose up in revolt, and to save Godoy's life, the kindly King tried to abdicate in favour of his son Ferdinand V11. However, Napoleon stepped in and forced Godoy to watch the ceremony in Bayonne where he took on the crown of Spain himself. Thus the over-indulgent King and his love-besotted Queen were deposed and sent into exile, where Godoy joined them.

The shamed and foolish Godoy was to live on in France and Italy in both poverty and disgrace for another fifty-eight years. Every day of them, he probably regretted joining the Bodyguard.

Berry **GORDY**

The French explorer Antoine Cadillac landed on a deserted bank of the Detroit River in 1701. He could scarcely have imagined the music in the city there two centuries later.

Detroit passed from the French to the British, and in 1796 became part of the United States. In 1837, the new state of Michigan abolished slavery, and Detroit became important on the escape route for slaves fleeing from the South – the 'Underground Railroad'.

Always a haven for African-Americans, Detroit was then transformed forever by the automobile industry, and especially by Henry Ford, who deliberately recruited robust plantation workers for his new 'assembly line' methods. Detroit's African-American population rocketed, with the employment first provided by Ford, then General Motors, and later Chrysler. The city had truly become the home of the gigantic American car industry – 'Motortown'. Not surprisingly with such a population, Detroit also became a centre for music; Blues, Gospel, Jazz and Jump Blues.

Berry Gordy, grandson of a white plantation owner and one of his black slaves,

'Cross over' black music to white audiences

was a car assembly line worker, and then a jazz shop owner. In 1959, he borrowed $800 from his family to start a record company called 'Tamla', later 'Motown', in a modest house at 2648 Grand Boulevard, which he less modestly called Hitsville USA. His ambition was to 'cross over' black music to white audiences. Elvis Presley had softened up the market by singing Rhythm and Blues like a black man. And the Rolling Stones used the songs of Muddy Waters, Bo Didley and other black bluesmen. Gordy felt he could go a lot further.

Cleverly, he hired experts to train his artistes as professionals, with coaching including deportment, dancing and enunciation. Soon, all through the '60s and into the '70s, star after star with hit after hit were pouring out of 'Motown'; Smokey Robinson, Stevie Wonder, The Contours, The Temptations, The Isley Brothers, The Marvelettes, Gladys Knight and The Pips, The Spinners, Martha Reeves and the Vandellas, Mary Wells, Jimmy Ruffin, The Jackson Five, Marvin Gaye and Tammy Terrell, Brenda Holloway, Kim Weston and, of course, The Supremes.

Diana Ross lived near Gordy's friend Smokey Robinson and worked as a secretary at Motown before she, Mary Wilson and Florence Ballard were allowed to record 'Where Did Our Love Go?' – a smash hit that was followed by five consecutive 'number one' records, a feat unmatched even by The Beatles. Multiple

Diana Ross of the Supremes

spots on *The Ed Sullivan Show* helped The Supremes to become glamorous role models for African-American women, inspiring among others, a young Oprah Winfrey. 'Motown' rivalled the British invasion of The Beatles and The Rolling Stones with The Sound of Young America.

Sadly the glamorous, positive and hip image created by 'Motown' did not always reflect the real motor town. In 1967, a police raid on a drinking club started a riot that exploded into one of the biggest in American history. Among those who eventually fled the city was none other than Berry Gordy, who moved the company to Hollywood in 1972, eventually selling it for $61 million.

Detroit suffered badly when the American car industry declined. But at least the Motown Museum is still there, at 2648 Grand Boulevard – a memorial to one of the most innovative American musical periods, and a form of music that is still very much with us.

John **GORRIE** and Willis **CARRIER**

Thousands of years after we learned to use fire to heat things up, people turned to trying to cool things down. The Chinese were first to flood fields to form ice for food preservation. The Turks brought their system of storing ice to the borders of Europe, and soon most French chateaux or English mansions had insulated 'icehouses'. Roman aqueducts fed cooling fountains and Arab wind towers captured the breeze.

In America, frozen water from northern lakes was cut into blocks and transported south by steamboat so that 'Southern gentlefolk' could sip iced mint juleps, even in summer. Whole new food industries in meat, fish and fruit were created by refrigerated railroad cars, 180,000 of them, cooled by ice hoppers. Fast 'reefer' trains had priority over passenger expresses.

Mechanical refrigeration, rather than expensive seasonal ice, had been examined by many pioneers, mostly British and French. But it was two Americans who helped launch the refrigeration revolution – the 'fathers of cool'.

Dr. John Gorrie lived in Florida, studying the ravaging tropical diseases of yellow fever and malaria, whose name, 'mal-aria' in Italian, reflected the erroneous belief that 'bad air' created the disease. He tried to make his patients better, or more comfortable, by suspending buckets of ice above their beds. However, he soon turned to creating ice artificially, eventually patenting a refrigeration machine which worked by the compression and rapid expansion of gases – exactly like modern refrigeration. He made ice, but never made any money out of it. It would take another inventor to take cooling to a new level.

Willis Carrier was born on a farm in Erie County, New York in 1876. His mother, a Quaker, happened to have a love for disassembling things such as sewing machines and clocks to see how they worked, and she passed this on to her son.

Willis was determined to become an engineer. Graduating from Cornell in 1902, he joined a heating company, earning just $10 a week. One customer was Sackett-Wilhelms, a Brooklyn printing company, and he noted that the expansion of the paper caused by varying heat and humidity was playing havoc with the pinpoint calibration needed for colour printing. His 'air-conditioning' solution solved the problem perfectly, and the word quickly spread to other companies requiring high manufacturing quality – film, tobacco, food-processing and textiles. He patented his 'Apparatus for Treating Air' in 1906 and with his own company laid down the four principles for modern air-conditioning:

Willis Carrier with his first 'Apparatus for Treating Air'

temperature control, humidity control, airflow regulation and air cleaning.

The invention's advantages for human comfort soon became apparent. When Carrier's air-conditioning was installed in a Detroit department store, business boomed, as did the summer attendance in the Rivoli Theater in New York. Competitive success meant that banks, hotels, theatres, shops and passenger railroads could soon not live without it. And, with such comfort in public buildings, having houses equally cool and pleasant could not be far behind. Carrier's home air-conditioner, the 'Weather-maker' was launched in 1928 and was an immediate success.

In warm climates, air-conditioning would rapidly be regarded as essential and its influence cannot be overstated. It has powered an economic and political shift, not only in America's 'Sun Belt', but all over the world. People can now live and work in places that were once virtually uninhabitable because of heat and humidity. Without it, whole industries would be impossible, notably computing or deep mining, and shiny desert miracles like Dubai could not exist.

And in Spain, sadly for many, nobody has to go home for an afternoon siesta any more.

James **GRAHAM**

Thousands of brave men of many nations fought at Waterloo. But the one the Duke of Wellington singled out as 'the bravest man at Waterloo' was Corporal James Graham of the Coldstream Guards, born in County Monaghan, Ireland.

The brilliant, ambitious, destructive Napoleon had finally abdicated and been exiled to Elba. Escaping, he marched into France with more and more troops joining him. In Paris, he offered the Allies peace, which was rejected, so he swiftly devoted his huge energy to rebuilding his veteran army into a formidable force, ready to strike at the foreigners invading France. In the distance were the Russians and the Austrians, closer were 128,000 Prussians under Blücher, as was a polyglot army under the Duke of Wellington, of 106,000 Dutch, Belgians and Germans and less than 32,000 British. Napoleon decided that he must first destroy his nearest enemies. He must never let Blücher and Wellington combine.

Napoleon secretly crossed the Sambre River at Charleroi, taking Wellington and Blücher by surprise. The French were just held at Quatre Bras, but at Ligny the Prussians were badly mauled and nearly retreated north-east, away from Wellington. But on Blücher's insistence they retreated close to Wellington. Without this, both Allied armies might have been defeated piecemeal, as Napoleon had indeed planned.

A year before, Wellington had chosen the ridge of Mont St. Jean, south of Waterloo. Now he arranged his forces there, anchored by three farmhouses, Hougoumont, La Haye Sainte and Papelotte. Napoleon began the battle by attacking Hougoumont, manned by Foot Guards, Dutch infantry and German riflemen. This attack was intended to be heavy, but only a diversion – to compel Wellington to shift troops, weakening his centre. But it was the French who were sucked in, due to the courage of the defenders, with some of Britain's finest troops, the 1st, 2nd and 3rd Guards, now the Grenadier, Coldstream and Scots Guards. Commanding the Coldstream was Lt. Col. James Macdonnell, a huge Highlander. When General

'Closing the Gates at Hougoumont, 1815' by Robert Gibb RSA © National Museums Scotland

Müffling, the Prussian liaison officer, appeared worried, Wellington drily remarked, 'You do not know Macdonnell'.

After losing 2,500 men in vicious fighting, the French Generals – Reille and Jérôme Bonaparte, Napoleon's brother – now made it a point of honour to capture the chateau. Another 8,000 French were sent. Now the North Gate was threatened.

With an axe, the huge Lieutenant Legros, *'l'enforceur'* (the wrecker), smashed through the gate, followed by forty Frenchmen. Macdonnell saw the danger and rushed to close the gate with three officers and several Guardsmen, including James Graham and his brother. Macdonnell and Corporal Graham heaved their shoulders against the doors with screaming Frenchmen resisting them. Graham dropped a crossbar into place, but a Frenchman tried to climb over. A musket was handed to Graham and he calmly shot the intruder. Legros and every Frenchman lay dead in the courtyard, except one young drummer boy, thankfully spared.

An impatient Napoleon ordered the chateau shelled, setting Hougoumont ablaze, but the Guardsmen resolutely fought on from the burning buildings. Graham suddenly asked his Colonel if he 'could be excused'. Knowing his courage, Macdonnell was surprised, until Graham explained that his brother was lying wounded in a burning building, requesting 'permission to drag him to safety before returning to his post'.

After fighting for hours, feeling all alone, the defenders of Hougoumont were suddenly ordered to join in the general advance. The stubborn defence of the building had exactly fulfilled its purpose, and the Duke of Wellington appreciated it. 'No other troops could have held Hougoumont other than British – and only the best of them. The whole battle turned upon the closing of the gates.'

Later, John Norcross, the rector of Framlingham in Norfolk, wrote to the Duke asking him to nominate a soldier to receive a pension from his farm. Graham was chosen. Then Norcross died and left £500 for 'the bravest man in England'. This time the Duke nominated Macdonnell, who, however, decided to share it, 'because Graham, who saw with me the importance of the step, rushed forward and together we shut the gate'.

So, a Scotsman and an Irishman were honoured for being the bravest Englishmen.

Maundy **GREGORY**

When, in 2005, Tony Blair and his arch-fundraiser Lord Levy were embroiled in selling 'peerages for loans', there were many who said that 'it was as bad as David Lloyd George and the antics of Maundy Gregory'.

In fact, Maundy Gregory – in spite of being best known for his selling of peerages – was a much more unpleasant and sinister figure than Levy or Blair could ever be.

He was born in Southampton in 1877, the son of a clergyman. Initially, he thought to follow in his father's footsteps, but was soon to start on a much less honourable career. His biographer, Richard Davenport-Hines, described him as being 'short, paunchy, bald, rubicund, monocled and epicene. He wore ostentatious jewellery and his manner was grandiose, mysterious, watchful and confidential'.

According to his own doubtful testimony, Gregory was recruited by Vernon Kell, head of MI5, to keep an eye on foreign suspects and 'to fight Bolshevism'. He certainly

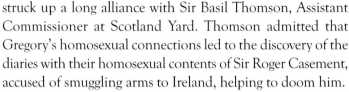

struck up a long alliance with Sir Basil Thomson, Assistant Commissioner at Scotland Yard. Thomson admitted that Gregory's homosexual connections led to the discovery of the diaries with their homosexual contents of Sir Roger Casement, accused of smuggling arms to Ireland, helping to doom him.

In 1918, Gregory began the enterprise for which he is infamous. Lloyd George's Liberal party was short of funds, so, for a commission, Gregory started selling honours. Knighthoods cost £10,000 (£310,000 today), baronetcies four times more. Gregory earned today's equivalent of £3 million and with his new-found riches bought the Ambassador Club in Soho and the Deepdene Hotel in Surrey, soon to be known as 'the biggest brothel in south east England'. Amazingly, this dubious character became quite friendly with the likes of the Duke of York – later George VI, and Lord Birkenhead.

When the scandal of the honours sales resulted in the 1925 Honours (or Prevention of Abuses) Act, Gregory started selling foreign titles and papal honours. But the honours selling led to something much more sinister. In 1918, a former Member of Parliament, Victor Grayson was, correctly, suspected of being connected with the Irish freedom movement Sinn Fein, and Gregory was asked to spy on him. Grayson soon discovered this, and he told a friend 'Just as he spied on me, so now I'm spying on him. One day I shall have enough evidence to nail him, but it's not going to be easy'.

Then at a public meeting in Liverpool, Grayson accused David Lloyd George of corruption with the sale of honours, describing it as a national scandal. He added 'It can be traced right down to 10 Downing Street, and to a monocled dandy with offices in Whitehall. One day I will name him'.

Grayson was never able name Gregory or 'nail' him. First he was beaten up in The Strand – obviously to scare him off. Then he disappeared, never to be seen alive again. Thus one threat had been removed.

In 1932, Gregory was in trouble – being pressed to repay £30,000 for a barony that was never delivered. He asked a retired actress, Edith Rosse, with whom he was living, for a loan. She refused, saying she 'needed it for her old age'. Almost at once she died, and under Gregory's supervision, was buried in a leaking coffin in a shallow, waterlogged grave. Even the forensics expert, Sir Bernard Spilsbury, could not detect the poison from which she probably died. Gregory duly inherited her money, from a will scribbled on the back of a menu.

Still in financial trouble, in 1933 Gregory tried to sell one last knighthood illegally and was arrested for corruption under the 1925 Act. Politicians were terrified of his possible testimony and arranged for him to receive the tiny sentence of two months in jail and a £50 fine. He was driven straight from prison to France, with a generous allowance.

After the 1940 invasion of France by the Germans, Maundy Gregory was arrested by them, but died in hospital of alcohol withdrawal symptoms. A remarkably unattractive character.

Herschel **GRYNSZPAN**

A small, shy seventeen year old boy called Herschel Grynszpan walked into the German Embassy in Paris in November 1938 and asked to speak to someone. A minor diplomat, Ernst vom Rath, ushered him into his office and was shot five times in the stomach, later dying of his wounds. Nowadays we would probably call it terrorism, but this act of desperation by a completely unknown youth was to trigger some of the most horrific and significant events in history.

Herschel's parents were Polish Jews who had settled in Hanover in 1911 and set up a tailoring business. But in 1930s Germany with anti-Semitic pressure building, they had tried to send Herschel to Palestine. But he was too young, so he was sent to an uncle in Paris, where he lived in a small Jewish enclave. Soon his Polish passport and his German entry papers had expired, so he was now an illegal.

In October 1938, as the Nazis tightened their grip on the Jews in Germany, they expelled 12,000 Polish Jews. But Poland refused to accept them, so they were then stuck on the border, only kept alive by the Polish Red Cross. Among them were the Grynszpans, who wrote to Herschel begging for help. When his uncle could not give him any money, Herschel took his own savings, bought a pistol and went off to shoot vom Rath.

This was a godsend for the Nazis, looking for an excuse to increase their persecution of the Jews. Propaganda Minister Josef Goebbels used the 'holy' anniversary of the Munich Beer Hall Putsch to make an inflammatory speech, telling Germans to 'take matters into their own hands'. The tragic result was *Kristallnacht* ('the night of broken glass'), with thousands of Jewish shops and businesses wrecked, along with 200 synagogues.

Ninety Jews died and 30,000 were shipped to concentration camps, the sinister first public phase of the Holocaust.

Herschel, the unwitting cause of all this, was jailed, mortified by what he had unleashed. The American journalist Dorothy Thomson raised money for his defence, refusing Jewish cash lest it help the Nazis' 'Jewish conspiracy' theories. The case dragged on in Paris until World War II, but when France was defeated by Germany, Herschel was shipped to Berlin. Strangely, his show trial was delayed by the German judiciary, especially when his defence might have been that vom Rath was homosexual and that they knew each other. Untrue, but embarrassing enough for even Goebbels to pause.

Having shared a special hut at Sachsenhausen concentration camp with Kurt Schuschnigg, Austria's former Chancellor, Herschel Grynszpan was interviewed by Adolph Eichmann in 1943, after which, like millions of others, he was never heard of again.

Just as when Charlotte Corday idealistically stabbed Marat, unleashing the real 'Terror' of the French Revolution, poor Herschel's action only worsened the fate of his own people.

Goldworthy **GURNEY**

It's hard to tell if Goldsworthy Gurney's most dramatic invention would ever have caught on, or for how long it would have lasted. In the event, it never had a chance — the victim of a perfect example of 'nobbling' by vested interests.

Goldsworthy Gurney was rather a good example of the kind of English gentleman scientist that the Victorian period produced. When the family first arrived with William the Conqueror, they were called the Counts de Gourney. By the time Goldsworthy was born in 1793, they were rich and well-connected. He became a surgeon, but displayed remarkable ability in scientific invention. He built a house at Bude in Devon, after which his oxygen-enhanced 'Bude Lights', which illuminated the House of Commons for the

next 60 years, were named. It was there too that he designed his steam carriage of which three went into regular service in 1830 between Gloucester and Cheltenham. The future looked bright, but within months dirty tricks intervened. Local horse-carriage owners used their political connections to persuade parliament to apply a toll on each journey of £2 (£140 today) on steam carriages compared with 2 shillings for horse-drawn carriages. Then his rivals covered a stretch of road with a foot of gravel, into which, being heavy, they sank, stopped Gurney's steam carriages literally in their tracks and he was bankrupted.

But Gurney's influence on steam power did not die with his road vehicles. He also created something less visually dramatic, but more long-lasting – the blast pipe or steam jet which, while forcing air out of a chimney at great speed, also had the effect of drawing air through the tubes in a boiler. This, starting with George Stevenson's Rocket, made steam locomotives much more efficient and would be used for the next 150 years.

The railways put paid to Gurney's steam carriages forever. While knighted by Queen Victoria for his other work, Sir Goldsworthy Gurney must have felt some measure of sweet revenge that railways did in the horse carriage trade as well.

He would also have been pleased to know that hospital trolleys are named after him.

Ludwig **GUTTMANN**

After the huge success of the Paralympics in London in 2012, quite a few people may have vaguely heard of Ludwig Guttmann. The events were sold out; 4,000 athletes competed from 147 nations, and all over the world millions of us watched with awe. Yet for Ludwig Guttmann they would have been so much more, 'his impossible dream'.

Such a stirring demonstration of international co-operation had unlikely roots. Born in German Silesia in 1899, Guttmann became a doctor and first encountered spinal cord injuries among miners. He was Director of the Jewish Hospital in Breslau when, in November 1938, came *Kristallnacht*, the Nazi-sponsored violent attacks across Germany on Jews and their property. Guttmann now did something supremely brave. Ordering his staff to admit anyone without question, he then took the suspicious Gestapo men from bed to bed, inventing diagnoses for each patient, so plausibly that 60 of the 64 were saved from concentration camps. Next day, he took a warm coat and stout boots into the hospital, fully expecting to be hauled off himself.

Harsh new racial laws very soon meant that Guttmann could only treat Jews. Whatever his international reputation, Guttmann sensibly realised that time was running out and made his way with his family to England.

In Oxford, he continued his spinal injury research at the Radcliffe Infirmary, and in 1943 the Government, fearing huge battle casualties after D-Day, asked him to set up the National Spinal Injuries Hospital at Stoke Mandeville in Buckinghamshire. There, he single-handedly revolutionised the care of paralysed servicemen. Before that, they were condemned as 'incurable', immobilised in plaster, developing sores and bladder and kidney infections. Nobody wanted such cases, and the nurses were embarrassed and revolted by the smell of urine and rotting flesh. Guttmann, hugely compassionate, got patients out of plaster, changed the food, turned them every two hours to reduce sores, and made them sit up, get out of bed and learn new skills. The mortality rate dropped from 80 to 20 per cent. All this was achieved against vested interests and blinkered opposition by Guttmann's inspiring mixture of charm, tenacity and bloody-mindedness.

Then came a dramatic moment. Seeing patients playing an impromptu game of wheelchair hockey, he suddenly realised that sport might boost fitness, increase self-esteem and restore dignity. The same day that the 1948 London Olympics opened, Guttmann organised the first 'Stoke Mandeville Games for the Paralysed'. By 1952, there were 130 international competitors, and in Rome in 1960 the International Stoke Mandeville Games were held proudly alongside the Olympics.

Guttmann was knighted in 1966, and died in 1980. Four years after his death, the International Olympic Committee retrospectively called all his Games since Rome 'The Paralympics'. This most compassionate of men would have been truly amazed by how his dream has triumphed.

Ruth **HANDLER**

Considering she is only eleven and a half inches tall, Barbara Millicent Roberts is doing rather well to be voted 'one of the most influential people who has never lived'. But then 'Barbie', as she is better known, has been around for sixty years and has been, for millions of little girls, the most important friend in their lives.

Ruth Handler was the wife of the co-founder of toy company Mattel. Watching her daughter Barbara playing with paper dolls, she noticed that the little girl was giving them adult roles. Up until then nearly all dolls had looked like babies or infants. Why not create an adult version? There might be an untapped gap in the market. She became even more convinced when she saw a German doll called 'Bild Lilli', based on a comic strip in the newspaper *Die Bild Zeitung*. 'Lilli' was a savvy, professional girl whom children could dress in miniature clothes.

Ruth re-worked a 'Lilli' doll, calling it 'Barbie' after her daughter Barbara. Her creation first appeared at the 1959 American International Toy Fair in New York, billed as a 'Teenage Fashion Model', sporting a black and white bathing suit, a ponytail hairstyle, open-toed shoes and sunglasses. She was a smash hit. 300,000 Barbies were sold that year, the first of hundreds of millions.

Ruth Handler had created Barbie just when young girls were becoming more and more exposed to fashion, celebrity and glamour through films and television. Moving with the times, Barbie's first look and wardrobe was of movie stars like Marilyn

Monroe, Rita Hayworth and Elizabeth Taylor, then the cool elegance of Grace Kelly and Jackie Kennedy, the 'flower power' of the Woodstock era, the 'big hair' and shoulder pads of the 80s, the 90s supermodels and even political contenders for the Oval Office.

Barbie has appeared in 50 nationalities and in 120 careers. She has owned 50 pets, several vehicles, has friends of all races and a boyfriend Ken (named after Ruth's son) in an on-off relationship of 52 years. Huge care by top designers goes into each new look and outfit, and using so much material that, even in 1/6th scale, Mattel is one of the world's top fabric manufacturers.

Barbie's success story has been marked by controversy, with parents worried about 'their kids growing up too early' and, more serious, the danger of anorexia, which Mattel had to address by widening Barbie's waist in 1997. Saudi Arabia has even banned Barbies, describing them 'as Jewish dolls, with their revealing clothes and shameful postures a symbol of the decadence of the perverted West'.

As a joke in 1993, a group called the 'Barbie Liberation Organisation' secretly changed the voice boxes of 'Teen Talk Barbie' with ones from 'G.I. Joe' dolls. It must have been a shock for little girls to hear their Barbies grunt 'We've got to knock out that machine-gun', and to small boys hearing their rugged heroes lisp, 'I love shopping' and 'Can we ever have enough clothes?'

Erich **HARTMANN**

It may come as a surprise to many that it took only a handful of 'kills' for a World War II fighter pilot to be called an 'Ace'. And even legendary Allied aces had quite low scores. 'Paddy' Finucane, an Irish pilot, shared the top spot with 'Sailor' Malan of South Africa, both with 32 victories. Another 'Battle of Britain' legend, the legless Douglas Bader had only 23. Among Americans, Richard Bong in the Pacific led with 40, while among his Japanese enemies the top scorer was Hiroyoshi Nishizawa with 87.

So it comes as a real shock to discover that the Germans had 76 pilots with over 100 kills, and quite a few with over 200. Even more astonishing is that the dubious accolade of the top-scoring fighter ace of all time goes to a baby-faced young Luftwaffe pilot called Erich Hartmann with the staggering total of 352 aerial victories.

At the beginning of the war Hartmann was not even old enough to fight, only joining his first fighter squadron in 1942 on the Eastern Front. Aged 20, he appeared even younger – nicknamed 'Bubi', or 'the kid'. After a couple of near fatal scrapes due to over-enthusiasm, he soon adopted his maxim 'fly with your head, not your muscles'. His extraordinary career started during the battle of Kursk, Germany's last and unsuccessful offensive against the Russians, which showed that she was both losing the war and air superiority. But by August 1943, Hartmann had shot down 50 enemy aircraft, and by the end of that month another 48. At the end of that year his incredulous superiors were triple-checking his tally of 159, but the figures proved real and they continued to mount. 'If you wait until the other plane filled your entire cockpit window, you don't waste a single round'. Such close-range firing caused him to crash land many times, his plane damaged by the debris of exploding enemy aircraft.

'Bubi' Hartmann, called 'The Blond Knight' by the German press and 'The Black Devil' by his fearful Soviet opponents, fought in the air an incredible 825 times. For those who might claim that most of his victories were against the 'inferior' Soviets, his two combat missions against Americans are sobering. On 21st May 1944 he shot down two P-51 Mustangs, and a month later four – in a single mission lasting only a few minutes.

At the end of the war, Hartmann was handed over to the Soviets who tried to coerce him into co-operating and joining the new East German air force. He was tortured and force-fed during a hunger strike, but was eventually repatriated after ten years, becoming a Colonel in the West German air force. His last act of courage was denouncing the safety record of the American F-104 Starfighter, which killed a shocking 115 German pilots in accidents.

For some German aces, the reason for their high scores was simple. 'Allied pilots were retired after a number of missions. We Germans flew and fought all through the war. If we didn't die, we became very good at it'.

Erich Hartmann certainly did.

Herman **HAUPT**

The most influential weapon of the last two centuries might not be the rifle, the machine-gun or the aeroplane, but surprisingly the steam engine – especially in the hands of Herman Haupt.

Until 1830 armies were limited in size by crude supply by horse-drawn wagons, and in speed by the pace of marching men. They campaigned in summer to 'live off the land' and battles would usually last just one day. Railways were to change that forever.

Only sixteen years after the opening of the world's first railway – the Liverpool and Manchester – troops and supplies were being moved by train, by the Prussians, the Austrians and by then the British in the Crimea. But it was in America that the railways' impact on warfare would truly change the future. With 30,000 miles of track, the country lurched into its tragic Civil War in 1861 and the railroads would prove decisive.

The 'wizard of railroading' was Herman Haupt. Graduating from West Point in 1835, he had resigned his commission to become a civil engineer. He became an expert on bridge building and design, working for the Pennsylvania and Southern Railroads. Not only was Haupt a thorough railway expert, but also a hard worker, stubbornly pigheaded, and exactly what the Federal government needed as Brigadier General in charge of the Railroad Bureau. He transformed the

speed of repairing destroyed track and bridges. In awe, President Lincoln exclaimed: 'That man Haupt has built a bridge over which loaded trains are passing every hour, and there is nothing in it but beanpoles and cornstalks'.

But it was not Haupt's ability to build bridges 'faster than the Rebs could burn them down' that was his true legacy, but his management of railroad movement. He had two ruthlessly imposed rules: the military should not interfere in railroad operations, and freight cars must be emptied and returned promptly – and not used as warehouses. If his rules were followed, Haupt could supply 200,000 men along a single line, ten times more than if his rules were broken. This railroad genius only stayed in uniform for a year, but it was a crucial year. Many battles and campaigns were won by his well-organised use of railroads to rush reinforcements and supplies to the vital point. Railroads would also increase both the length and intensity of warfare forever – and foreign observers soon noticed.

Herman Haupt

Within just months, the Prussians now created their own *Feldeisenbahnabteilung* (Field Railway Department), helping them to beat first the Austrians and then the French. Railways would enable the British to defeat the Dervishes in the Sudan and the Boers in South Africa. The Japanese, in 1904, went to war precisely because the Russian Trans-Siberian Railway was a strategic 'dagger aimed at our heart'. Alfred von Schlieffen's famous Plan, to invade France in 1914, was a railway plan, over 14 routes with 11,000 trains.

The Great War then became ever bloodier, because any attack, as at the Somme or Verdun, was not only defeated by the defensive power of artillery and machine-guns, but also by the railways. When advancing, soldiers became weaker, struggling across broken ground with declining supplies of ammunition, food and water, while their opponents became stronger, retreating back on to the plentiful supplies delivered by the railways, thus prolonging the murderous stalemate of the trenches.

For another fifty years railways were crucial. After Pearl Harbor, they fulfilled a huge supply role in America in World War II, with 75,000 locomotives hauling two million freight cars, faithfully following Haupt's rules 'No car shall be loaded without the assurance that it can and will be unloaded at destination'. In Russia the paucity of lines and their different gauge meant that, apart from their elite Panzer forces, the Germans invaded the Soviet Union mostly on foot or with 620,000 horses and were surprisingly and thoroughly 'outrailroaded' by the Russians

Thanks to Herman Haupt, railways shaped not just warfare – but history itself.

? George Dewey **HAY**

A log cabin in America's Ozark mountains not only changed the life of George Dewey Hay, it transformed the world of music. On a newspaper assignment at Mammoth Spring, Arkansas, Hay was taken by a farmer up a track to a 'hoedown' in a barn. There he saw the mountain people dancing to guitar, fiddle and banjo until dawn – and never forgot the enjoyment of that night.

George Hay then became quite a personality. He enlivened drab court reports in Memphis's *Commercial Appeal* newspaper by creating a humorous column called 'Howdy, Judge' – earning the nickname, 'Solemn Ole Judge'– despite being still in his twenties. Then the newspaper created its own radio station, and Hay became such a star that he was recruited to WLS-AM Chicago, where, based on the music in that log cabin, he created the 'National Barn Dance' show. Soon, he was the most popular radio announcer in America.

A new radio station in Nashville took him on as Radio Director, with the intention of starting another 'barn dance' show. Within days, in November 1925 he featured 78-year old 'Uncle' Jimmy Thompson – a Tennessee fiddle player – and was dumbfounded by the enthusiastic cables and calls that flooded in.

Hay could announce that 'due to listeners' interest, we will feature one or two hours of old time tunes every Saturday night'. At first, this smash hit programme was called *WSM Barn Dance*, but in December 1927 it followed NBC's classical *Music Appreciation Hour*. Hay now came out with his immortal words: 'For the past hour, we have been listening to music taken largely from Grand Opera. From now on, we will present the Grand Ole Opry'.

Hay presided over his baby until he retired in 1951, attracting the cream of country performers. The Opry house rule was a minimum of 26 appearances per year, giving new acts a helpful contract and much-needed exposure.

Dolly Parton, beamed to the desert troops

In 1938 the Opry had found a really big star, Roy Acuff, whose records sold massively through the 1940s, a period when Opry began to attract a host of 'big stars with string bands'. The legendary Hank Williams joined in 1949, and the list of artists became a Who's Who of Country music: Williams himself, Jim Reeves, Dolly Parton (with a debut at 13), Flatt and Scruggs, Johnny Cash, and the Carter family.

As more radio stations syndicated the music, Opry put Nashville firmly on the map as the undisputed home of Country music. Capitol Records arrived in 1950 and soon attracted other major record companies, providing the smooth distinctive 'Nashville Country Sound'. This reached its fullest development in the 1960s, when even mainstream acts such as Bob Dylan (notably with his *Nashville Skyline* LP) and the Byrds flirted with country music.

The rise of rock'n'roll both threatened and strengthened the Country music scene (Elvis Presley himself was a country boy who fused this music with the black man's blues). The Grand Ole Opry was the only barn dance radio programme to survive this cultural upheaval. Indeed, it went from strength to strength.

Commercial and stylised as it is, Country is beautifully crafted, has stars with great voices, and remains the most popular music in America, even bigger than pop and rock 'n' roll.

'Keep it as simple as sunshine', George Hay advised. He was right.

Leona **HELMSLEY**

Donald Trump, the American billionaire property tycoon, was more than blunt in his opinion: 'She is a horrible, horrible human being'. He was referring to Leona Helmsley, and thousands, maybe millions, of people agreed with him.

Lena Rosenthal was born to very poor Polish parents in New York in 1920, and after toying with several names, she settled on Leona. A striking and attractive woman, after two marriages she found herself aged 42 with no job, no money, no college education and a son to feed. She turned to real estate in which her brand of brash salesmanship excelled. At a property ball, she engineered a meeting with the fabulously rich Harry Helmsley, the 'King of real estate'. Within minutes 'he was leading Leona smoothly and gracefully across the dance floor in a perfect waltz'. Just weeks later she was a Senior Vice-President in Harry's company and his lover. Soon they were married, Leona having gone literally from 'rags to riches'.

It was Harry's dream hotel, the Helmsley Palace, which propelled Leona to fame, or rather, notoriety. Having been put in charge by her doting husband, Leona dominated the hotel and appeared in advertisements trumpeting headlines like 'THE ONLY PALACE WHERE THE QUEEN STANDS GUARD.' But the dark side of her personality emerged. A fanatic for detail, she treated the staff of the Helmsley Palace and their other hotels appallingly. She fired people, screamed obscenities and reduced grown men and women to jelly. Soon dubbed 'The Queen of Mean', she did not even seem to care.

But her behaviour finally brought her down. Typically, she treated the contractors on their magnificent new house, Dunnellen Hall, just as badly, who exasperated, mailed a parcel of invoices to the *New York Post*. This revealed that, by pretending the work was on Helmsley commercial properties, the Helmsleys had been avoiding income tax. 'We don't pay taxes. Only the little people pay taxes.' This remark did not endear her to the eventual judge and jury, who sentenced her to 18 months in jail – Harry being now too ill to stand trial.

Harry having died in 1997, she was one of the richest women in the world. But after unpleasant fights with family and employees, and rivals like Donald Trump, Leona did not have the longest list of friends and only had her dog for company, called 'Trouble'. When she died in 2007 she left him $12 million. Hardly a dog's dinner.

Fletcher **HENDERSON**

Of the many successful American musical exports, 'Swing' was one of the greatest – a mixture of co-ordinated big band music and improvised jazz. Two famous names, Louis Armstrong and Benny Goodman, were pivotal to its creation, but they were linked to one far less familiar today – Fletcher Hamilton Henderson.

After World War I, people in America wanted to enjoy themselves and dance. In a country divided by race, African-Americans would dance to all-black jazz bands, while white folks danced to white bands. Paul Whiteman, one of the first 'big band' leaders, signed up brilliant white instrumentalists like Bix Beiderbecke and singers like Bing Crosby. But there were no wild sounds or inspired improvisations. For that you had to listen to the jazzmen who had come north from New Orleans. And playing in 'King Oliver's Creole Jazz Band' in Chicago was one of the greatest trumpet players ever – Louis Armstrong.

A superb instrumentalist, Louis was also a great improviser, spontaneously inventing new melodies as he played. Bandleaders like Paul Whiteman flocked to Chicago to hear him. One was mesmerised – Fletcher Henderson, the leader of the 'other' big band in New York, the black one, who exclaimed, 'I've heard a guy who can really swing', the first time anyone had used the word.

Fletcher Henderson, good-looking and mild-mannered, was born into a middle-class Atlanta black family. His respectable piano teaching mother had urged him to avoid 'low music', and he had arrived in New York to take a master's degree in chemistry. However he soon realised his race would block his scientific aspirations and drifted into music management and arrangement.

Now he had the best black dance band in New York and, after listening to Louis Armstrong, he realised he could do something that a white bandleader never could. He hired Armstrong and it electrified his band.

While Armstrong played for him, Henderson and Don Redman, his excellent arranger, wrote down the notes and the swing era was born – the interplay between the brass and reed sections, sometimes in 'call and response', sometimes with supporting riffs – and now with solos inspired by Louis Armstrong.

Louis only stayed a year, but the seeds had been sown. Henderson employed some of the finest talent and became one of America's most successful arrangers. This was fortuitous. As the Depression deepened, his band folded. And financial problems forced him to start selling his arrangements to others. This was to be the vital link in the growth of swing, because

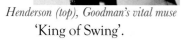
Henderson (top), Goodman's vital muse one of them was Benny Goodman, soon to be dubbed the 'King of Swing'.

Benny Goodman was an obsessive musical perfectionist and a clarinet virtuoso. With dance halls folding due to the Depression, people still wanted to dance, albeit at home. So NBC created the radio show *Let's Dance*. Armed with Fletcher Henderson's masterful arrangements, Benny Goodman won the competition to become its dance band – making him famous.

Capitalising on the success of *Let's Dance*, he went on tour – a big shock because audiences were initially tiny. But at the Palomar Ballroom in Los Angeles, everything changed. The time zone meant that the West Coast kids had been able to listen to *Let's Dance* at 7.30 in the evening and they turned out to be wildly enthusiastic. 'You couldn't get to within 50 feet of the stage'. Many people think that August 21st 1935, beamed across

America, was the beginning of the 'Swing Era'.

Swing bandleaders like Goodman, Count Basie and Artie Shaw became the first popular music superstars, earning £500,000 a week in today's money. Conservative critics soon denounced swing as something 'that would make people want to have sex' – always an excellent catalyst.

Fletcher Henderson had turned out to be the key link at the right place and time.

Benjamin **HENRY**

No 'Western' film would ever be without them – the lever-action, repeating rifles that we call Winchesters. James Stewart even starred in one film called *Winchester '73*. In fact, the rifles were originally the creation of the gunsmith Benjamin Tyler Henry. A small number of his Henry repeating rifles appeared during America's Civil War and were a great success, so valued that many were paid for by Union soldiers saving up for them. Capable of 28 rounds a minute, Confederate troops, then still armed with muzzle-loaders, cursed the 16 shooter, 'That damned Yankee rifle that they load on Sunday and shoot all week'.

After the war, Henry rifles played a prominent role in several fights with the Plains Indians, and indeed captured or traded rifles helped the Sioux and Cheyennes to wipe out George Custer's command at the Little Big Horn.

It was Horace Smith and Daniel Wesson, later famous for their revolvers, who had given Benjamin Henry his designing break, hiring him to improve their 'Volcanic' repeating rifle and, crucially, its ammunition.

'That damned Yankee rifle that they load on Sunday and shoot all week!'

Their largest shareholder was a clothing manufacturer called Oliver Winchester who eventually re-organised the company into the Winchester Repeating Arms Company. The Henry rifle was further improved in 1866, not least with the addition of a safety catch, and became the 'Winchester' – dubbed 'the gun that won the West'.

However, it was thousands of miles away from the 'Wild West' of America that Winchester rifles played their most significant military role. In 1877 at Plevna, an obscure place in Bulgaria, just 15,000 Turkish troops armed with Winchesters drove off 150,000 invading Russians three times – with terrible losses for the Russians.

It was a demonstration of devastating defensive firepower seemingly lost on the military leaders who would command 60 years later in World War I.

Ivan **HIRST**

Tap 'Ivan Hirst' into YouTube and you see an interview with an elderly, modest Englishman. Sitting beside him is a green model of a Volkswagen 'Beetle'. Only four of these miniatures were made – one presented to Adolf Hitler. Appropriate, because Ivan Hirst saved Volkswagen for the world and Hitler had made it happen.

Many car German designers had thought of creating small, affordable cars, and *Volkswagen* or 'People's Car' was their generic term. But the real impetus to produce one came when Hitler became annoyed at the Berlin Motor Show that depression-hit Germany only produced expensive cars and had not switched to smaller and cheaper models. Over tea with Ferdinand Porsche in 1934 he himself sketched the distinctive curves of a car that would cost only 1,000 Reichsmarks and do 40 miles a gallon, also laying the foundation stone of a huge new factory. The car's unusual rounded shape soon earned it the affectionate name *Käfer* or Beetle, and it was simple as well as cheap and practical.

Soon 336,000 Germans eagerly paid for stamps in a *Kraft durch Freude* (Strength through joy) savings scheme for their cars to be produced at a new town called Stadt des KdF-Wagens. But only a handful of German civilians ever received them. War intervened and the giant factory was needed for military vehicles.

With Germany beaten in 1945 the Allies pondered what to do with the huge Volkswagenwerk. Initially, Volkswagen was to be broken up and its machine tools sold off. But many experts argued for the plant to be taken over by the British motor industry, despite being three times larger than any British factory, '*Both the car and the factory in which it is produced are wonderful achievements in their respective spheres.*'

Enter young Major Ivan Hirst, born into an engineering family from Oldham in Northern England, who had fought in France as an infantry officer and later ran advanced workshops repairing tanks. Hirst now found himself in what was called Wolfsburg, in charge of a gigantic, apparently wrecked factory. He was vaguely told, 'Just take charge. Sit there.' But Hirst noted that most of the machinery was unscathed, and he decided not to 'sit there', but to make cars again. He had a passion for cars, a genius for improvisation and a fresh, friendly approach that would enable him to win over the demoralised, starving Germans.

Major Ivan Hirst

Hirst and his team cleared away the wreckage and started to cobble together a few 'beetles'. By painting one car in military green, he cleverly persuaded the British Army to start buying Volkswagens, soon ordering 20,000. However, Sir William Rootes, Chairman of Britain's Society of Manufacturers and Traders (SMMT), was disparaging. 'It's quite unattractive to the average motor car buyer,' adding to Hirst the immortal words, 'If you think you are going to build cars in this place, you're a bloody fool, young man.'

Nevertheless, the Control Commission sent three vehicles to Britain to be evaluated with a recommendation: 'The Volkswagen would appear to offer a possible solution of a cheap utility vehicle which would be acceptable to Britain and in overseas markets.'

Ivan Hirst painted one car green, and impressed the British army.

Various members of the assessment team agreed, 'an extremely cheap car, exceptionally good and very popular.' But British engineering snobbery and arrogance intervened. Ford of Britain and Humber were negative and assessed the car as 'noisy' and 'uncomfortable.'

Faced by such lack of enthusiasm, it was in vain that the Control Commission's Colonel Boas spoke passionately to a S.M.M.T. meeting 'I have an intimate knowledge of this car and factory, and think that it is a first-class car and a novel piece of engineering. It would form the nucleus of a national motor industry in England.' The answer to this perspicacity was sad. 'British designers have nothing to learn in this branch of the industry.'

Other countries *were* interested. France, the United States, Australia and Brazil – everyone except the British. While the British decided not to acquire Volkswagen, they let Hirst keep it running, with the limited objective of stopping rival countries obtaining it. But with its novel

'If you think you're going to build cars in this place, you're a bloody fool, young man!'

design and cheapness, the Beetle spread its wings. Exports were climbing and plants to assemble cars were set up in Ireland and Brazil.

For a while, complacency reigned. The Board of Trade calmly reported, 'It is doubtful if German production and marketing could challenge our strong position in most markets.' Echoed by the Control Commission, 'German exporters can never be expected to compete seriously with the United Kingdom.'

Too late did the British car industry wake up, complaining that its markets 'were being unfairly attacked by our former enemy.' It had only itself to blame.

In 1949, Ivan Hirst's job was done and he went back to Britain, while Volkswagen was handed over to a trust controlled by the German government. Just five years later, the millionth Beetle (or Bug, Coccinelle, Käfer, Fusca etc) rolled off the line. In 1972 it overtook the Ford Model T with 16 million sales, finally achieving over 21 million in 2000. Today its shape has been revived and sales are booming again.

In stark contrast, Britain's car industry has shrunk beyond recognition. And Volkswagen, the little car and the big factory spurned by the British, now owns Audi, NSU, SEAT, Skoda, Bugatti, Lamborghini and even the quintessentially British Bentley.

James **HOBAN**

It is the most talked about, most photographed residence in the world – a large Neo-classical building whose occupant is the most powerful man on earth, the President of the United States. Its official, mundane address is 1600 Pennsylvania Avenue – but the world knows it as The White House. It was created by a carpenter from a little thatched cottage in Ireland – James Hoban.

Born in 1758, Hoban was brought up on the Earl of Desart's estate in Kilkenny before being given an 'advanced student' place at the Dublin Society's Drawing School, where he excelled, later becoming the assistant to the prominent architect Thomas Ivory. He emigrated to the United States and set himself up as an architect in Philadelphia in 1777, marrying and having ten children.

In South Carolina, he designed several prominent, graceful buildings, notably the Charleston County Courthouse. George Washington on his Southern Tour, much admired these buildings and now persuaded Hoban to return to Philadelphia – then the temporary national capital – while the 'Federal City' in the District of Columbia was being planned.

In 1792, a competition was held to design a 'Presidential Palace', which George Washington felt should 'have the sumptuousness of a palace, the convenience of a house, and the agreeableness of a country seat'. James Hoban beat eight other contenders, and was awarded a prize of $500.

The building was to be part of the new city rising from the swamps near the Potomac River called Washington, which then had only one, unpaved, road. It took seven years to build and the first residents were John and Abigail Adams who virtually froze in their first winter. President Thomas Jefferson, the next occupant, quickly installed coal fires in 1801.

There is a famous myth about how the White House received it name: 'In 1814, the British captured and burned much of Washington, including the President's House, which was then repainted white to cover the scorching'.

The truth is that the building, to protect its porous sandstone against freezing, had first been whitewashed by Hoban as far back as 1798, and by 1811 many people were already calling it the 'White House'. After the 1814 fire damage, James Hoban was in charge of its reconstruction, and no doubt the improved white lead paint he ordered ensured that the nickname stuck – President Theodore Roosevelt making it the official title in 1901.

Hoban had become Superintendent of all Washington's public works and oversaw the construction of many important buildings. And amongst all the prominent Irish emigrants, with that one famous building it was Hoban who left us the most enduring image. Yet how many people, even in Ireland, know his name?

John **HOLLAND**

Ireland's long struggle to free herself from Britain has been marked by a heady mix of bravery, false hopes, sacrifice, tragedy, daring, treachery, political miscalculation and inventiveness. It produced evocative poetry, powerful literature and sad songs. Less well-known was something that went from a marine curiosity to one of the world's great strategic weapons – the submarine. As the U-Boat, it nearly brought Britain to her knees in two World Wars. In American hands it did the same for Japan in the Pacific and it has since maintained a nuclear standoff that has served the world quite well.

The 'father of the submarine', John Philip Holland was born in a cottage in County Clare in Ireland in 1841. Although his father worked for the British Coastguard, the boy spoke little English until he went to school. He initially considered becoming a priest, but instead became a teacher. Already fascinated by the idea of a submarine, he built a working clockwork model. Meanwhile, his brothers were now embroiled in the independence movement, and when two of them went to America with his mother, John followed them to Boston in 1873.

Two years later he submitted his first design for a one-man submarine powered by pedals to the US Navy Department, but it was dismissed as 'impractical'. However, his brother Michael now came up with a group that had good reason to be interested – the 'Fenians'.

The 1848 'Young Ireland' revolt led by William Smith O'Brien had ended in farce. A veteran of that revolt, James Stephens, realised that success demanded arms and military skill, and ten years later founded the 'Fenian Brotherhood', both in Ireland and New York. In 1867, a really dangerous Fenian plot for thousands of Irishmen in the British Army to revolt was betrayed. But the movement was still looking for a way to strike at the British.

John Holland both sympathised with the Irish cause and needed money to

develop his submarines. Thus, after showing a working model, he was delighted to receive money from the Fenians' 'Skirmishing Fund'. Built in some secrecy, his *Holland 1* was 14 feet long and its trials impressed the Fenians enough to finance a larger boat. *The New York Sun* found out and dubbed it 'The Fenian Ram', although the 19 ton, 31 foot submersible was never meant to ram British ships, instead to fire a pneumatic 'dynamite gun'. In the event, the Fenians began to quarrel amongst themselves and their submarine was never used in anger.

However, other backers emerged, not least a naval officer, Lieutenant Kimball, and a competition was announced by the US Navy, demanding a rather unrealistic 15 knots on the surface. Holland's resulting design was the massive *Plunger*, which needed a huge, hot steam engine that fried the crew – a design dead-end.

Fortunately, John Holland convinced his colleagues in his 'Holland Torpedo Boat

102

Company' to allow him to go back to his principles and build a prototype at their own expense. *Holland VI* was 53 feet long, weighed 75 tons and was powered by a petrol engine on the surface and an electric motor for submerged running. His successful diving and surfacing tests were achieved on March 17th 1898 – St. Patrick's Day.

After the mysterious sinking of the USS *Maine* led to war with Spain, Assistant Secretary of the Navy Theodore Roosevelt recommended that the Navy buy the submarine, noting 'Sometimes she doesn't work perfectly, but often she does, and I don't think in the present emergency we can afford to let her slip'. However, the Navy still did not buy Holland's boat, and – virtually broke – he had to sell out to others to keep going, the company becoming the 'Electric Boat Company'.

A year later *Holland VI* performed flawlessly in a decisive Navy trial. A few days later, Admiral George Dewey, the 'Hero of Manila Bay', affirmed 'if the Spanish had two of these things, I could never have held it with the squadron I had.' Opposition collapsed.

On April 11th 1900 – celebrated as the birthday of the US submarine service – the Navy at last bought *Holland VI*, soon increasing its order to seven more. Other navies ordered boats, notably the Royal Navy whose first submarine was called, ironically, *Holland 1*.

But John Holland was being squeezed out of his own company and had serious disagreements with colleagues who thought of submarines as surface ships that could be occasionally submerged. 'The Navy does not like submarines because there is no deck to strut on!' Disillusioned, he left the company in 1904 and died ten years later, just as Holland-type submarines began to make their devastating impact on naval warfare.

Howard **HUGHES** Sr.

Most people think they have heard of Howard Hughes, picturing the rich and handsome playboy in Hollywood, the director of *The Outlaw* film, the designer of Jane Russell's sensual bra uplift, the intrepid aviator who set records and created the giant wooden 'Spruce Goose' seaplane and the owner of TWA – and finally the billionaire recluse who descended into madness.

But there was another Howard Hughes, the father, who was far more influential than his bizarre son, and left a legacy which lasts to this day.

By the beginning of the 20th century, the oil industry was becoming the most important in the world. Led by the Royal Navy, the world's ships were turning to oil and the internal combustion engine was about to make automobiles, trucks and buses the transport of the future. Anything that made the finding and production of oil quicker and cheaper would be a godsend– and a money-spinner.

In spite of the oil found with rotary drilling in Titusville and Spindletop, one of the key problems was producing oil from greater depths and from under hard rock formations. Existing 'fishtail' drill bits suited only soft formations, whereas most oil is trapped between multiple layers of hard rock.

Howard Hughes, Sr. was born in Lancaster, Missouri, into a cultured family. His sister was 'Jeanne Greta', a grand opera and concert singer, his brother Rupert was a well-known novelist and screenwriter, while Felix, his youngest brother, was an opera singer.

Hughes was a classic entrepreneur, trying and failing at many endeavours before eventually finding success. He had entered Harvard University in 1893 and after two years began to study law at the University of Iowa. Without completing his law course, he started to practise with his father, marrying an heiress, Allene Gano.

Seeing the problems at Spindletop, he began to focus on the shortcomings of the 'fishtail' bit. Experimenting carefully, by 1908 he and his partner Walter Sharp had built a wooden model of a bit with two rotating cones.

His legal experience told him to file the patents for the 'Sharp-Hughes Rock Bit', and in 1909 he was granted two patents for the world's first rotary rock bit equipped with two rolling cone cutters. It was to revolutionize rotary drilling by making it possible to cut through medium and hard rock formations at ten times the speed of any other bit.

Hughes and Sharp secretly tested the prototype at Goose Creek Oilfield in 1909, where the first offshore drilling for oil in Texas was occurring. Telling the rig crew to leave, they took the bit from a locked wooden box and started drilling. The new Sharp-Hughes rock bit penetrated 14 ft (4.3 m) of hard rock in 11 hours, which no previous equipment

had been able to penetrate at all. This helped to make Goose Creek one of the great oilfields of the Gulf Coast and it propelled Hughes and Sharp to fame and riches, and by 1914 the dual-cone roller bit was being used in eleven U.S. states and in 13 foreign countries – a near-monopoly as complete as Watts' dominance of the all-important steam engine market a century before.

After Hughes Senior's death in 1924, his only child Howard R. Hughes, Jr. assumed sole ownership. From 1934 right up to 1951 Hughes' market share approached 100%. Howard Junior became – without much effort – the wealthiest person in the world. It also enabled him to indulge in his foibles, great and small.

After decades of innovation, Baker-Hughes is one of the great oil service companies, and all over the world versions of the famous bit are still being used, making it one of the most enduring inventions ever created.

It is a pity we remember the extraordinary and eccentric son and not the more deserving father.

Albert **JACKA**

It was a unique tribute. In the little town of St Kilda, a coffin was carried by eight other Australian holders of the Victoria Cross, watched by tens of thousands. Australia's greatest war hero, Albert Jacka, was being laid to rest. Far more of us would know that name if he had been awarded – as he deserved – not one but three Victoria Crosses – a historic event blocked by British military conservatism and Australian jealousy.

In Sarajevo, 8,000 miles away from Australia, a young Serbian had killed an Austrian

Archduke, and 'Bert' Jacka decided to fight for the 'Old Country' and the Empire. Typical of Australia's troops, he was intensely independent, outspoken, even sometimes 'difficult'. But, as one historian put it, 'some of the best men in the trenches were those who had given most trouble in training.'

After nine months, Acting Lance-Corporal Albert Jacka, aged 22, was in Gallipoli, rocky and inhospitable, facing brave and skilful resistance by the Turks, with losses just as bad as they were on the Western Front. At the vital 'Courtney's Post', the two front lines were only yards apart and on the night of 19 May 1915, the Turks attacked.

While others withdrew, Jacka doggedly held his position and continued to fire. An officer tried to help, but was instantly killed. Another, Lieutenant Crabbe, gathered volunteers to help Jacka, but the first man to move was wounded three times in seconds. Stopping Crabbe and the others from suicidal exposure, Jacka decided to go it alone and charged the Turks, shooting five and bayoneting two. At dawn, Crabbe found him surrounded by bodies. 'Well, I got the beggars, Sir!' Jacka was the first Australian recipient of the Victoria Cross.

By August he was a Company Sergeant-Major, and after 26,000 Australian casualties, the Allies withdrew in the cold of winter that December.

Now commissioned as a Second Lieutenant, Jacka then performed his second memorable feat. During the Somme offensive, the Australians had captured the shattered village of Pozières, losing thousands of men. During the German counter-attack, a grenade rolled into Jacka's captured German dug-out, and he and the survivors of the blast staggered out to find themselves 200 yards behind the second wave of advancing Germans. What is more, the nearest Germans were escorting 42 Australian prisoners to their rear. Jacka, with just seven men, did not hesitate, instead launching himself at the 60 Germans. Two of his comrades were killed, all the others were wounded. Incredibly, Jacka was wounded seven times, but picked himself up and personally killed 12 of the enemy. The Australian prisoners were freed, the Germans surrendered and the ridge was retaken.

His stretcher-bearer boasted, 'Here's the bravest man in the Aussie Army' and C.E.W. Bean, the Australian historian, called it 'the most dramatic and effective act of individual audacity in the history of the Australian Imperial Forces'. But sadly his own Company Commander had been hundreds of yards away and his Battalion Commander, for some reason, played down Jacka's action. So he 'only' received a Military Cross.

After convalescence, Jacka was soon back in action with his 14th Battalion, now long known as 'Jacka's mob'. At Bullecourt, he crawled in darkness into 'No Man's Land', capturing two Germans. More important, he noted that the thick German barbed-wire had not been cut by the British artillery. He desperately warned his Brigadier that next day's Australian attack would be 'pure murder', but his advice was ignored and the Australians were indeed murdered. Once again, he was recommended for a V.C. by his own Battalion Commander, but the Brigadier, perhaps ashamed, downgraded it to M.C.

Extraordinarily, the AIF's commander then secretly ordered 'that Jacka's report be expunged from the records of the AIF and he is to be systematically ignored both in regard to decorations and promotions'. Which is why another brave action at Polygon Wood, where he became de facto Commanding Officer, was not rewarded even with the recommended DSO. Nor was he promoted beyond Captain.

In the last year of the war, he was badly gassed and finally arrived back in Australia to a rapturous welcome. He became Mayor of St Kilda but died, at 39 still a young man, of his war wounds.

There, each year on the 17th of January, a service commemorates a remarkable Australian whose name should be infinitely better known.

Leslie **JACKSON**

In April 1943, General Sir Harold Alexander was planning his final assault on Tunis, but the massive rock-strewn feature of Djebel Bou Azoukaz, 'The Bou', blocked his way. After two days of bitter fighting, the Irish Guards had secured the central mile-long ridge. But they had suffered terrible casualties. Four companies had been reduced to one, and many of the officers and NCOs had been killed. Just 173 men were on their feet.

It was vital that they held off the vicious German counter-attacks.

Lance-Corporal Patrick Kenneally saw below him a whole company of Germans forming up to attack. Leaping to his feet, he charged down the rocky hill, firing his Bren light machine-gun from the hip. The German attack broke up in confusion (and probably disbelief).

What was unbelievable is that two days later Kenneally did it all over again, and with the same victorious result. This time he was wounded, but continued to hop around the battlefield, supported by a Guardsman and firing his Bren gun, refusing to give it up 'as he was the only one who understood it'.

He proudly received his Victoria Cross from his Army Commander (who was also Colonel of the Regiment), General Alexander. Almost certainly, 'Alex' thought he was giving it to a fellow Irishman.

Later, on the radio, Prime Minister Winston Churchill paid tribute to the gallantry of the Irish, telling his listeners about 'Lance-Corporal Kenneally and other heroes I could cite'.

However, the irony of all this was that Kenneally was not Irish at all. 'John Patrick Kenneally' was in fact an assumed name. He was actually more English than Churchill, being Leslie Jackson, the illegitimate son of an 18-year old daughter of a Blackpool chemist. His father was apparently Neville Blond, a wealthy Jewish Manchester businessman, later the Chairman of the English Stage Company and husband of Elaine Marks, the Marks &

Spencer heiress. So the young man was half English, half Jewish.

Always keen on adventure, Leslie had joined the Royal Artillery on his 18th birthday, and found himself at Dollis Hill in London. He went 'absent without leave' and was detained at Wellington Barracks. He was so impressed by his gaolers, the Irish Guards, that he applied for a transfer – which the Royal Artillery refused. So he deserted and went back to civilian life.

Now working on a building site with a team of Irish builders, John Patrick Kenneally, who was going back to Ireland, gave him his identity card. Thus he was free to turn up at the Manchester recruiting office to join the Irish Guards, a regiment formed in 1900 on Queen Victoria's orders because she considered the 'bravery and performance of my Irish soldiers' to be one of the few positive highlights of the Boer War. The Irish Guards, 'the Micks', became one of Britain's finest and best-loved regiments, famous for its disciplined bravery and also acts of impulsive personal gallantry. So it was hardly surprising that 'Patrick Kenneally' should be feted as 'a typical Mick, loving a good fight'.

Even in a tightly regulated organisation like the Army, things like names may not always be what they seem.

? Mary **JACOB**

It took a French Queen to trap women and their breasts into extreme discomfort and an American to set them free.

For 350 years, women had endured the tyranny of the corset, a device of steel and whalebone, created by the wishes of Catherine of Medici, the wife of King Henry II of France. Incredibly, she decreed that no women with thick waists could attend the Royal Court. This arbitrary decision led, throughout the 1550s, to women narrowing their waists in aid of royal fashion right down to a mind-boggling ten inches. This bizarre idea soon spread and fashion-conscious women became condemned to centuries of laced up torture, their breasts pushed upwards by the rigid device. Women were continually fainting and having to be revived at social events with 'smelling-salts'. Worse, their unnatural shape was a real health risk to them, let alone their unborn babies.

In the 19th century, improvements were attempted. In 1875, George Best and George Phelps created the tortuously-named 'Union Under-Flannel, no bones, no eyelets and no laces or pulleys under-outfit'. Rather more catchy was the 'Breast Supporter' of Marie Tucek in 1893, with 'separate pockets' for the breasts. Six years later, Hermione Cadolle launched an 'aid to health' called the 'Bien-être' or 'Wellbeing'. However, none of these really caught on.

A New York socialite, Mary Phelps Jacob, was in the right place and at the right time to create the first true 'bra'. In 1913, she was due to go to a big social event, but found that her corset's whalebone reinforcements were showing through and wrecking the appearance of her sheer evening gown. So she and her maid took two silk handkerchiefs and some pink ribbon and it did the trick. Friends and family began to ask for similar devices and then a stranger offered a dollar for one. As a result she decided to create a business, first patenting her 'Backless Brassiere', named after the old French word for upper-arm.

But she soon became bored with administration, selling her patent for just $1,500 to manufacturers called Warner Brothers – who were to make millions from her invention. Its success was guaranteed when America entered World War I in 1917, because the US War Industries Board appealed to women to stop wearing corsets, thus saving a hefty 28,000 tons of steel – enough to build two battleships or ten million rifles. (A patriotic move similar to the World War II fabric-saving appeal to adopt two-piece swimsuits, ultimately creating the bikini).

HELLO BOYS.

Ida Rosenthal created Maidenform in 1928, but more importantly, devised bust cup sizes. Now women could not only live in comfort but their breasts could be enhanced and promoted as two of their greatest assets. As Eva Herzegova in the 'Wonderbra' posters (above) would controversially say much later, 'Hello Boys'.

? Jenny **JEROME**

Of all the 'Dollar Princesses' – the wealthy American girls who came to Britain to marry a title – Jenny Jerome was the most glamorous, unconventional and easily the most influential.

Jenny was born in Brooklyn in 1854 and grew up into a really beautiful woman, but as one admirer put it 'more of a panther than a woman in her look'. Aged 20, she met Lord Randolph Churchill, the second son of the Duke of Marlborough. They were engaged within three days and married in April 1874. Only eight months later, Winston Churchill was born.

The young couple were the toast of London. Lord Randolph was a rising political star and Jenny was so beautiful that pictures of her were sold to the public like pin-up postcards. She could have been regarded as a matrimonial mercenary, but had such charm and wit that 'Society' took to her. As another 'Dollar Princess', Consuelo Vanderbilt, Duchess of Marlborough put it, 'her grey eyes sparkled with the joy of living and when her anecdotes were risqué, it was with her eyes as well as her words that one could read the implications'.

Unfortunately, there was soon something else risqué in their lives. Randolph had contracted syphilis and Jenny would no longer sleep with him. However, she did sleep with many others including even the Prince of Wales. When he later became King, Jenny got on famously with Queen Alexandra in spite of her affair, which the Queen knew all about.

Winston had been turned over to a nanny, Mrs Everest, and scarcely ever saw his parents. Indeed, even by the cold-hearted standards of that age, both parents neglected their son. He was often terribly unhappy, especially when snatched from his beloved Mrs Everest and sent off to prep school. *'Darling Mummy, I despair. I am so wretched'* he wrote every day. There is always something truly pathetic about his pleading letters to his mother. He later recalled 'she shone for me like the evening star. I loved her dearly, but at a distance'.

Later, scraping into Harrow, Winston remained miserably at the bottom of his class. However, at The Royal Military Academy, Sandhurst, things changed dramatically. Winston became a superb horseman and fencer and was commissioned into the cavalry. Even then his father wrote to him cruelly, 'You will become a mere social wastrel and degenerate into a shabby, unhappy and futile existence'. Lord Randolph, who was sickening of his 'unmentionable' disease, could not have been more wrong. When he died, Jenny, typically unconventional, married an army officer the same age as her son.

The next five years sound more like a racy novel than the normal career of a young British officer. Winston was under fire in four different wars. First it was Cuba, fighting with the Spanish ('there is nothing more exhilarating than being shot at without result'). Then it was against Pathan tribesmen on the North-West Frontier. At the battle of Omdurman in the Sudan, he galloped in the last cavalry charge of the British Army. In Natal, as a journalist he was captured by the Boers and then daringly escaped, becoming a national hero. He then rejoined the cavalry, fought in several battles, wrote his third book and was elected to Parliament where he was to serve for an incredible 65 years.

Now Jenny came into her own. The years of neglect ended and she devoted her life to helping the rising star. She was Winston's political mentor, more like an older sister than a mother.

In 1921, Jenny slipped in her new high-heeled shoes and broke her ankle. She contracted gangrene, her leg was amputated and she died. Winston was devastated.

However, her influence would live on in Winston during his finest hour, the first three years of World War II. His optimism, dynamism, warmth and wit would give him powers of persuasion which not only helped him to beat his foreign enemies but also his defeatist Cabinet colleagues, his suspicious party, the petty-minded Commons, the media, his generals and the often striking trade unions. Most of his great qualities came from his feisty, independent American mother.

William **JOYCE**

For the British awaiting the Nazi onslaught in 1940, there was one person even more hated than Hitler: 'Lord Haw-Haw', the insidious voice on the radio – 'Germany calling, Germany calling'. Unknown to his listeners, his real name was William Joyce.

The Joyces are one of the celebrated 'tribes of Galway,' but William's father emigrated to the United States, so William was born in Brooklyn, before the Joyces returned to Ireland, then part of the United Kingdom. They were pro-British, and with Ireland beginning to fight for her freedom, in 1921 they thought it better to be in England. William was good-looking, intelligent, blue-eyed, fair-haired and patriotic. When he tried to join the Officers Training Corps, his father assured the authorities that, while William was born in New York, 'the whole family was British'.

In 1924, Joyce joined an anti-Labour, anti-Communist movement called the British Fascisti, and in a fracas, a 'Jewish Communist' tried to cut his throat – scarring Joyce's face for life. Despite such activities, he acquired a First in English at Birkbeck College and a wife, Hazel. Soon however, he fell under the spell of Sir Oswald Mosley and joined his British Union of Fascists. Hoping to visit Hitler with Mosley, Joyce made a fatal error, stating he was born in Galway. Little did he realise what passport number 125943 would do to him.

Joyce, now Mosley's Propaganda Director, made his name as an orator. At a smart 'Blackshirt' event at the Park Lane Hotel in 1933, a witness recalled, 'Never before have I met a personality so terrifying in its dynamic force, so vituperative, so vitriolic. We listened in frozen hypnotism to this cold, stabbing voice.'

Similarly, at another meeting in Scotland, a young girl, Margaret White, was fascinated by his oratory. Soon, with Joyce divorced from Hazel, they were married in February 1937. But the British Fascists were losing political ground and income, as public opinion recoiled from both Mussolini's attack on Abyssinia and Hitler's belligerency. Joyce duly lost his job, and Margaret and he became language tutors. As war clouds gathered, Joyce knew he would be interned, and agonised between Southern Ireland and Germany. Fatally, he decided to renew his passport and leave for Germany.

In Berlin, the couple's German friends were not sure what to do with them – until someone suggested the radio that Propaganda Minister Josef Goebbels was then using to undermine foreign countries. At the *Reichsrundfunk* radio station, Joyce met Norman Baillie-Stewart, the 'officer in the Tower', jailed for spying, who with his upper-class accent, was really the first 'Haw-Haw'. But soon Joyce was the star, beaming propaganda towards Britain. With his clever scripts and effective delivery, he became *the* 'Lord Haw-Haw', at one stage reaching 14% of the British population. But many more also claimed to know what 'Haw-Haw' had said – the buildings to be blitzed, the local roads to be 'widened' by bombs, and above all, his apparent uncanny knowledge about which High Street clocks were wrong! As the Luftwaffe wrecked Britain's cities, 'Haw-Haw' went from a public joke to public enemy. Hitler, Goebbels and Goering were distant, almost cartoon figures, but 'Haw-Haw' spoke in insidious, sneering English to the British in their own homes. Simple people even thought he was personally directing the war against them.

As the losing war for Germany dragged on, it was scant consolation for the Joyces that William was awarded the *Kriegsverdienstkreuz* (War Service Cross) personally signed by Hitler. On April 30th 1945, in Joyce's last broadcast, drunk, he slurred, 'You may not hear from me again for a few months. I say, Ich liebe Deutschland! Heil Hitler, and farewell.'

War ended, and in the British zone of occupation Joyce was recognised, arrested and soon on his way to England. Now his 1939 British passport doomed him as a British and not an American citizen. Found guilty of treason, this hated but fascinating man was hung in January 1946.

Henry **KAISER**

There are those who might associate Henry Kaiser with Kaiser Aluminum or Kaiser Steel or Kaiser-Jeep or even his Healthcare Foundation and hospitals. But his most staggering achievement must be the 'Liberty Ship'.

Born in 1882 in New York, Kaiser by the 1930s was a major force in industry and construction, building roads and dams including the Hoover Dam. He also turned to building ships for which he pioneered new mass production techniques, including welding instead of traditional rivets. He was destined to be the right person in the right place at the right time.

In 1936, war clouds were gathering. America began to prepare, and ordered 50 naval auxiliary ships, but few of these were built. The big boost came from Britain in 1940. Desperate to replace merchant vessels being sunk by German U-Boats, the British ordered 60 'tramp steamers' from American yards, initially to a British design and using coal-fired engines. Under Kaiser, modified and improved ships with oil-fired boilers were built in sections welded together. By eliminating skilled riveting, the ships could be produced far faster and more cheaply. A whole new workforce could be quickly trained. Indeed, when America was plunged into war in December 1941 and her men enlisted, women could do the work.

President Roosevelt launched 14 ships on one day in September 1942. The first was the SS *Patrick Henry* and he quoted the revolutionary Patrick Henry's famous 1775 speech, 'Give me liberty or give me death'. The name 'Liberty Ship' caught on.

The time to build a 'Liberty Ship' dropped rapidly from 230 days to an average of 42, with some produced much faster. The SS *Robert E. Peary*, as a startling publicity stunt, was built in an amazing four and a half days.

Soon the 'Six Companies' and their 17 shipyards under William Kaiser's direction were building Liberty ships far faster than the enemy could sink them, sometimes three a day. Eventually a colossal total of 2,710 would roll down the slipways, and played a major role in winning the war.

After the war, 2,400 Liberty ships survived, of which 526 formed the basis of the shipping fleets and wealth of the Greeks like Aristotle Onassis. Now only two operating ships survive, and many of us have seen inside one of them, because the engine room of the SS *Jeremiah O'Brien* was filmed as the engine room in the blockbuster, *Titanic*.

Duke **KAHANAMOKU**

At the 1924 Paris Olympic Games, Duke Kahanamoku just failed to win his third Gold Medal as the fastest swimmer in the world. Now 34, something of a veteran, he was pipped by a 20 year old kid called Johnny Weissmuller, who went on, of course, to be much better known – as 'Tarzan'.

However, the Hawaiian was now destined to leave the pool and the record books to become famous in his own right – as the man who single-handedly made the sport of surfing popular.

He was certainly born in the right place – Waikiki Beach. He inherited his name 'Duke' from his father, who had been thus christened when Prince Alfred, Duke of Edinburgh had visited the Hawaiian Islands back in 1869.

As a teenager, every day Duke would go out surfing, on a traditional board, made of Koa wood, and huge by modern standards – 16 feet long.

One day he left the beach to compete in a swimming race in Honolulu Harbour, and proceeded to break the 100 yards freestyle world record by a whopping 4.6 seconds. This was so extraordinary that the Amateur Athletics Union at first refused to ratify the record, claiming, rather rudely, that 'the timers must have been using alarm clocks, not stopwatches!'

But Duke quickly confirmed his position as the fastest swimmer on earth, breaking many more world records and winning Olympic Gold medals at Stockholm in 1912 and Antwerp in 1920, before retiring after that silver against young Weissmuller.

He then gave swimming exhibitions all over the world, crucially deciding to include surfing demonstrations. These were an instant success. His thrilling show at Freshwater Beach in Sydney is acclaimed as the real starting point of all surfing in Australia, especially when he chose a young spectator, Isabel Letham, to ride in on a wave on his board, celebrated by his statue staring out to sea.

It was also because of Duke that surfing first started in America – in Santa Cruz, California. With his proximity to Hollywood, he also played in several films, publicising the new sport.

At nearby Newport Beach, his fame was further enhanced after rescuing eight fishermen from a capsized boat from which many perished. His surfboard enabled him to make repeated, quick trips out to the wreck. The Police Chief described this feat as 'the most superhuman surfboard rescue the world has ever seen'. Many beaches now have surfboard lifeguards.

Duke was Sheriff of Honolulu for nearly thirty years, and uniquely, he is fêted in both the Swimming and Surfing Halls of Fame.

When, in 1968, Duke Kahanamoku died, his coffin was taken in a long motorcade to his beloved Waikiki Beach and buried at sea. His statue still stands on that beach, often adorned with traditional *leis* of flowers.

It is very seldom that someone 'creates' a sport. But it can certainly be said that Duke did exactly that, and the sport that he started is now immensely popular, not only on the huge waves of the Pacific, but even in the rather more modest surf of Cornwall and Ireland.

Vijay **KAKKAR**

When we hear the words 'Deep Vein Thrombosis' (DVT), perhaps most of us immediately picture long flights, in which a handful of passengers have developed blood clots in their veins – often fatal when they reach the lungs – in what is called 'pulmonary embolism'.

If we were told that methods had been devised to save 300,000 people a year from dying from such blood clots, and jumped to the conclusion that such potential deaths were related to air travel, many of us would simply stop flying. In fact, the figure relates to another danger – patients undergoing surgery, and, for them, the risk is really that severe.

An Indian Professor, Vijay Kakkar, has spent 35 years identifying and solving the problem of what he calls the 'Cinderella of clinical medicine and surgery'. At King's College, London, as a Research Fellow, he witnessed in 1965 two patients die in quick succession after what seemed successful surgery. As he began to realise the enormity of the problem, he decided to devote the rest of his life to answering several key questions: 'Can the risk of DVT be diagnosed earlier? Can it be prevented by some method? And can re-occurrence be avoided?'

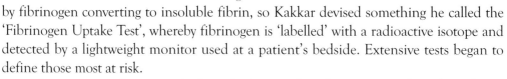

Professor Kakkar started a unique research facility, The Thrombosis Research Institute, funded by King's College, London. Its first task was to detect the danger. Blood clots are caused by fibrinogen converting to insoluble fibrin, so Kakkar devised something he called the 'Fibrinogen Uptake Test', whereby fibrinogen is 'labelled' with a radioactive isotope and detected by a lightweight monitor used at a patient's bedside. Extensive tests began to define those most at risk.

It was not as if surgeons had not been struggling for years to reduce thrombosis, with physiotherapy and elasticated stockings, but Kakkar nevertheless estimated that 25% of patients were still developing thrombosis. Another possible remedy was blood-thinning agents. But these could cause serious bleeding during and after operations, which is why many surgeons were very wary about their use.

Heparin, however, might be the answer. Heparin was originally derived from dog liver cells (hepar , Greek for liver), but now mainly from pig intestine and cow lung tissue. A naturally-forming anticoagulant, heparin is only fully effective for one hour, so that it needs to be injected frequently or as a continuous infusion. Thus, patients with a suspected thrombosis are routinely put on a 'Heparin Pump'.

In 1969, Vijay Kakkar now sought to use heparin in very small and controlled doses as a prophylactic treatment before, during and after surgery. With one company, CHOAY in Paris, providing free heparin supplies, he now carried out extensive trials that indeed indicated that heparin could be used to prevent thrombosis related to surgery. But, in spite of such trials, one of which covered several countries, and the presentation of the results at major medical events, there was great scepticism among surgeons. It would take years to break down this resistance.

One of the workload problems of administering heparin frequently was eliminated by the next improvement at the end of the 1970s, the creation of 'low molecular weight heparin' doses. Trials again indicated that this has prevented at least 50% of patients at risk. As it has become standard practice and with tens of millions of patients now treated annually worldwide, this means that Vijay Kakkar's pioneering work is indeed saving 300,000 people a year. Yet how many of them know his name?.

Mikhail **KALASHNIKOV**

In 1941, Sergeant Mikhail Kalashnikov was lying in hospital, badly wounded after one of the battles in the titanic struggle between the Soviet Union and the German invaders. Of peasant stock, one of 19 children, he heard his wounded comrades complain about Soviet rifles, and he submitted designs for sub-machine guns and rifles. Later he entered a competition to design an assault rifle that would suit the mucky conditions of the Eastern Front, eventually creating the most ubiquitous small-arms weapon the world has ever seen – as well as one of its most potent symbols.

In most armies, infantrymen had single-shot rifles, each section (or squad) had a light machine gun, and for real fire power, a separate platoon with medium machine guns. However, trench warfare in World War I featured firefights at much closer range, highlighting the need for fast-firing, lightweight weapons (indeed, Al Capone's 'Tommy Guns' had first been designated as 'trench brooms').

The trouble with most submachine guns was that they used pistol ammunition – too light – while guns using conventional rifle ammunition were too heavy. So all armies experimented with 'intermediate-power' ammunition and weapons. It was the Germans who first found the solution with their *Sturmgewehr 44* or 'storm rifle', a name coined, typically, by Adolf Hitler himself.

Soviet soldiers, desperately fighting the Germans, asked for a similar weapon and that's when Kalashnikov entered the competition. After several trials and many changes, his design won in 1947.

He had not needed to 'reinvent the wheel', and the AK-47 used features from many foreign weapons. It could fire single shot or automatic, was simple to operate, cheap and easy to manufacture. With generous clearances, it kept on firing even when full of mud and sand and did not have to be accurate at long ranges – its sights usually set at 'point blank'.

The AK-47 swept the world. It armed all the Soviet 'Warsaw Pact' armies and the huge Chinese Army, plus 70 foreign armies, as well as various rebel movements and even criminal gangs. Over 100 million have been produced so far, most legally or under license, but incredibly no less than one million are made illegally each year. The pirates of Somalia can obtain an AK-47 for just $30, and in Kenya the exchange price over 20 years has dropped from 15 to 4 cows per gun.

Confirming how its rulers obtained their power, the AK-47 now features in the official flag of Mozambique, while Zimbabwe has one in its coat of arms. Unsurprisingly, Hezbollah uses it on its flag, as do the Iranian Revolutionary Guards. In general, it is a symbol of anti-Americanism, so Hollywood often arms its 'terrorists' and 'gang members' with the weapon.

Kalashnikov has no regrets about the effect his weapon has had on the world. 'It is the Germans who are responsible for the fact that I became a fabricator of arms. If not for them, I would have constructed agricultural machines – or lawnmowers. If someone asks me how I can sleep at night knowing that my arms have killed millions of people, I respond that I have no problem sleeping, my conscience is clear. I constructed arms to defend my country.'

Ingvar **KAMPRAD**

Ingvar Kamprad's sales talent showed early. At the tender age of five he was selling matches from his bicycle in the village of Agunnaryd in southern Sweden, and soon learned that he could buy them in bulk cheaply in Stockholm and sell them at a good profit. He then graduated to Christmas tree decorations, pencils, ball-point pens, seed and fish. A studious boy, when he was 17 in 1943 his father gave him some cash for doing well in his studies. Instead of blowing it on something trivial like most teenagers, Ingvar decided to start a company which he called IKEA, made from his initials IK, his family farm Elmtaryd, and his home village, Agunnaryd.

At first, young Ingvar's IKEA company continued the pattern of his childhood trading, adding wallets, picture frames, watches, jewellery and nylons. But then he began to expand by advertising, persuading the local milkman to deliver the resulting orders to the railway station.

In 1948 came the decisive move, when Ingvar Kamprad decided to make what he was going to sell, choosing furniture, produced locally. This went well, and three years later the first of his catalogues appeared, soon to be followed by the first IKEA showroom in 1953. It was there that he saw a fellow worker helpfully removing the legs of a table to fit it in a customer's car. This was the defining moment for IKEA. The idea of flat packs and allowing customers to assemble the furniture themselves at home was born – now the heart of the company's business.

Ever since, IKEA's progress and success have been extraordinary and unstoppable, with its combination of good design, new materials and very affordable prices. The company has steadily expanded, not just in Europe, but in countries like distant Australia in 1975, Canada the next year and the USA in 1985. Only months after 1989, the 'Year of Revolutions' and the collapse of the 'Iron Curtain' and Communism, IKEA stores were opening in Hungary, with Poland and the Czech Republic following in 1991. And Communism in China appears not to be a problem, IKEA's Shanghai store opened successfully in 1998.

At sixty, Ingvar Kamprad retired from Group management to become an advisor in 1986. Millions of us can thank our lucky stars that young Ingvar did not decide to use his father's birthday present to buy some snappy new skis.

Gary **KILDALL**

Gary Kildall could have been one of the richest men on earth. But unfortunately he decided to fly off and let his wife handle things – the biggest and most tragic business blunder in history.

Computing was changing fast. Gone were IBM's Thomas Watson, estimating that five computers in the world would suffice, or Kenneth Olsen of Digital stopping any development of personal computers because he did not see 'any reason why anyone would want to have a computer at home.'

Intel's invention of the microprocessor or chip changed everything. Now computers did not have to weigh tons and fill whole rooms. In 1974, young kids with long hair and/or beards met on Wednesdays at the 'Homebrew Computing Club', a hall rented from Stamford University in what became 'Silicon Valley'. Young men like Steve Jobs and Steve Wozniak of Apple and 19-year old Bill Gates and Paul Allen of Microsoft shared their triumphs. Soon the Personal Computer or PC was on its way – out of their garages and into millions of homes and offices.

Gary Kildall, of Norwegian seafaring stock was, like Bill Gates, brought up in Seattle, but was up the road from Silicon Valley in Monterey when he heard about Intel's commercially available microprocessors. Experimenting with them, he was the first to realise that they were fully capable computers rather than equipment controllers, and he created the first high level programming for microprocessors. With his wife, Dorothy, he set up Digital Research Inc in his California house to market, fairly successfully, his operating systems.

Now IBM, the world's leading mainframe manufacturer, wanted to get into the booming personal computer market, and also to do this secretly and fast. One August day in 1980 they called Bill Gates and said they were flying to Seattle and would like to come in next day 'to talk about Microsoft products.' This was like a visit from the Queen or the Pope, so Gates quickly looked for a suit to wear. Jack Sams of IBM described arriving, *'We were waiting in the front and this young fella came out to take us to Mr Gates' office. I thought he was the office boy, but, of course, it was Bill Gates.'*

After agreeing to sign IBM's standard non-disclosure agreement (swearing them to secrecy), Bill Gates (below) then had to reveal that he did not have one of the key things IBM was looking for – an operating system. But in a spirit of friendly co-operation, he called his friend Gary Kildall. 'I'm sending some guys down. Treat them right, they're important guys.'

So next day, the three IBM executives flew south and turned up at the small house in Pacific Grove, California, the headquarters of Digital Research. But Gary Kildall, the genius who had created the CP/M (Control Program/ Microcomputer) operating system, was not there to greet them. Flying off to deliver software to someone else was not 'treating IBM right'. Nor was his wife Dorothy, refusing to sign the non-disclosure agreement. Jack Sams of IBM recalls the chaotic, frustrating day in the tiny house, even when Gary turned up and joined the discussion. *'So we spent the whole day in Pacific Grove debating with them and with our attorneys and her attorneys and everybody else about whether or not she could even talk to us about talking to us. We left.'* And they went back to Bill Gates.

This time, Gates did not hesitate. He agreed to find them an operating system and turned to Tim Patterson, who quickly wrote QDOS (Quick and Dirty Operating System), which IBM called PC DOS 1.0. Gates paid just $50,000 dollars for the rights. It was based on Gary Kildall's CP/M and months later, when he discovered this, there was a furious confrontation at a Seatttle restaurant between the two friends. But Kildall knew he could not sue Microsoft without suing IBM, a daunting task. So, to avoid trouble, he agreed to licence his system to IBM at a high royalty. But when IBM's PC was launched, he was stupefied to find that IBM was charging $240 for his CP/M and just $40 for Bill Gates' DOS.

The result was inevitable; hundreds of millions of computers running Microsoft's software, and Bill Gates becoming the richest man in the world, worth $40 billion and climbing. Gary Kildall sold his company for $120 million and died aged 52 after a fall on the floor of a bar.

If only he had not flown off that morning.

Alberto **KORDA**

In March 1960, Alberto Korda attended a huge memorial service for 136 men killed by a Belgian ammunition ship blowing up in Havana harbour. Fidel Castro harangued the crowd with 'Che' Guevara beside him. Korda, as the main photographic chronicler of the Cuban revolution, snapped two quick frames of Guevara with 'a look of noble anger on his face.' One was to become the most recognised image in the history of photography, appearing on millions of posters, cards and T-shirts, the universal icon of protest. As an icon it was undeserved, and what is more, we might never have seen it because Korda's newspaper, *Revolución*, actually turned it down as 'too dreamy'. So Korda just stuck it up on his bathroom wall, where it stayed undiscovered for seven years.

Korda, whose real name was Alberto Díaz Gutiérrez, had become Cuba's leading fashion photographer. 'My main aim was to meet women.' A master in black and white, he became the official and personal photographer of Fidel Castro and his Cuban revolution against the Batista regime, taking many photos of 'Che', but none as iconic.

'Che' himself was not even Cuban, born Ernesto Guevara Lynch in Argentina. Among those of Irish descent, he was to make nearly as much trouble in South America as his namesake, Eliza Lynch. Passionate about literature, especially poetry, he studied to be a doctor. In spite of his asthma, he was an excellent rugby player, although he so rarely washed that we might have known him by his other nickname, 'Chango' or pig!

In 1951, he embarked on his famous motorcycle journey through South America. This trip shocked him about the continent's general level of poverty, hunger and disease. Blaming capitalism and the Americans, he resolved that only a 'well-armed struggle against imperialism' would succeed.

He obtained his chance in Cuba. Guevara impressed Castro by his 'competence, diplomacy and patience' – skills he was not always to show. However, Castro also supported his deputy's brutal ruthlessness in shooting waiverers. In late 1958, Guevara, outnumbered and surrounded by Batista's troops, brilliantly won the battle of Santa Clara and it was this victory that persuaded Batista that he should go.

Once in power, Guevara was put in charge of the feared La Cabaña Fortress prison and there took his revenge by firing squad on anyone opposed to Castro's revolution. After the American-backed 'Bay of Pigs' invasion he was able to rub in the salt at a conference – by passing President Kennedy a note, 'Thanks for Playa Girón. Before the invasion, the revolution was shaky. Now it is stronger than ever.' He then, perhaps over-confident, became the architect of the disastrous Cuban-Soviet alliance that led to the 'Cuban Missile Crisis', a failure for both Castro and the Soviets.

He then failed in Africa and then in Bolivia, where he was surrounded and wounded, shouting, 'Don't shoot! I am Che Guevara and worth more to you alive than dead.' The Bolivian President disagreed and ordered him shot.

Just two months earlier, Giangiacomo Fetrinelli, pretending to be a revolutionary but actually a publisher, had dropped in to Korda's house. Convinced that in Bolivia 'Che' was doomed, he persuaded Korda to give him the negative of the photograph on the bathroom wall for nothing. With Che's death, millions of images were sold within weeks.

Whether all those young people, looking at Che staring down from their walls, knew his real story is debatable. Apart from one battle, arguably he was a failure all his life – as a politician, or as a guerrilla trying to export revolution. It was in marked contrast to other Irishmen, like Bernardo O'Higgins, who really did help to liberate South American countries.

Poor Korda received virtually nothing from his famous photograph, which earned millions, because Castro had not signed up for the Berne Convention protecting intellectual property.

But just at the end of his life, he had one little victory. In Britain's High Court, he prevented Smirnoff from putting it on a Vodka bottle. He probably thought it was one capitalist insult too far.

Ivar **KREUGER**

In March 1932, a man was found shot dead in a Paris apartment. He was Ivar Kreuger, the 'Match King' and reportedly the third richest man in the world. He left a note saying *'I have made such a mess of things that I believe this to be the most satisfactory solution'*. What was this mess? And why did the 'Kreuger crash' rock the investment world and push it even further into depression?

The trouble with Kreuger was he was both a genius and a swindler. As the great economist John Kenneth Galbraith wrote *'Boiler-room operators, peddlers of stock in imaginary Canadian mines, mutual-fund managers whose genius and imagination are unconstrained by integrity, as well as less exotic larcenists, should read about Kreuger. He was the Leonardo of their craft'*.

Ivar Kreuger was born in Sweden in 1880 and his father was an industrialist with several match factories. Ivar started his business life conventionally and respectably, creating Sweden's best construction company. He then turned to the match business (matches were then an important and essential product) and built a huge monopolistic empire based on the new 'safety match'. Soon he controlled all the match production in Scandinavia and then 75% of world match production. He really was the 'Match King'.

But he also bought into banks, mining companies, railways, timber and paper companies, film distributors and real estate firms, as well as household names like S.K.F. bearings and the Ericsson phone company, amazingly ending up controlling 400 companies. This led to a life of luxury with many houses and apartments and even a private island, as well as several yachts on which he hosted stars like Greta Garbo, Douglas Fairbanks and Mary Pickford.

But much of this was achieved with bluff, extraordinary luck and even outright dishonesty. Falsified accounts, forged signatures or whole documents played their role, as well as dummy companies and the creation of exotic new financial instruments, of which some are used today. He was even regarded as something of a hero, lending money to several needy countries, including even France and Germany, and this was often in return for favours like the country's match monopoly.

However the financial fallout and pressures after the 1929 Wall Street crash and the worldwide depression, began to affect Kreuger's house of cards, and by 1931 rumours were spreading that all was not well. He turned to Sweden's central bank, the Sveriges Riksbank, for new loans to prop him up, but the bank now very sensibly demanded a full-scale meeting furnished with a complete statement of accounts.

It was the day before that meeting that Ivar Kreuger was found dead.

Jan **KUBIŠ**

In a park in Prague in June 1942, Alois Denemarek met his boyhood friend Jan Kubiš, who seemed distracted. 'Look, things are a bit tense here at the moment.' Not surprising, because Jan had just succeeded in killing the most hated man in Czechoslovakia - Reinhard Heydrich.

Until his death, few British or Americans would have heard of him, but of all the Nazi leaders, the icy, blond and slit-eyed Heydrich was arguably the most evil and dangerous of all. He was born into a comfortable, highly musical family. However, a musical career was not for the young Heydrich. With his family's wealth ruined by inflation, he joined the Navy and – a serial seducer – slept with the daughter of a powerful shipyard director. Spurning her when he fell for his future wife, Linda von Osten, he was cashiered out of the Navy.

Linda persuaded him to approach the fledgling Nazi party and her husband soon became the brutal right arm of Heinrich Himmler. Most people were simply terrified of him, seeing him as ' a young, evil god of death'. They had good reasons. It was the brilliant, ruthless Heydrich who helped to destroy Röhm and the SA in 'the night of the long knives'. He also unleashed *Kristallnacht,* the first public attack on the Jews, and engineered the fictitious assault on Gleiwitz radio station – the excuse to attack Poland that started World War II. Even more significant, it was Heydrich who chaired the notorious lakeside Wannsee Conference which planned the 'Final Solution' for 11 million Jews, and who commanded the 'Jewish expert' Adolph Eichmann, who succeeded in killing six million. The Slavs were likely to be next.

By 1942, Heydrich had created an unique power base: second in command of the SS, head of the *Sicherheitsdienst* (SD) and of the *Reichssicherheitshauptamt* (RSHA), the overall security umbrella of the Reich. This coldly complex man also had a reckless streak. On the Luftwaffe reserve, he flew combat missions in several campaigns – once forced down behind Russian lines. Hitler forbade any more risks – or thought he had.

When Heydrich was sent to Prague as Czechoslovakia's brutal master, he cleverly started to use his 'sugar and whip' method – combining harshness with rewards – and vital Czech production actually started to rise. In response, the British backed a Free Czech attempt on Heydrich's life, and Jan Kubiš was one of the team flown in.

Sergeant Kubiš, (left), like Josef Frantisek, (page 73), had already fought with the Poles and then the French, winning the *Croix be Guerre*. Now he waited by the roadside with his friend Josef Gabcik.

Heydrich's overconfident contempt for the Czechs was to spell his doom. In his open green sports Mercedes, he saw Gabcik struggling with his jammed Sten gun, and foolishly ordered his driver to stop. Then Kubiš threw a grenade that drove debris deep into Heydrich's body. His wounds were to turn septic and kill him in what many would say was well-deserved agony.

While publicly praising 'the man with an Iron Heart', in private Hitler was devastated and also furious with his possible successor. *'Such heroic gestures as driving in an open, unarmoured vehicle are just damned stupidity. That a man as irreplaceable as Heydrich should expose himself to unnecessary danger, I can only condemn as stupid and idiotic'.*

Within days, Kubiš and the others were betrayed, and trapped in a church where, in a long firefight with 700 avenging Germans, they all died. The Nazis took a terrible revenge for the death of a favourite son. The innocent villages, Lidice and Lezaky, were razed and most of the inhabitants annihilated, the Germans gloatingly filming their work. Thousands of Czechs died.

'Children of Lidice' Marie Uchytilovo

But the bravery of Jan Kubiš, the strongest act of defiance in occupied Europe, meant that the Czechs felt no longer felt like slaves, and began to resist with pride. Years later Alois Denemarek told the BBC, 'Even though it cost the lives of my family and thousands of others, that's nothing compared with what we would have suffered had Heydrich been allowed to live.'

Henrietta **LACKS**

Johns Hopkins Hospital in Baltimore was the only one near to where Henrietta Lacks lived that would treat black patients, and there in 1951 she was diagnosed with a cancerous tumour. Born in Virginia, she had taken her name from a white family called Lacks who had once owned her ancestors as slaves.

Just after giving birth to her fifth child, Henrietta had mysteriously started bleeding. When she was found to have cancer, a small part of her cervix was removed for examination and given to Dr George Otto Gey. Henrietta Lacks was about to become, literally, immortal. Dr Gey was to discover that

Henrietta's cells 'did something we'd never seen before. They could be kept alive and grow.' Henrietta sadly died a few months later, but her cells lived on, freely donated, *initially*, by Dr Gey to the medical world. At first they were coded 'Helen Lane' or 'Helen Larkin' cells, but Henrietta's real name emerged a few years later and to this day they are called 'HeLa cells'. Most doctors, researchers and pathologists would know the name HeLa cells, but be completely unaware of the unwitting role of Henrietta Lacks in saving the lives of others.

The first, most urgent and spectacular such use of HeLa cells was by Jonas Salk testing his vaccine that saved much of the world from devastating polio in the 1950s. But

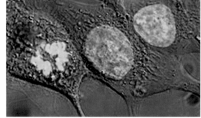

since then, the cells have been used in innumerable experiments, including those for cancer and AIDS, and with no less than 60,000 scientific articles published about their use, with 300 new ones added each month. After Dr Gey's initial generosity, her cells have been sold commercially for millions of dollars, yet shockingly her family has received nothing.

All over the world, there are millions of people who owe their health, and even their lives, to an unknown woman dying in a Baltimore hospital over half a century ago. And many, if they knew about Henrietta might – at the same time as being thankful – find themselves reflecting on the morality of it all.

Hedy **LAMARR**

Hedy Lamarr was once regarded as the world's most beautiful woman, but far fewer of us know her as a woman with remarkable brains as well as beauty, responsible for a breakthrough we value today.

Born Hedwig Kiesler in Vienna in 1913, twenty years later she created a sensation in a Czech film called *Ecstasy*, in which she not only appeared nude but simulated an orgasm in close-up, its shocking realism aided by her being stabbed with a safety pin in the rear by the director.

That same year she had married the much older Friedrich Mandle, an obsessive armaments millionaire whose lavish parties both Hitler and Mussolini attended. Mandle tried to buy up copies of *Ecstasy* in a vain attempt to limit its distribution. But one side-effect of the young actress's unhappy marriage to Mandle was to awaken her scientific interest in weapons.

In London Louis B. Meyer of MGM hired the 'Ecstasy Lady', but insisted she change her name, choosing Lamarr after a star who had recently died. 'Hedy Lamarr' went on to make 18 films, often cast as a glamorous, exotic seductress and opposite stars like Charles Boyer, Clark Gable and Spencer Tracy. Her biggest success was with Victor Mature in *Samson and Delilah*, the world's highest-grossing film in 1949.

It was during World War II that Hedy made a scientific advance that echoes to this day. She had been impressed with her neighbour George Antheil's experiments with the

automated control of musical instruments, and hit on the idea of creating frequency-hopping as a secret method of making radio-controlled torpedoes harder to jam. In 1942, she and Antheil were granted a patent for a device using a piano roll to change between 88 frequencies.

In the event, the US Navy did not adopt it – until twenty years later when it was used by American ships during the 'Cuban Missile Crisis', and after her patent had run out. However, Hedy did not completely lose out commercially, because in 1998 a Canadian technology company acquired 49% of her patent. And her frequency-hopping idea is now the basis for modern spread-spectrum technology like Bluetooth and Wi-Fi networks.

The beautiful star with the clever mind had a tempestuous life. Married five times, she was arrested for shoplifting in 1966, prompting her to write next year in her autobiography 'I figured out that I had made – and spent – some thirty million dollars. Yet earlier that day I had been unable to pay for a sandwich'.

Nevertheless she did make some extra pocket money out of the name that Louis B. Meyer had given her. She sued Mel Brooks for millions for the unauthorised use of it in the film *Blazing Saddles*.

Dominique-Jean **LARREY**

Since the dawn of time, to be wounded in battle was often a sentence of death – by shock, infection, disease and primitive surgery. Luckily for those unfortunate enough to have to fight, there would eventually be several pioneers in what many military men would dismiss as a hidden and inglorious part of warfare.

'If ever the soldiers erect a statue, it should be of Baron Larrey, the most virtuous man I have ever known.' Thus spoke Napoleon of his legendary Chief Surgeon.

While born poor, Dominique-Jean Larrey was a nephew of a surgeon and had studied hard, then trained under the famous surgeon Pierre-Joseph Dessault in Paris. Enlisting first in the Navy, he found that he suffered from chronic seasickness. Soon after transferring to the army in 1792, the 26-year-old Larrey realised that the battlefield was a terrible place for a wounded man if he were to have any chance of survival, and that it was essential to remove the wounded men as soon as possible. Thus, he designed *Ambulances Volantes* or 'flying ambulances' – light, horse-drawn wagons backed by a team of a medical officer, a quartermaster, a Sergeant, a drummer boy (carrying the bandages) and 24 men. His ambulances could evacuate the wounded back to proper hospitals within minutes. Soon the whole French army followed his lead, as later on did foreign armies.

Larrey was also a calm and brilliant surgeon. He worked so fast –

to minimise the terrible shock before anaesthetics – that he completed 200 amputations in just 24 hours after the bloody battle of Borodino, and no less than 300 at the crossing of the Berezina River, where the pitiful remnants of the *Grande Armée* just escaped from Russia. There, immensely popular, he was passed to safety over the heads of the soldiers.

While serving his Emperor in no less than 60 battles, Larrey pioneered new techniques and wrote books on military surgery influencing the world's medical profession. Unusually, he tended with equal care to both friend and enemy, increasing the universal respect for him on all sides. This would pay dividends.

At the height of the Battle of Waterloo, the Duke of Wellington peered through the smoke and suddenly asked, 'Who is that bold fellow?

'It's Larrey', someone answered.

'Tell them not to fire in that direction; at least let us give the brave man time to gather up the wounded.' He then doffed his hat.

'Who are you saluting?' enquired the Duke of Cambridge.

'I salute the courage and devotion of an age that is no longer ours', then replied Wellington, pointing at Larrey with his sword.

Only a few hours later, his lifetime of helping enemy wounded was to save Larrey's own life. Captured by Wellington's allies, the Prussians, he was to be executed. But a Prussian doctor intervened – a former student of Larrey – and then pointed out to Marshal Blücher that Larrey had recently saved the life of Blücher's own son.

Larrey was therefore released, and went on to become the most popular surgeon in France, boosted by the 100,000 francs willed to him by Napoleon, because 'he is the worthiest man I ever met.'

Luckily for the wounded, three lessons – removing them from battlefields quickly, looking after them in sanitary conditions and cutting down infection – have vastly improved their chances of survival.

Of those wounded in World War I, 45% then died; in World War II it was down to 30%; in Korea, Vietnam and the Falklands the figure was 24%, and today in Afghanistan and Iraq, it has dropped to 10%.

Gérard **LEMAN**

General Leman was a brave and resourceful officer, the military tutor to his king, Belgium's Albert 1. By August 1914, he had few illusions that Belgium's neutrality would be respected and he knew how important the town of Liège, and even more so, its railway line, were likely to be.

In many ways, the legendary German 'Schlieffen Plan' was a railway plan. The American Civil War had proved that railways, with their ability to move masses of men and supplies rapidly, had transformed warfare. Germany had so embraced the concept that only her top military graduates went to the all-important Railway Department.

General von Schlieffen, the Chief of Staff, had personally spent 15 years studying in detail both Germany's and her neighbours' railway systems for his proposed great sweep through Northern Europe, designed to defeat France in weeks, before turning on Russia – as the Kaiser over-confidently boasted, 'Lunch in Paris, dinner in St. Petersburg'. Schlieffen had plotted every station, point, bridge and wagon, to move 11,000 trains with four million men and their horses, supplies and ammunition.

Liège was the key, not only blocking the best way into Belgium, but also straddling the main railway line that Schlieffen needed from Germany to Brussels and Paris. The Belgians fully grasped its strategic significance, and built a defensive ring of 12 forts whose overlapping fields of fire meant that if one fort fell, its neighbour's guns could still dominate the gap. General Leman (right) brought this defensive system to full effectiveness.

The Germans smashed through 'neutral' Belgium's border on 4th August, 1914, and next day attacked Leman's defences. However, they were bloodily repulsed time and again. The clock was ticking, and after two days of costly failed assaults, a German brigade infiltrated between two forts, capturing Liège itself. It made no difference to Leman. His forts valiantly held out and still interdicted the all-important railway.

The over-rigid Schlieffen Plan became fatally delayed. But waiting were huge 14.5 inch howitzers called 'dicke Bertha', 'Big Bertha', (below) named after Bertha Krupp. The

squat, black 93-ton guns were hauled into Liège and began to hurl their one-ton shells a mile into the sky. These sliced down through the forts' concrete roofs and then exploded with devastating force. Leman himself had both legs crushed by masonry, but was patched up and continued to be driven between the forts to encourage his men. Then a shell hit Fort Loncin and its magazine, burying the garrison, who were all wounded or killed. Leman was dragged out, asphyxiated by fumes, 'Respectez-vous le General, il est mort', his men entreated a German Captain. But Leman came to, murmuring, 'It is as it is. Please put in your dispatches that I was unconscious.'

His stubborn defence imposed a vital delay to the German sweep through Belgium and France, spoiling the whole enterprise. France was not knocked out of the war, the French and British counter-attacked near Paris and trench warfare began. Germany's troops were not 'home by Christmas' and she was condemned to a long, bloody, ruinous war.

General Leman returned after four years captivity to a hero's welcome in Belgium. This was richly deserved.

Jules **LEOTARD**

The word 'leotard' is familiar enough – for the one-piece, skin-tight garments worn by dancers, gymnasts, skaters, acrobats, athletes, actors and legions of keep fit enthusiasts. They can be any colour, simple or with flashy decorations, and can also be worn with ballet skirts and tights.

It is curious that the man they were named after, Jules Leotard, had been dead for 16 years before the name became common, and he himself would have used the French word 'maillot'. Indeed, Jules Leotard should really be known for something else he invented – the flying trapeze – which thrills circus audiences to this day.

Leotard was born in Toulouse in 1842, the son of a gymnastics instructor. At first he turned his back on this physical heritage, passing his legal examinations to become a lawyer. But at 18 he was drawn back to experimenting with trapeze bars and ropes.

Soon he was the star of the *Cirque Napoleon*, and inspired the 1867 popular song:

'He'd fly through the air with the greatest of ease,
That daring young man on the flying trapeze.'

With the lyrics by British writer, George Leybourne, and music by Gaston Lyle, *'That daring young man on the flying trapeze'* has since been recorded by such stars as Burl Ives, Don Redman, Eddie Cantor, Les Paul & Mary Ford, and even Bruce Springsteen.

Three years after the song first appeared, Leotard died in Spain at just 28 years old, and not in a dramatic trapeze accident but from an infection.

While it is better to be remembered for something, Leotard would surely have preferred to be known for his daring on the trapeze than for a simple and everyday exercise garment.

James **LIND**

Scurvy is a hideous disease. It starts silently with fatigue, poor appetite and weight loss. Then bruises appear on the skin and the gums begin to bleed. Soon the joints become painful and swollen as their cavities fill with blood, haemorrhages turn the whites of the eyes red, the teeth fall out and the breath becomes foul. Anaemia, fever, incontinence and paralysis follow. Death comes slowly but dignity goes long before. And all this through lack of a simple chemical in the diet – ascorbic acid, Vitamin C.

Vitamin C is essential for collagen production and iron absorption in the body. Most animals are able to synthesize the vitamin, but humans cannot, and must obtain it from outside sources like citrus fruits, tomatoes, peppers, spinach, broccoli, several other vegetables and surprisingly, oysters.

Scurvy emerged as a major maritime problem with the advent of voyages of exploration. Before the end of the fifteenth century most sea trading was in small vessels sailing close to land. But global commerce led to journeys lasting weeks or months away with the difficulties of preserving fresh food. It became a major cause of death, with Vasco da Gama losing 50% of his crew on his way to India in 1491, and Magellan 80% on his circumnavigation in 1521. Scurvy had become *'the plague of the sea, the spoyle of mariners'*.

In 1739 James Lind, a young Scottish physician, joined the Navy as a surgeon's mate. After service in the Mediterranean and the West Indies, he was promoted to surgeon of HMS *Salisbury* in the Channel Fleet in 1747. During his years aboard ship he had observed the effects of scurvy on crews, especially Admiral Anson's catastrophic circumnavigation in 1740 in which 1,400 out of 1,900 men had died. Lind, already aware that eating citrus fruits might have an effect on scurvy, wished to prove it and on HMS *Salisbury* he set up one of medicine's first clinical trials.

Lind selected 12 sailors suffering from scurvy, and divided them into six groups of two. They received the same basic daily diet, but to one group he added a quart of cider, to another group twenty five drops of sulphuric acid, and group 3 had six spoonfuls of vinegar, group 4 half a pint of sea water, group 5 two oranges and group 6 a mixture of garlic, mustard and horseradish, mercifully combined with barley water. It was Group 5 that responded. Within days one sailor was fit for duty and another had almost recovered.

Lind retired from the Navy, returning to marry and practise medicine in Edinburgh. In 1754 he published A *Treatise of the Scurvy* and three years later On the Most Effectual Means of Preserving the Health of Seamen. In both books he carried out a systematic review of what had been written on the topic by others – again not something that medical writers had done before, and in both he recommended giving sailors citrus fruits on long voyages.

Amazingly, it took forty years for his advice about this to be taken seriously by the Navy. However, eventually the message got through. More and more captains took citrus fruits with them on long voyages, and when in 1793 an East India fleet well-supplied with lemon juice reached Madras scurvy-free after nineteen weeks, the Lords of the Admiralty conceded. In 1795 they introduced lemon juice to all fleets and scurvy vanished from the Royal Navy. The battle against an enemy which, in Lind's words, had 'caused more deaths in the British fleets than French and Spanish arms combined', was finally won.

The Navy's issue of oranges, lemons or limes earned the British the nickname 'limeys', still used by Americans today.

Hugh **LOCKE KING**

One man's pique at a supper party was to change the sport of motor racing and create the world's first motor racing circuit. A wealthy landowner, Hugh Fortescue Locke King, was bemoaning the 20 mph speed limit on Britain's roads, meaning that no British competitors could practice for the Targa Florio road race in Sicily of 1905. Indeed, he had to go to the Continent to see a motor race at all. By the end of supper, he had volunteered to build a track on his estate at Brooklands.

Allocating 300 acres of swampy meadows and farmland, he thought it would be like building a golf course, budgeting only £22,000. But when Colonel Holden of the Royal Engineers took charge, a 100ft wide track emerged with two long, super-elevated bankings. 2,000 workmen worked 3 shifts, 6 days a week, with 20 steam shovels and seven miles of railway. 30 acres of woodland were levelled, 350,000 cubic yards of earth moved and 200,000 tons of concrete poured.

This colossal undertaking wrecked the health of Locke King and nearly bankrupted him, but his loyal wife Ethel took over and her family chipped in. The final cost was £150,000 – £13 million today.

When racing started in July 1907, horse racing was copied. It was called a 'Motor Ascot'. Cars were kept in 'the Paddock', 'weighed in' at the extremely elegant clubhouse, handicapped, and the drivers even wore coloured smocks like jockeys.

Australian Selwyn Edge then used Brooklands to race for 24 hours, at the speed of 66mph, a record that stood for 17 years. Soon it was the place to beat speed records. While K. Lee Guinness was the last to create a World Landspeed Record actually at Brooklands, 135.75mph, from then on it was Brookland's influence that took Sir Malcolm Campbell and his Blue Birds to world records elsewhere.

Other circuits had been built in imitation, but Brooklands will always be remembered for its uniquely British sporting atmosphere – in vivid contrast to the professional commercialism over at Indianapolis. There were races of all classes, speed trials and record attempts – and all by amateurs. With its tennis courts, putting greens, restaurants and 'society' in elegant clothes, it was more like Ascot or Henley than a modern motor racing scene. 'The right crowd and no crowding' snobbishly proclaimed the advertising. You could not imagine a more flagrantly British, upper-class and elitist slogan if you tried. Some of the drivers' names give us the feel of it all; Sir Malcolm Campbell, The Duke of Richmond and Gordon, Sir Henry Birkin, Lord Montague of Beaulieu, Lord Brabazon of Tara, Sir Henry Segrave, Earl Howe, Count Zborowski and, among the ladies, Barbara Cartland, the romantic novelist, later to be famous as the step-grandmother of Diana, Princess of Wales.

But these amateurs were very serious. You have to admire the fastest of all, John Cobb, in his 24 litre Napier Railton, high on the bumpy Byfleet Banking lapping at 143mph, or the fastest woman, Gwenda Hawkes, whose 'Ladies Lap Record' was 135.95mph – ten miles an hour quicker than that year's fastest driver at Indianapolis.

World War II ended all motor racing, with factories for Hurricane fighters and Wellington bombers. But Brooklands is still there, and open to the public. The Members' Banking may have weeds growing through it, but the Clubhouse is restored magnificently (including a Barbara Cartland Room), together with the sheds and many of the historic cars and memorabilia. It is a unique tribute to one man's dream.

Ben **LOCKSPEISER**

There is a theory that the British are great at inventing things, but then blow it by not being able to go on develop and to manufacture them. There is no more tragic example than Britain's aviation industry after the Second World War. But in this case, the blame can be laid firmly at the door of a succession of ignorant, cowardly or dishonest decisions by governments – both Labour and Conservative.

During World War II, Britain created the second biggest aircraft industry in the world. Under-resourced, under fire and under siege, Britain managed to build 125,000 planes. The United States, five times bigger, safe from bombing and with huge resources, built 300,000. Even more remarkable was the advanced nature of Britain's scientific achievement – far ahead in radar, electronic navigation, specialised weapons and also jet engines, all of which was shared with its larger ally.

In 1943, for instance, the Miles Aircraft Company was issued by the government with an amazingly advanced specification. Working with Frank Whittle's Power Jets Ltd, Miles was asked to produce an aircraft that could fly at 1,000 mph at 36,000 feet. (This at a time when a Spitfire could manage 430 mph, and Germany's secret jets could just top 500 mph). By 1946 the Miles M52 was ready to fly. Then a shattering note to cancel the whole project arrived from Sir Ben Lockspeiser, the very official who had first commissioned it. It was ostensibly on cost grounds, but Sir Ben later revealed that he privately believed that planes could not fly super-sonically, and might never do so! He also said publicly that, 'he had not the heart to ask pilots to attempt it', in spite of a crowd of enthusiastic test pilots who volunteered, including a German former Messerschmitt 262 test pilot, then a prisoner of war.

In the usual spirit of friendly co-operation, Miles sent all the M52's test data to the United States. Just one year later, benefiting from this wonderful technical windfall, Chuck Yeager rocketed the Bell X-1 (right) to Mach 1.06.

The Miles M52 incident was sadly typical of the pattern of what was to come. Rolls-Royce, with its Nene and Derwent jet engines, was way ahead of the world. The Russians were desperately trying to catch up, unsuccessfully using captured German engines that suffered from lack of power and reliability. Imagine their amazement when Britain offered to sell her technology! As usual, Soviet dictator Josef Stalin was highly suspicious, fearing a trick, 'What a fool one must be to sell one's own secrets'. What fools indeed! First, Soviet scientists were given free access to visit all

Britain's aviation factories, especially Rolls-Royce. Then dozens of Rolls-Royce engines were sold and shipped to Moscow. Russian aviation jumped two years, all its engines copies of Rolls-Royce ones. The skies above Korea were filled with Russian MIG15s and American F-86 Sabres, using British technology.

For the next two decades, the litany of British Government vacillations and last-minute cancellations continued, and with them the gradual destruction of a great industry.

The Hawker P.1081 fighter, the thin-wing supersonic Hunter, the delta-winged Fairey FD (becoming the French Dassault Mirage), the supersonic Harrier, all were victims.

This sorry story was repeated in the commercial market. The Vickers V1000/VC7 cancellation left the way open for the massive success of the Boeing 707 and DC8. The smaller DH121 and the AVRO 776 were cancelled, and the Boeing 727 dominated that market. Several Westland helicopters were cancelled, so everyone uses American Chinooks and Hueys.

The double-decker VC10 might well have rivalled the Jumbo Boeing 747. And with British transport planes scrapped, we now only use the C-130 Hercules.

Reflecting Lockspeiser's decision, the greatest tragedy was the TSR.2, (below) a super-fast bomber and reconnaissance aircraft way ahead of its time. Prime Minister Harold Wilson decided to cancel TSR.2. Its replacement, the American F-111, then arrived years late and cost more than TSR.2, the prototypes of which were broken up for scrap.

The terrible thing is that nearly all of these cancellations by successive governments occurred at the last minute, when all the work was done. They cost a fortune and wrecked a superb industry.

Leopold **LOJKE**

Who was to blame for the horrors of the First World War? A belligerent German Kaiser locked in an arms race with the British? Or the French, still thirsting for revenge from their 1870 defeat by the Germans? Or the ramshackle Austro-Hungarian Empire with its restless Balkan states? After all, Prince Otto von Bismarck had once remarked that a world war would start 'with some damn fool thing in the Balkans.' But even in his wildest dreams he could not have imagined one starting with a chauffeur's driving mistake.

In June 1914, Archduke Franz Ferdinand, then heir to the throne of the Austro-Hungarian Empire, was to visit Sarajevo in Bosnia-Herzegovina. Members of Serbia's secret 'Black Hand' waited to assassinate him. The designated killers were suffering from tuberculosis and were told to kill themselves after their attempt.

Franz Ferdinand arrived at the railway station on Sunday 28th June and his cavalcade set off for a reception at City Hall. Seven members of the Black Hand were in the crowd, and one threw a grenade at the Archduke's car. The driver, Leopold Lojke, took evasive action and the grenade bounced off the back of the Archduke's car and rolled underneath the one behind, exploding and wounding two of its occupants.

The Archduke leaves City Hall

The assassination appeared to have failed, and a furious Franz Ferdinand interrupted the Mayor's welcome. 'What is the good of your speeches? I come to Sarajevo, and I get bombs thrown at me. It is outrageous!'

After the reception, the Archduke insisted on visiting the injured at the city hospital. His host, General Potiorek, decided that the motorcade should take an alternate route to the hospital, avoiding the city centre. However, the driver of Ferdinand's car, Leopold Lojke, was not told of the change of plan and so took the original route.

Turning into Franz Joseph Street, General Potiorek, in Ferdinand's car, noticed the mistake and shouted at the nervous driver, who stopped the car and reversed slowly out of the street. By chance, sitting in a café was Gavril Princip, one of the young assassins, consoling himself over the morning's failure. He could not believe his luck. He rushed out with his revolver, and as Lojke tried to accelerate, shot at Franz Ferdinand, hitting him in the neck. His second shot killed the Duchess Sophie, who had flung herself across her dying husband to protect him. Princip was arrested (right) while poor Lojke was given the task of sending the dreadful news by telegram to the Austro-Hungarian Emperor, the German Kaiser and the Archduke's children.

Europe went into shock. Four weeks later the Austrians presented impossible demands to the Serbian government. Britain offered to mediate, which the German Kaiser decided was 'insolent.' The Austrians, encouraged, declared war on the Serbs. Russia, Serbia's ally, mobilised, as did France and Germany. In every country, 'mobilisation' now meant huge, complex railway plans. Once ordered, they were almost impossible to stop. Europe began to steam to war.

On 1st August the Kaiser declared war on his cousin Czar Nicholas. Two days later, he declared war on France, and just 24 hours later German troops stormed into Belgium. The British came back from a sunny August Bank Holiday and were amazed to find themselves at war with Germany. The world had lurched into the most horrible war in its history. Killing millions, it would engulf monarchies, destroy Empires, bring Communism to Russia and then the world, and lay the seeds of Fascism and the Nazis.

Only 19, Gavril Princip languished in jail for four years, dying of his T.B. He must have wondered what he had unleashed. But at least he was deliberately sent to create havoc. A simple driving mistake by poor Leopold Lojke, the chauffeur, had the most devastating influence on the history of the world.

Lojke was given 400,000 crowns by his Emperor and bought an inn, where he often showed his guests the blood-stained braces of the Archduke.

? Jean-Jacques **LUCAS**

In 1805, Jean-Jacques Etienne Lucas was acknowledged to be the most efficient and resourceful officer in the French navy, which he had joined aged 15. Now 39, he was still tiny at 4ft 8, and was about to be the nemesis of an opponent not much taller – Admiral Nelson.

On land, Napoleon was the master. Nearly every country in Europe had been beaten in battle – all except England, protected by twenty two precious miles of water and the Royal Navy. But Napoleon was determined to invade, and thousands of his troops waited in Boulogne. 'The Channel is a mere ditch, and will be crossed as soon as someone has the courage to attempt it.' So he ordered Admiral Villeneuve to join him and clear the Channel of British ships so that his army could cross. *'Come to the Channel. Bring our united fleet and England is ours. If you are only here for 24 hours, all will be over and six centuries of shame and insult will be avenged.'* British Admiral Jervis dryly commented 'I do not say they cannot come, I only say they cannot come by sea.'

After an unsuccessful feint to the West Indies, Villeneuve joined a Spanish navy even more ramshackle, sick and ill-trained than his own. A frustrated Napoleon had struck camp to begin his march across Europe to conduct the brilliant Austerlitz campaign against the Russians and Austrians. The logic for a battle was gone, but Napoleon had ordered a now humiliated Villeneuve out anyway. The scene was set for one of the decisive battles of history.

Villeneuve's formidable adversary, Admiral Horatio Nelson, was already a legend. In a long and brilliant naval career, he had lost an eye before his victory at Cape St Vincent and later his right arm. Off Copenhagen he had ignored his vacillating superior's signals by famously holding his telescope to his missing eye.

While Napoleon had 2,000 ships, they had been blockaded in their ports for years by a Royal Navy which constantly patrolled, with nothing to do but watch and endlessly practise seamanship and gunnery, able to fire at twice the rate of the French.

Captain Lucas understood this problem perfectly. Commanding the 74-gun *Redoutable*, he decided that his crew would be at least superlatively trained in the one skill they could practice – musketry. He also taught his 40 selected marksmen that it is much more effective to kill an officer, and preferably a senior one, rather than just an ordinary soldier or seaman.

Off Cape Trafalgar, the breeze on 20th October 1805 was so light that the two great fleets approached each other at walking pace. So there were six hours to prepare – and to worry. On the *Victory*, Dr William Beatty, the ship's surgeon, quietly expressed his unease that the four shiny stars embroidered on the Admiral's uniform would mark him as an obvious target, and that he should change into a plain coat. 'Take care, Doctor, what you are about,' warned the Admiral's secretary. 'I would not be the man to mention such a matter to him.' Beatty tried but failed to do so, hovering near the Admiral.

Courtesy of Richard Grenville

Eventually, it was the *Victory*'s Captain, Thomas Hardy, who raised the question, suggesting that the decorations might catch the eye of a sniper. Nelson replied, 'I am aware it may be seen, but it is now too late to be shifting a coat.' It was to be a brave and foolish decision. In fact, at 11 o'clock, Nelson did take the time to go below, praying and writing letters and his diary for an hour. He could have changed his coat in seconds.

An hour later, the *Victory* cut straight into the French line and was soon locked by collapsed spars and lines in a murderous embrace with the smaller *Redoutable*. Captain Lucas's training paid off. '*A heavy fire of musketry opened, in which Admiral Nelson fought at the head of his crew. Our firing was so much superior to his, that in less than a quarter of an hour we had silenced that of the Victory altogether. More than two hundred grenades were flung on board her, her decks were strewn with the dead and wounded. Admiral Nelson was killed by the firing of our musketry. Immediately after this, the upper deck of the Victory became deserted, and she again ceased firing.*'

Victory was near defeat and capture

Victory was in real danger of defeat and capture, but out of the smoke came the British *Temeraire*, whose devastating point-blank broadsides killed and wounded half of *Redoutable's* crew and reduced her, as Lucas reported, to 'a heap of debris'.

While the *Victory* was saved by the sudden intervention of the *Temeraire*, Nelson had indeed been hit by one of Lucas's well-trained snipers. Two hours later he was dead, one of Britain's great tragic heroes.

Surrounded by ships, Lucas finally struck his colours and surrendered, and British and French sailors then struggled manfully together to save the brave *Redoutable*, but she finally sank, shot to pieces and having sustained the worst casualties of the battle, with 300 killed and 222 wounded out of 643 men.

Of all Britain's opponents on that day, Captain Lucas had performed intelligently and courageously, and thoroughly deserved the praise that Napoleon eventually heaped upon him.

Victor **LUSTIG**

Victor Lustig's whole attitude to life made him the perfect confidence trickster. 'I really don't understand honest people. They lead desperate lives, full of boredom.' It was a view which would lead him to 45 aliases, 50 arrests in the United States alone and one of the best-known con tricks of all time – and, eventually, to Alcatraz.

Born in Bohemia, now the Czech Republic, in 1890, Lustig became fluent in five languages and an excellent player of billiards, bridge and poker. He first applied his wits and charm to fleece the rich on the magnificent liners on Transatlantic cruises. When World War 1 intervened, Lustig went to the United States where he became a European 'Count'. In Missouri he bought a farm with Liberty Bonds, persuading the bank to give him cash for some of the bonds, then switching envelopes and escaping with both bonds and the cash. Arrested in New York, he then persuaded the lender to 'avoid a run on the bank', by releasing him and giving him another $1000. This was just one of dozens of such brazen con tricks and cucumber-cool escapades.

In May 1925, back in Paris, Lustig dreamed up the scam that made him famous.

He read that the Eiffel Tower, one of the world's great landmarks, was costing the French government so much to paint and maintain that it was exploring the idea of dismantling it.

Within hours a forger friend had created letterheads from 'The Deputy Director-General of Posts and Telegraphs'. Lustig wrote to six leading scrap metal dealers inviting them to a meeting to 'discuss a government contract'. At the prestigious Hotel Crillon, he explained that the Eiffel Tower, part of the 1889 Paris Exposition, had never been intended to be permanent and was now costing so much that it must be scrapped. But, as this might be highly controversial and unpopular, they must all be sworn to secrecy. 'The Deputy Director-General' then drove them in rented limousines to inspect the Tower with its 15,000 pre-fabricated parts. Lustig noticed that André Poisson, anxious to be in the big league of Parisian business, was the most gullible and over-eager, and it was Poisson whom he chose as the 'mark', inviting him back four days later to be awarded the contract. At the meeting, Lustig also discussed the lifestyle that a Minister was expected to lead, and revealed 'how little he was paid'. Poisson understood and quickly supplemented the $125,000 contract cheque with a hefty bribe. Lustig and his accomplice, 'Dapper Dan' Collins, left on the train to Vienna that very evening.

For a month, they scanned the French newspapers for news. There was nothing. Insecure and humiliated, poor André Poissin had decided it was better to absorb his loss and keep quiet.

Then Victor Lustig did something unbelievable, but certainly typical. He returned to Paris and repeated the whole scam with six new scrap merchants. But this time the 'mark' did go to the police and Lustig only just made it back to America.

Graduating from selling his 'Rumanian Boxes' that appeared to transform paper into $1000 bills, he went into serious counterfeiting, but was caught by the FBI in 1935. And after a daring escape, he was finally sent to Alcatraz for twenty years, but died of pneumonia after twelve of them.

Trying to sell the Eiffel Tower *once* is astonishing enough. But twice?

Eliza **LYNCH**

In 1855, Francisco Lopez was in Paris on a buying trip, but not for the usual things.

Under orders from his father, the military dictator of Paraguay, he was there to purchase arms and munitions. One night, he dropped in on the salon of a beautiful, blonde courtesan with a statuesque figure – Eliza Lynch. It was a visit that was to cost half his countrymen and women their lives.

Eliza had arrived in Paris in 1849 from Cork, soon after the Irish Famine. Married off to a French army officer at just fifteen, after three boring years in Algiers she returned to Paris alone and was soon successfully selling her charms to rich and influential men.

Deciding to attract a foreign 'sugar daddy', into her salon came a rather ugly, short man with brown teeth and a cigar – Francisco Lopez – who fell in love with her. Told of his 'paradise' in Latin America, she readily agreed to go back with him to Paraguay.

Arriving with crates of Parisian gowns, china, furniture and even a piano, Eliza was shocked to find a hot, humid and run-down capital, Asunción, whose aristocratic women plainly regarded her as the 'Irish whore'. However, she bore him six children, and the couple built a 'palace' – the first two-storey building in Paraguay. When his father died, Lopez became President and demanded that his mistress be accorded the courtesies due to a wife. This seems rather petty and provincial and he could then have settled down to the lifestyle of a typically corrupt, incompetent Latin American dictator.

But Lopez worried that tiny Paraguay could be swamped and dismembered by its two large neighbours, Brazil and Argentina, and even by Uruguay. He was probably right, but, unfortunately for his country, it was the last thing he was to be right about. His paranoia was fuelled as Eliza then filled his strange mind with grandiose ideas of military glory and becoming 'Emperor and Empress' of the whole of South America.

With the largest army in South America, 30,000 men, but with no proper officers, Lopez attacked both Brazil and Argentina. By May 1865, he had managed to force his neighbours into a triple alliance against him, his forces now outnumbered ten to one. Eliza tried to help by recruiting 'Amazon' regiments of women with lances, leading them into battle on a white horse. She took also pleasure in confiscating the jewels of her haughty rivals 'for the cause', and promptly shipping them off to Paris for her future private plans.

With Lopez now a hugely fat megalomaniac, it became even more dangerous to be his friend than his enemy. His armies destroyed by their continuous and suicidal attacks, he now turned on his own elite. Suspecting a conspiracy, he ordered the killing of his two brothers, his brothers-in-law, cabinet ministers, officers, bishops, policemen and even hundreds of members of the diplomatic corps.

When his mother revealed that Lopez was illegitimate, with no right to be President at all, he finally cracked – ordering the population of Asunción into the jungle like Pol Pot in Cambodia a century later. Demanding to be recognised as a saint, he shot the 23 bishops who disagreed. He even ordered what remained of the national treasure of gold to be thrown off a cliff, killing all the witnesses.

He had his mother publicly flogged, ordering her execution. She was luckily saved by his military collapse. Now, with a handful of troops, Lopez was trapped and killed as he waddled into the water to swim across a river.

She helped to wreck a country

The couple had managed to reduce Paraguay's population from 525,000 to 221,000 – a feat unmatched by Hitler, Stalin or even Genghis Khan. Paraguay's neighbours duly took great chunks of the country.

Eliza, not slow to realise her situation, under the gallant 'protection' of a Brazilian General made it back to Paris, where she lived in comfort on the proceeds of her rivals' jewels. Most would agree that, for an unknown emigrant girl from Cork, she had been nothing short of an unmitigated disaster.

Ernst **MACH**

There are many scientists and engineers who must have been justifiably pleased that their names became irrevocably associated with one of their breakthroughs – Sir Henry Bessemer with his steel-making 'converter', Christian Doppler with his 'effect', Nikolaus Otto with his petrol engine 'cycle', Michael Faraday with his electrical 'cage' and Albert Einstein with his 'relativity'.

Similarly, there are dozens of noted physicians who proudly attached their names to the diseases or ailments they discovered, although they might have flinched at the gloom their names were later to spread: Alzheimer's Disease, Bell's Palsy, Down's Syndrome, Parkinson's Disease, Asperger's Syndrome and Hodgkin's Lymphoma.

We also live with many measurements reflecting the names of scientific pioneers – for instance, the 'curie' for radioactivity, or the 'roentgen' for X-rays. Earthquakes and tsunamis suddenly make us pay attention to Richter and his 'scale'. Pop music enthusiasts might be surprised that the 'decibel' comes from old Alexander Graham Bell, while many of us struggle to decide whether to use the temperature scales of Daniel Fahrenheit or Anders Celsius.

And while sophisticated laboratories and factories may worry about George Ohm's electrical resistance, Heinrich Hertz's frequency measurements or Isaac Newton's degrees of force, few of us can ignore in our everyday lives the 'volts' of Alessandro Volta, the 'watts' of James Watt or the 'amps' of André Ampère.

Which brings us to Ernst Mach. An Austrian physicist, he was highly regarded. His 'Mach Bands' added to our knowledge of eyesight and he discovered how the sense of balance in the ear worked. His 'Mach Principles' were used by Albert Einstein in formulating his Theory of Relativity. However, Mach was curiously limited by not believing in things he couldn't see, like atoms. But he could see in his photography the shockwaves around a supersonic bullet, which is why most of us know his name from the relative speed of aircraft.

Anyone lucky enough to fly in Concorde may remember that it cruised at Mach 2.02.

Iain **MACLEOD**

There are those who remember the name Iain Macleod because of politics, but millions more of us should really know him because of a card game.

Iain Macleod was born in 1913 in Lewis in the Western Isles of Scotland and was educated first at a Grammar School and Fettes College, then at Edinburgh and later Cambridge. Wounded during World War II - and with his injury combined with spondylitis in his back, he would live in permanent pain.

As a rising Conservative politician, Winston Churchill made Macleod Health Minister in 1952, who memorably announced the link between smoking and cancer while chain-smoking throughout the press conference. Churchill may have been an admirer, but not all were. MacLeod's rapid decolonisation of much of Africa earned him the damning jibe from the Conservative right, 'too clever by half', as did his liberal views on the death penalty, abortion and homosexuality. It was Macleod who coined the phrase 'stagflation' and it was his money-saving policy on scrapping school milk that unfairly earned a young Education Minister the name 'Margaret Thatcher, milk snatcher'.

In 1970, Macleod was rushed to hospital from No. 11 Downing Street, where he lived as Chancellor of the Exchequer, and he died of a heart attack – some calling him 'the best Prime Minister we never had'.

However, his legacy lives on way beyond politics. He was always a brilliant Bridge player and had even lived off his winnings before entering politics. He was also a member of the team that won the coveted Gold Cup in 1937 and later wrote a bestseller called *Bridge is an Easy Game*.

The game he was describing so brilliantly in his book grew out of Whist – invented in Britain in the 16th century and soon popular worldwide. It came back via Turkey to Britain in 1890 complete with the 'dummy' and the 'auction'. A highly mental game, Bridge can be played at any level and in Britain competes in popularity with golf and angling as a participant hobby. Most of its millions of enthusiasts play by the 'Acol' system of bidding, without realising its origin. In fact, it was created in 1934 by Iain Macleod and his friends in a small Bridge club in leafy Acol Road, off the Abbey Road in London's Hampstead.

Few people now remember Iain Macleod the politician, and almost no Bridge players know why they call their bidding system 'Acol' and who thought it up.

'Owney' MADDEN

As a gangster, Owen 'Owney' Madden attracted none of the notoriety of the likes of Al Capone. But he was to prove one of the most successful, and, at least in music, the most influential. Born in Leeds in 1891, he remained sentimental about his native Yorkshire all his life, retaining both his British passport and North Country accent and even saving *Yorkshire Post* clippings.

Madden arrived in New York aged 11 to stay with his widowed aunt Elizabeth O'Neil, and it did not take him long to join the 'Gopher Gang', one of the most notorious Irish gangs terrorizing the streets of 'Hell's Kitchen'. Known as 'That banty little rooster from hell', slim, dapper and charming, he was a vicious thug, soon known for good reason as 'the killer', and terrifying other gangsters. In 1912, shot 11 times in a fight with the rival 'Hudson Dusters', he refused to testify. 'Nothing doing. The boys'll get 'em.' Indeed, two years later he was jailed for shooting 'Duster' Patsy Doyle.

In January 1923, while in Sing Sing prison awaiting parole, he sat thinking, with three things on his mind. First was the potential of New York's Harlem.

Harlem had been built as a property speculation with fine buildings and broad tree-lined avenues, intended for middle-class whites. But in 1905, there was a property slump. Ruin beckoned. However, African-American tenants were attracted from overcrowded parts of New York and saved the speculators. Thus Harlem became, almost overnight, the largest black community in the United States. Prosperous, it quickly became a musical centre, especially for jazz and blues. Its nightspots took off and soon whites began to come up to Harlem – as they called it, 'slumming it'.

And one of the reasons they came was to drink, the second thing on Owney's mind. 'Prohibition', the well-meaning law, far from reducing drinking had created huge numbers of illegal 'speakeasies', far more than the previously legal bars. And Owney was going to need an outlet for his 'bootleg' beer.

Finally, he had noted the growing success of all-black shows like *Shuffle Along*, *The Creole Show*, *A Trip to Coontown* and *Darktown Follies*. So he decided to combine his opportunities and create a unique nightclub in Harlem with the finest African-American talent, but entirely for white audiences.

Madden bought Harlem's Club de Luxe from Heavyweight Boxing Champion Jack Johnson and re-opened it as 'The Cotton Club'. There entertainment would be a dazzling fast-paced revue with the finest jazz music, superb male dancers and beautiful 'high-yaller' octoroon chorus girls, ('*Tall, tan and terrific*'). With elegant and polite staff, Owney's club quickly became a smash hit despite its dubious connections.

In 1927, its bandleader Andy Preer suddenly died, and the Cotton Club was desperate for a replacement. 'King' Oliver turned the offer down, and someone suggested 'Duke' Ellington. He still had a week booked in Philadelphia, but Madden made the theatre owner an offer that he couldn't refuse: 'Be big or you'll be dead'.

'Duke' Ellington (named for his immaculate dress sense) was the son of a White House butler. His talent, always changing and innovative, was to cover four decades. But it was the Cotton Club that propelled him to fame, because a local radio station, and then the Columbia Broadcasting System transmitted the 'Cotton Club Sound' across the nation. Everyone in the country knew about the club, and every visitor to New York just had to visit it. 'All of me', 'Mood Indigo', 'Creole Love Call' and 'Black and Tan Fantasy' became hits among people across the world who would never have thought of themselves as jazz enthusiasts. And Madden actually ended up owning 20 clubs, including the legendary Stork Club, whilst also becoming a major force in boxing promotion.

In 1932, cooperating with 'Dutch' Schultz, Madden kept Vincent 'Mad Dog' Coll, a vicious killer from Count Donegal, on a public pay phone long enough for three men to pump 15 bullets into him. Now New York was becoming too hot for Madden, so he abandoned it to the Italian Mafia and retired to Arkansas in 1935, dying there peacefully thirty years later, a forgotten man, but who gave us the unforgettable Ellington.

? André **MAGINOT**

It was all too easy, after the extraordinary collapse of France in 1940, to accuse her military of being hide-bound by 'Maginot Line thinking'– surely one of the most unfair remarks in the lexicon of warfare. And the man who created that Line should be spinning in his grave at the injustice of it all.

André Maginot was born in Paris in 1877, but significantly, spent his youth in Alsace-Lorraine, the provinces that border the Rhine and Germany. With inhabitants from both countries, their ownership has always been a source of bitter dispute. And it was on the Lorraine front that young Maginot fought as a Sergeant at the horrific battle of Verdun, where 400,000 French men died or were wounded. He was awarded France's highest decoration for bravery, the *Médaille Militaire*. Wounded, and limping for the rest of his life, with his beloved childhood home destroyed and with a strong distrust of Germany, it is scarcely surprising that he would take a special interest in preventing Alsace-Lorraine from being invaded again.

Thus it was as Minister of War that he pushed his government into creating a huge line of defensive fortification along the border. This was an extraordinary system of concrete forts, with inter-locking fields of fire, linked by underground railways, (right) complete with air-conditioned galleries, mess halls, hospitals, even suntan rooms to keep the thousands of defenders healthy. It was dubbed the 'Maginot Line', although much of it was built during the tenure of Paul Painlevé, Maginot's successor. Maginot never actually saw the Line finished, dying of typhoid fever in 1932.

And, in the event, eight years later the Maginot Line was bypassed by the Germans plunging their Panzers through Belgium and the Ardennes to victory. As a result, people have, ever since, ridiculed the Maginot Line as a symbol of out-of-date thinking. But they would be very wrong – especially if they considered the original written objectives for the Line:

- To *avoid a surprise attack and to give alarm.*
- To *cover the mobilisation of the French army (2 – 3 weeks).*
- To *save manpower (France had 39 million inhabitants, Germany 70 million)*
- To *protect Alsace-Lorraine and their industrial basin.*
- To *be used as a basis for a counter-offensive.*
- To *push the enemy to circumvent it by passing through Switzerland or Belgium.*
- To *hold the enemy while the main army could be brought up to reinforce the line.*
- To *show non-aggressive posture, and compel the British to help France if Belgium is invaded.*

Each one of these objectives the Line *precisely* fulfilled – except one – 'the basis for a counter-offensive'. Having watched how the Panzer divisions worked in Poland, it should have been as clear as day that the Germans would bypass the formidable Maginot Line to its north, and – as the French planned – be canalised through Belgium. Then the French would need a powerful armoured force to counter-attack and trap the thinly stretched

Panzer formations. Just imagine what would have happened to Rommel and Co if 500 French tanks and fighter-bombers had sliced sideways into them.

That is certainly what Winston Churchill *thought* would happen when he flew to visit the despairing French as their lines collapsed. 'Mais où est la masse de manoeuvre?' he demanded, assuming the existence of such a striking force. 'Aucune', they shrugged, 'There is none'. A horrified Churchill called it 'one of the biggest surprises of my life'.

That is why France fell, and why we should all stop blaming poor Maginot.

Adolf **MAHR**

When Ireland won her freedom from British rule in 1922, she also lost technical expertise and turned to the Germans and Austrians to fill some key posts. Adolf Mahr was one of these, and it was to lead him down some strange paths. One, as he claimed himself, was as 'Dublin Nazi No. 1'.

Adolf Mahr was in his native Austria working as an archaeologist when he saw an advertisement for the 'Keeper of Irish Antiquities' in a Viennese paper. He travelled to Ireland for the interview and was appointed, moving his family into an elegant house in Dublin. He was soon a prominent figure in the 250 strong German and Austrian community.

With Mahr soon to become the leading Nazi in Ireland, it was ironic that his great benefactor was an Irish Jew living in San Francisco, with 170 letters exchanged between 1931 and 1939. Albert Bender, an insurance millionaire, had become a great arts patron in America and was equally generous to Mahr, who succeeded in opening the 'Bender Memorial Room of Far Eastern Art' in the National Museum. Eamon de Valera gave the speech of thanks and weeks later 'Dev' promoted Mahr to be Director of the Museum.

Mahr had joined the Nazi party in 1933, only weeks after Hitler became Chancellor. With roots in both Austria and Sudeten Czechoslovakia, he would be delighted that Hitler would join both to the Reich. And he would approve, too, of Hitler's treatment of Jews, while continuing his strange collaboration with an *individual* Jew, Bender, and, for that matter, welcoming his daughter's Jewish school friends to his home. In 1934 Mahr became *Ortsgruppenleiter*, or branch leader, of the German community and soon added the local Hitler Youth to his responsibilities. He treated the crew of the visiting German cruiser *Schleswig-Holstein* to a picnic and archaeology lecture. (This was the ship that, on a 'courtesy visit' to Danzig in 1939, was to fire the first treacherous shells of World War II).

With war clouds gathering, Mahr - officially an Irish civil servant - pretended to give up his Nazi leadership, while bizarrely being placed in charge of the protection of the national treasures in the event of invasion – by either Britain or Germany.

Partly to attend that year's Nazi Nuremberg Rally, in July 1939 the Mahrs left for a holiday in Germany and Austria. They were never to return to Ireland, because war broke out in September and their ship was blockaded.

Mahr, left, with his Irish Hitler Youth

Through his friend, Foreign Minister Joachim von Ribbentrop, Mahr started to work for the German Foreign Office. Now with Germany polishing its plans for the invasions of Britain and of Ireland ('Operation Green'), Mahr wrote Ribbentrop a long memo suggesting a propaganda radio service beamed at Ireland, *Irland-Redaktion* – rather like fellow-Irishman William Joyce's 'Lord Haw-Haw' programme to Britain. Mahr then became head of the service that would broadcast until the last days of the war.

However as time passed, life for the Mahrs deteriorated. The Battle of Britain made Germany's invasion of Ireland unlikely and Ireland became steadily less relevant. The Mahrs were bombed out of their homes, their son was drafted into the *Wehrmacht* and captured in North Africa, and Maria Mahr started blaming her husband for their plight. Mahr then suggested beaming anti-Roosevelt propaganda to the 6 million Irish-Americans in the US to try to stop him being re-elected. But soon the Mahrs were, like millions of Germans, trapped between the western invaders and the vengeful hordes from the Soviet east. With a last burst of Irish music, *Irland-Redaktion* went off the air.

Adolf Mahr was captured by the British and released, starving. He started to lobby to return and take up his old post in Dublin. But Irish military intelligence warned de Valera not to allow him back, and he never was – dying in Germany in 1951.

In 1946, as a little boy, I flew with my parents in an Aer Lingus Dakota to Dublin. Arriving at the little terminal, one of our passengers was greeted by several men with the Hitler salute. I was too young to realise what I was watching, but it seems that quite a few rather questionable Germans *did* make it back to Ireland.

Beatrice **MARCONI**

At the turn of the last century my great, great aunt, Beatrice O'Brien, was strolling in the grounds of Dromoland Castle in the west of Ireland. She turned to her mother, Lady Inchiquin, and proudly announced a startling fact:

'My new Italian suitor can send messages hundreds of miles'.

'Oh, that can't be right, dear.' replied her mother. 'Everyone knows you can't shout more than a hundred yards.'

She had obviously not been reading the newspapers or she would have known that Beatrice's fiancé, Guglielmo Marconi, had indeed succeeded in sending messages hundreds of miles – in fact halfway round the globe.

Beatrice was not the first Irish connection in Marconi's life. His mother, Annie, was the granddaughter of the founder of Jameson Whiskey. It gave him two advantages as an inventor – connections in high places in the British Isles and fluent English.

Marconi, born into a wealthy family in Bologna, demonstrated a great early enthusiasm for electricity. He based his work on Heinrich Herz, who had demonstrated that electro-magnetic waves could pass through the air and be detected at a distance. With his own homemade equipment, Marconi graduated from sending 'Herzian waves' from one room to another to signals right over a large hill.

But the Italians were not interested, so aged 21, Marconi left for England with his resourceful Irish mother. Now their connections and his fluency in English came into their own. In 1887, Marconi sent the first message across four miles of open sea in the Bristol Channel, and in 1899 he 'crossed' the English Channel with his signals.

In the United States, Marconi was given his first stroke of luck when the *New York Herald* sponsored him to report on the 1899 America's Cup yacht races. His visit to America inspired his greatest ambition – to cross the Atlantic with his signals and compete with the transatlantic cables. He set up a station in Cornwall, relay stations in Ireland and one in Newfoundland, receiving a message from England, 2,200 miles away. The next year his first signal was sent from the U.S. to Europe, a greeting from President Theodore Roosevelt to King Edward VII.

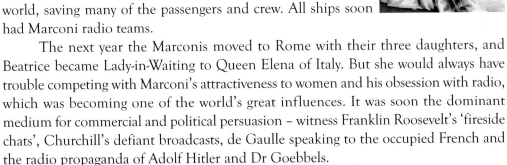

In 1904 Marconi met 'Bea' O'Brien (right) and fell in love, dropping the second of his two American fiancées. After initial opposition, Lady Inchiquin began affectionately calling him 'Marky' and the couple were married in a huge London society wedding. Typically, the honeymoon was cut short by Marconi's business. In fact, 'Bea' was always going to have trouble competing with Marconi's wireless, which was becoming a huge success.

He had established a news service for liners and also a transatlantic radio-telegraph service, and a first success was the on-board arrest of the suspected murderer, Dr. Crippen.

Then a disaster in 1912 made Marconi truly famous. When the *Titanic* hit an iceberg, it was the two men of the Marconi radio team who stuck to their posts and informed the world, saving many of the passengers and crew. All ships soon had Marconi radio teams.

The next year the Marconis moved to Rome with their three daughters, and Beatrice became Lady-in-Waiting to Queen Elena of Italy. But she would always have trouble competing with Marconi's attractiveness to women and his obsession with radio, which was becoming one of the world's great influences. It was soon the dominant medium for commercial and political persuasion – witness Franklin Roosevelt's 'fireside chats', Churchill's defiant broadcasts, de Gaulle speaking to the occupied French and the radio propaganda of Adolf Hitler and Dr Goebbels.

Militarily, too, radio became vital. Heinz Guderian – inventor of *Blitzkrieg* – made

his fast-moving Panzer divisions so effective by putting a radio in every tank. Radar, or radio-location, was key to the 'Battle of Britain'. Radio code-breaking has changed the course of history.

And the televisions and mobile phones we all use? They, of course, are another result of the pioneering efforts of Guglielmo Marconi (left).

After 22 years of marriage, Marconi and Beatrice were sadly divorced. She married an Italian aristocrat, and when Marconi re-married, his 'best man' was no less than the dictator Benito Mussolini.

However, Beatrice continued to give him advice for the rest of his life and when he died in 1937 she silently watched from the crowd, unnoticed, as he lay in state.

The man who had sent messages hundreds of miles had sent us into a new era.

? Hiram **MAXIM**

Even though he lived most of his life in England and was knighted by Queen Victoria, Sir Hiram Maxim was American, born in Maine. A prolific inventor, we might have remembered him for his mousetrap or his pocket inhaler for asthmatics. As he wryly said, 'It will be seen that it is a very creditable thing to invent a killing machine, and nothing less than a disgrace to invent an apparatus to prevent suffering!'

As a pioneer in electricity, Maxim had been 'bought off' by his rival Thomas Edison, who had sent him to Europe. But in 1882 a friend in Vienna memorably suggested, 'Hang your chemistry and electricity! If you want to make a pile of money, invent something that will enable these Europeans to cut each other's throats with greater facility.'

Maxim knew that an automatic, repeating weapon was the answer. He had followed closely the progress of Dr Richard Gatling's multi-barrelled, hand-cranked 'machine-gun'. This had its flaws, as when nervous soldiers turned the crank too fast:

'The Gatling's jammed and the Colonel dead
And the regiment blind with dust and smoke.'

Maxim had noticed the heavy kick of a rifle firing, and decided to use that recoil to eject the spent cartridge, feed a new one, close the breech and release the firing pin, all in a continuous automatic cycle.

Now with only one barrel, he needed to cool it in a distinctive water jacket and he fed the gun with continuous belts of ammunition. In his own workshop in Hatton Garden, London's jewellery district, 200,000 rounds were fired off, some by luminaries like the Prince of Wales and other members of the nobility. At one stage, he protested, 'My dear Sir, this gun costs £5 a minute to fire. You provide the cartridges and

I'll provide the gun!'

Maxim's machine-gun was bought by most countries. The British used it with deadly effect in her drive for Empire. At Omdurman in the Sudan in 1898, 10,000 Dervishes died and a mere 47 British. As the poet Hilaire Belloc was ironically to write:

Whatever happens, we have got

The Maxim gun and they have not

Amazingly, generals on every side still underestimated the power of the machine-gun, especially in a deadly combination with barbed wire. General Douglas Haig had even written 'The machine-gun is an overrated weapon.' But his attack on the Somme was to prove him tragically wrong, with 57,000 British casualties on the first day alone. Whole proud regiments were obliterated by single German machine-guns.

As the battle drew to a close in November 1916, 'a quiet scientific gentleman living in Kent' died peacefully. About one and a half million men, British, German and French, had died or been wounded rather less peacefully by his weapon in just that one miserable and indecisive struggle. And it has been estimated that, in World War 1 alone, five million men died from Maxim machine-gun fire.

Maxim, some might think, should have stuck to mousetraps.

John **MAXWELL**

John Maxwell first showed his arrogant and callous indifference to those he despised on the bloody battlefield of Omdurman, where many thousands of Dervishes lay wounded. A young Lieutenant Winston Churchill, just after one of the world's last cavalry charges, vehemently objected to Major Maxwell's orders not to help the wounded Dervishes, but to 'finish them off or let them die'. Maxwell contemptuously replied, 'A dead fanatic is the only one to extend any sympathy to.' Eighteen years later Maxwell was to indulge such cruelty again, and this time with more far-reaching results.

Maxwell in fact enjoyed a reasonably good military career, awarded the DSO in the Sudan and 'Mentioned in Despatches' several times. In April 1916, the 'Easter Rising' occurred in Dublin. 1,200 men and women seized key buildings, but the British recovered their composure and poured in 30,000 reinforcements, with an armed cordon tightened around the city centre. Major-General Sir John Maxwell arrived from England to take 'firm charge', promising maximum severity with indifference to damage. Thousands of soldiers concentrated on the 255 Irish volunteers fighting on from the General Post Office. The insurgents tunnelled out from the burning building and set up positions in nearby houses. After six days, to avoid any more loss of life, they finally surrendered. Eighty-two rebels were dead, along with 256 civilians and 157 soldiers, with 2,600 injured. Whole areas of Dublin had been devastated.

Many bewildered Dubliners thought that these men and women were at best misguided and at worst traitors to the thousands of Irish fighting for the British against the Germans. Some prisoners being marched off were cursed by the crowds and pelted with vegetables.

'The GPO 1916', courtesy of Thomas Ryan RHA

However, General Maxwell was soon to change all that, arresting 3,430 men and 79 women. Convening 'Field General Courts Martial', he ignored the 'Defence of the Realm Act', ruling that courts should be in public, with 13 members, a professional judge and proper defence lawyers. Rather, they were held in secret with Maxwell and his officers as judge and jury. On 2nd May, 90 people were condemned to death, and the next day firing squads started shooting the leaders, one by one. James Connolly was too wounded to stand up and was shot strapped to a chair. James Plunkett was executed ten minutes after being married to his fiancée. A leading figure in Dublin society, The Countess of Fingall, coined the tragic phrase, '*It was like watching a stream of blood coming from beneath a closed door.*' One of Maxwell's officers even revealed his own misgivings to her. 'I have just done one of the hardest things I have ever had to do. I have had to condemn to death Padraig Pearse, one of the finest characters I have ever come across. There must be something wrong in the state of things that makes a man like that a rebel.'

The shootings caused mounting horror on both sides of the Irish Sea, together with severe political problems. John Redmond and John Dillon of the Irish Party at Westminster both stood up in Parliament and asked Prime Minister Herbert Asquith to stop the executions, Dillon saying in despair, 'You are washing out our whole life's work in a sea of blood!' The Cabinet began to panic.

It was too late. By the time the shootings were stopped on 12th May, with 15 already dead, the mood in Ireland had changed from apathy to revulsion. It had all taken less than three weeks. W.B. Yeats captured it in his memorable poem '*Easter 1916*', describing how all was '*changed, utterly changed*'.

When they did not get their promised Home Rule, in 1919 the Irish decided to fight in a war that lasted four years. In 1922, one of the survivors of the Rising, Michael Collins, helped to negotiate the Irish Free State. Another survivor, Eamon de Valera, fought a tragic civil war to repudiate the compromise partition of Ireland, with results that are with us to this day.

Sir John Maxwell, promoted to full General, retired comfortably. But his hasty, brutal and illegal actions had not only alienated Ireland for years, but, watched by a horrified world, had started the unravelling of an empire.

Ward MCALLISTER

Ward McAllister established one of the most curious social niches in history. He had made good money as a lawyer in California during the Gold Rush, visited Europe to study how titled nobility behaved, married an heiress and then fell in with a fabulously rich patroness, Mrs Caroline Astor. Under his influence, she began to completely dominate her social scene, in an era called 'the Gilded Age'. Caroline Schermerhorn came from wealthy mercantile Dutch stock and had married a real prize, William B. Astor Jr. from the richest family in the world. Four daughters and a son later, William ordered a huge yacht and sailed off to be one of the original millionaire playboys.

Caroline, with the marriage prospects of her daughters in mind, turned to McAllister, the 'Southern Gentleman'. Under his Svengali-like influence, 'the' Mrs Astor dictated how the rich in New York should behave. Indeed, it was the capacity of her ballroom that precisely determined how large 'Society' should be – just four hundred people. Soon 'Society' and the members of McAllister's 'Social Register' were involved in a rigid, snobbish ritual of balls, soirées, dancing classes and dinners, of which Caroline's weekly 'Mystic Rose' dinners were the most exclusive – elaborate feasts of ten courses on gold plates.

To Caroline and McAllister, there were obvious targets to be excluded from 'Society', including Catholics and Jews and brash new people from the mid-West. It also became vital for Mrs Astor to keep out some real super-rich new competitors, especially the Vanderbilts, the railroad millionaires. She succeeded for years, but power was shifting, Alva Vanderbilt was now preparing to welcome to her huge new Fifth Avenue mansion a thousand guests for the city's most expensive ball ever. The envy between the families had the city agog. Then Alva staged a knockout blow.

In one of the planned Star Quadrilles of 'approved young ladies' was Carrie Astor. After the girls had been practising dancing for weeks, Alva suddenly told Carrie she was no longer welcome 'because your mother has never called on me'. Desperate not to miss the ball, Carrie bullied her mother into paying a formal visit to Alva. The Vanderbilts had made it into 'Society', and Caroline Astor's unique power begun to slip for ever.

Ward McAllister's influence also waned after he published his book *Society as I have found it*. His social climbing began to annoy the very society he had nurtured and he died in 1895, dining alone and rather unmourned.

Randolph MCCOY

History is full of disputes between neighbours that lasted for years and created vicious bloodshed. But the ones we know were usually between countries. However, in America there was a feud in a tiny mountain area between two families that lasted for decades and became so famous that it entered folklore as a metaphor for such quarrels. Most Americans would know exactly what you meant if you said 'They were fighting like the Hatfields and McCoys'.

Both families originated in Northern Ireland and came to settle near the Big Sandy River straddling the border between West Virginia and Kentucky. The men served as comrades on the Confederate side in the Civil War – all except Asa Harmon McCoy who fought for the Union. At the end of the war, he was hunted down and shot by a gang of ex-Confederates led by Jim Vance, an uncle of the chief of the rival family, 'Devil Anse' Hatfield. Thirteen years later, in a bizarre dispute over a pig, another relative of both families was gunned down.

Then love intervened, with Roseanne McCoy made pregnant by 'Johnse', 'Devil Anse' Hatfield's son, who then abandoned Roseanne in favour of her cousin – even more complicated than the Montagues and Capulets in *Romeo and Juliet*.

For reasons people hardly remember later, the brutal killings continued, culminating in the 1888 'New Year's Night Massacre' when the Hatfields set fire to a cabin to kill Randolph McCoy, only succeeding in murdering two of his children and nearly killing his wife.

With the press from coast to coast recording every move, eventually the Governors of West Virginia and Kentucky both had to send in their state militias to restore order. The Adjutant General of Kentucky, Samuel Ewing Hill, arrived to investigate, giving rise to another American phrase, 'What in the Sam Hill is going on?' Gradually after more than a dozen deaths the feuding died down.

But this obscure family feud, left an indelible mark on America. Nearly a century later, it inspired the television game show *Family Feud* and in 1979 McCoy and Hatfield descendants competed on the show for a week – accompanied by a pig. Innumerable films, TV shows and even cartoons have alluded to the dispute. Tourism has cashed in too, with a Hatfield-McCoy 500 mile trail through the mountains and an annual Hatfield and McCoy Reunion Festival.

Most foreigners would still not have heard of all this, but for a television series that reached our screens in 2012, with Kevin Costner as 'Devil Anse' Hatfield, Bill Paxton as 'Ole Ran'l' McCoy and Tom Berenger as Jim Vance. With the History Channel's highest ratings, it was a huge success, winning several awards, although not all the critics approved. One described it as '*a bunch of bibulous knuckleheads who shoot at each other year after year – or on TV, hour after hour – and have no real idea why*'. It's probably a good description of 'going at it like the Hatfields and McCoys'.

Clyde McCoy

An important descendant of the feuding family was Clyde McCoy, a brilliant jazz trumpeter popular for seven decades. His 'wah-wah' sound, as in his huge hit *Sugar Blues*, was later copied by first Vox and then others as the 'Clyde McCoy Wah-Wah Pedal', one of the great innovative effects for electric guitars. (It's now called the 'Cry Baby').

William **McGREGOR**

Soccer or 'Association Football' is the world's biggest participant and spectator sport. An incredible 240 million people play it and billions watch it.

The idea of kicking a ball about is as old as history itself, and evidence of such 'footballs' has been found in Japan 3,000 years ago, then in China and ancient Rome. In Britain however, until the 16th century any such sport was frowned on by the authorities, partly because, like the new game of golf, it threatened vital archery practise. There was, too, a snobbish attitude towards a simple and popular game. In King Edward's reign (1307-1327), laws threatened prison. Judged to be vulgar and indecent, soccer was suppressed by English sheriffs following royal orders describing the game as 'a useless practise'. Henry IV and Henry VIII passed laws against the sport, and Queen Elizabeth I used to have soccer players jailed for a week.

It is curious, therefore, that in more modern times, the first organised football was played in the upper-class English public schools like Eton, Harrow, Winchester, Shrewsbury and Rugby, where in 1823 William Webb Ellis allegedly picked up the ball, eventually leading to the split between 'Rugby' football and soccer.

Gradually soccer became the favourite sport of the industrial towns of the north of England and the Midlands, with some players being secretly paid – illegally. Such 'professionalism' was first allowed by the Football Association in 1885, and three years later someone stepped forward to try to bring order to a somewhat chaotic world of clubs trying to organise their own fixtures.

William McGregor (right) was born in Scotland in 1846 and was working as a draper in Aston outside Birmingham. A genial and committed Christian, his pastor described him as 'a man of absolutely unblemished personal character'. He had become a director of his local football club, Aston Villa, and loved all sport, even trying to start a baseball league in Britain.

Now McGregor realised a similar league was needed for football. So he wrote to other clubs suggesting a league that would provide guaranteed fixtures each season. He also suggested a meeting on 23rd March 1888 at Atherton's Hotel in London to fellow directors of Blackburn Rovers, Bolton Wanderers, Preston North End and West Bromwich Albion. There he proposed a 'Football League', based on a similar one recently created by the American colleges, and his pioneer clubs were soon joined by Accrington Stanley, Burnley, Derby County, Everton, Notts County, Preston North End and Stoke. Based on the Woolwich military complex in London, Arsenal was the first southern club allowed in.

Soccer had become essentially a working-class sport, local and tribal, with players and spectators alike living and working within walking distance of the mine or the mill. The players were paid, but not much more than the miners and factory workers who watched them. However, McGregor had changed football from a pastime into a business.

Then, five decades after his death, television changed everything, with real money to be made out of winning televised competitions like the Champions League, League Cup, FA Cup and the televised Premier League matches. Players and managers could now be brought in – even from abroad. This was expensive, so sponsorship was needed, together with another phenomenon – very rich owners. Manchester United, once supported by a railway, was then backed by the Irish horse racing magnates John Magnier and J.P.McManus, and now by the American businessman Malcolm Glazer.

At Chelsea, someone really rich became the owner in 2003, Roman Abramovich, worth at least $11 billion. Sheik Mansour of Abu Dhabi with his 2008 purchase of Manchester City, spent $750 million on the club and another $1 billion in the surrounding area. Quite what William McGregor would have made of the modern game is anyone's guess.

Nadezhda von **MECK**

The relationship between Pyotr Tchaikovsky and his mentor Nadezhda von Meck must be one of the strangest in history.

Nadezhda was born into the rich Frolovsky family in 1831, and inherited a love of music from her father and of business from her mother. She became highly cultured, especially in music – playing the piano well herself.

Only 16, she was married off to Karl von Meck and while bearing him no less than 18 children, she bullied him into resigning from the Civil Service and grasping the opportunity of profiting from railways. With the Russian railway system expanding from just 100 miles of track in 1860 to 15,000 twenty years later, Karl duly became a multi-millionaire, but died suddenly in 1873 leaving his railway networks, cash and estates in Nadezhda's sole care. She became a recluse, even refusing to meet the relations of those whom her eleven surviving children were to marry. But she also became a major patron of the arts, especially music, and did attend concerts – incognito, even hiring Claude Debussy as a music teacher for her daughters.

It was in 1877 that she first wrote to the up-and-coming Pyotr Tchaikovsky, describing herself as a 'fervent admirer'. It was the first of 1,200, and their bizarre and intimate relationship by letter was to last 13 years. She also provided the composer with enough money to leave his professorship at the Moscow Conservatory and to compose full time, although he seemed somewhat embarrassed; *'Every time we write to one another, money appears on the scene'*.

If prodigious correspondence made her strange, so did other things. Not only a recluse, she was also an atheist, and revealed that she regarded sex as unpleasant and shameful. A cerebral, platonic relationship with Tchaikovsky suited her perfectly and she ruled that they should never meet. Their letters were highly intimate, and both characters were eccentric, capricious and neurotic. He dedicated his *Symphony No. 4*, to her and both worked to organise the marriage of her son Nickolai to Tchaikovsky's niece Anna. Nadezhda von Meck, of course, did not attend the wedding.

In 1890, a week after sending one of her loving and confessional letters, von Meck suddenly sent the composer a year's subsidy and a letter ending her patronage. This bizarre and abrupt break was probably due to tuberculosis. Unable to write because of the sharp pains and cramps caused by atrophy of her arm, she was hardly going to dictate to a stranger the kind of revealing letters she normally sent to her friend.

In addition, she was also in temporary financial trouble due to her son Vladimir's mis-management of her interests, prompting her family to pressure her into ending the drain of Tchaikovsky's subsidy.

Nadezhda von Meck died of tuberculosis in 1894 in Nice, surviving Tchaikovsky by only two months. Asked how she had endured his death, her daughter-in-law, Anna von Meck, baldly replied, 'She did not endure it.'

? Han van **MEEREGEN**

In the history of art, often either conservatism or the pretensions of the 'art establishment' have been made to appear ridiculous. Recently Damien Hirst even pricked his own bubble, demonstrating to us that, when not pickling sharks or fixing diamonds in skulls, he is hardly a great painter.

Han van Meeregen was, by contrast, a very good painter – but a very frustrated one. Time after time, he was savaged by the Dutch art critics, especially Dr Abraham Bredius, Holland's leading expert on Vermeer. So he decided to do something amusing. He would forge some Vermeers and see how long it would take for the 'experts' to discover the deception.

He went about his task carefully, using 17th century canvasses, specially-created paints, authentic brushes and a phenol

Why not forge 'Vermeers'?

and formaldehyde mixture that caused the paint to harden and crack. He then baked the paintings, and rolled them over a drum to crack them with a wash of black ink to fill in the cracks. His first triumph was 'Christ at Emmaus', which fooled the whole art world, including, to his great delight, his enemy Dr. Bredius. But, having achieved his objective, the painting was suddenly sold for millions and he had second thoughts. He would keep quiet.

So he began to paint and sell more 'Vermeers', as well as false works by Frans Hals and Pieter de Hoog. The chances of being discovered were reduced by the war, the occupation, and the black market. Then, in 1942, one of his 'Vermeers' was sold for 1.6 million guilders, making it one of the most expensive paintings ever sold.

The Nazis were ruthlessly looting works of art from every country they occupied. The greediest was *Reichsmarschall* Hermann Goering. Normally he just stole, but he paid a huge price for one of van Meeregen's 'Vermeers' – while paying the dealer, with some poetic justice, in counterfeit money!

It was the link with Goering that would expose the story of the prolific Dutch forger. The war over, the Allies were on the lookout for stolen treasures and art works. Hidden in

a salt mine in Austria, experts found in the 'Goering collection' a Vermeer, *'Christ with the Adulteress'*, (left) never seen before. The painting was traced back to Amsterdam, and eventually the Dutch police tracked down and interrogated Han van Meeregen. He was in deep trouble because selling national treasures to the occupying Germans was regarded by the Dutch as collaboration, and worse, treason, carrying the death penalty.

After days of questioning, he revealed the astounding truth. He had not sold a Vermeer, he had painted it. The police did not believe such a ridiculous story, so he offered to prove it. In three weeks, under the amazed supervision of police and art experts, he created another wonderful 'Vermeer', *'The Young Christ teaching in the Temple'* (right). As a result, the charge was dropped to forgery. During his trial in October 1947, polls showed that he became the second most popular person in Holland to Queen Juliana.

Sentenced to two years in prison, failing health meant he was sent to hospital where he died peacefully in December.

His little plan to embarrass the Dutch art world had mushroomed. He had become rich, then an international celebrity and finally a local hero.

Frank and Charles **MENCHES**

The hamburger is one of the most popular products in the world, with millions eaten every day. Few people know how the name arose, let alone of the two brothers who created it. They know it is not to do with 'ham', (because hamburgers are made of beef), so many simply assume they must come from Hamburg. They are partly right.

Hamburg is a huge city in Germany, and then there is small town of Hamburg in Erie County, New York State. It was this little town, and not the German giant, that gave its name to the most famous fast food in the world.

In 1812 the town of Willink was subdivided into three towns, Eden, Concord and Hamburg. Historians think the latter was just picked as a pleasant enough name from a map of Europe by the State Land Office.

In 1865, the Erie County Agricultural Society met to decide where to stage its famous annual Fair. After much debate, they took up farmer Luther Titus's offer of his land at Hamburg. The Fair has remained there ever since.

Twenty years later Frank and Charles Menches, two brothers from Ohio, arrived as usual to sell their hot pork sausage sandwiches at the Fair, bringing their new gasoline stove. Unlike wood and coal cookers, this was clean, and that year they were favoured by a new Fair ruling banning dirtier cookers – particularly resented by ladies with their white dresses. Thus the pair looked forward to a profitable visit. But a crisis threatened. Warm and humid weather had halted local pork butchering, so Andrew Klein, the butcher, offered them ten pounds of beef instead. A cautious Frank Menches decided he would only risk five pounds. When the patties of beef were cooked, Frank thought they seemed to lack something. 'Salt don't seem to develop the flavour'. His brother half-jokingly responded, 'Why not try sugar?' A little brown sugar was sprinkled on, and the effect was instant. Customers began to line up, and Frank wondered about a name for their new product.

One customer asked in German 'Gutte schmeck! Was ist?' (Good taste! What is it?). 'Hamburger' was Frank's reply. Within an hour he had tacked up a huge sign with HAMBURGERS written in charcoal. A star was born.

The Menches brothers and their hamburgers then rocketed to popularity thanks to their concession at the 1893 Chicago World's Fair, helped by their friend, the future U.S. President, William McKinley.

The success of the hamburger was phenomenal and soon swept the nation and the world, with Macdonalds and Burger King perhaps the greatest exponents of this very American export.

A good thing that the Menches' butcher ran out of pork.

Glyndwr **MICHAEL**

On 26th January 1943, a tramp was found near death in an abandoned warehouse near London's Kings Cross Station. In hospital, the doctors discovered that he had poisoned himself, either on purpose or by accident, by eating bread laced with poison to kill rats. This unfortunate fellow turned out to be Glyndwr Michael, an alcoholic Welsh vagrant, homeless and destitute, whose whole life had been miserable and lonely. Yet still unknown, in death he became one of the most influential people in World War II – because three months later he was to play a vital role in one of warfare's great deceptions.

With the Allies victorious in North Africa, Winston Churchill correctly wrote, *'Everyone but a bloody fool would know that it's Sicily next'*. But suppose the Germans could be fooled into thinking that the massive planned attack would instead be going to Greece? The idea to achieve such a deception was number 28 of 51 ideas put up by the future James Bond writer Ian Fleming to Flight Lieutenant Charles Cholmondeley, a tall gangling man with a splendid waxed moustache. He started working with the equally brilliant barrister Lieutenant Commander Ewen Montague on the idea, now codenamed 'Operation Mincemeat', of planting a dead 'British officer' with documents pointing to an attack on Greece.

And so it was that poor Glyndwr Michael's refrigerated body became 'Major William Martin, Royal Marines', floated on to the Spanish shore near Huelva from the submarine HMS *Seraph*, and attached by chain to a briefcase containing 'secret documents'. On the body, found by a fisherman, was superbly forged 'wallet litter' – love letters from Martin's 'fiancée', a jeweller's bill for an engagement ring, pompous letters from his 'father' and the Army and Navy Club and a rude one from his 'bank manager' with all sorts of other personal evidence about 'Major Martin'. In the briefcase were letters to General Sir Harold Alexander, commanding Allied forces in North Africa, which included the clear misinformation that 'Operation Husky' would attack Greece, not Italy.

As expected, Spanish Fascist police chiefs allowed German spies from the *Abwehr* to copy all the documents before blithely returning them to the British Attaché. Quickly the evidence went via *Abwehr* chief Admiral Canaris right up to Hitler, who became convinced that Greece was the next Allied target and who reassured Mussolini that any attack on Sicily would be feint. Sicily was thus left unreinforced, with Greece going from one to eight divisions, including three Panzer divisions, two of them, critically, from Russia, thus weakening Germany's Kursk campaign. '*Mincemeat swallowed whole*', Churchill was told by his code-breakers.

On the 9th July, the Allies stormed ashore in Sicily and soon captured the island, while the German troops in Greece stared out to sea uselessly.

The extraordinary story eventually emerged in 1950 when, to scotch rumours, Ewen Montague wrote the best-seller *The Man Who Never Was*, later made into a film. It took another half century for the words 'GLYNDWR MICHAEL SERVED AS MAJOR WILLIAM MARTIN' to be added to Martin's gravestone in the cemetery at Huelva. At last, he had achieved some recognition. In life, a tragic figure. In death, a hero.

Thomas **MIDGLEY**

'A greater influence on the environment than any other single organism in world history'. The environmental historian J. R. McNeil was not talking about bubonic plague, anthrax, ebola or genetically modified food. He was referring not to a bug but to a person, Thomas Midgley, a distinguished American scientist. And he was not being very complimentary, because Midgley helped to bring about two environmental scourges — lead in petrol and ozone-eating CFCs.

Thomas Midgley was born in 1889 in Pennsylvania, the son of an inventor. In 1916, working at a subsidiary of the giant General Motors, he discovered a cure for 'knocking'

in petrol engines, enabling them to have higher compression and better performance. Superior to other products, and also more profitable, was the additive Tetra Ethyl Lead or TEL. But no mention of lead was made on the petrol pumps promoting the successful 'ETHYL anti-knock compound'.

Midgley was awarded a prize by the American Chemical Society in 1922, but he knew perfectly well the dangers of lead poisoning. Indeed, the very next year he had to take a paid holiday to cure himself of its effects. Within months, there were two deaths at the Deighton, Ohio TEL plant, and the next year no less than eight people died at the TEL plant at Newport, New Jersey. In spite of this, Midgley conducted a dramatic press conference pouring TEL on himself and breathing it in to demonstrate its 'safety'. The New Jersey health authorities then closed down the Barway TEL plant after several cases of hallucinations, insanity and five more deaths. Midgley had, meanwhile, sneaked off to Europe for a year, again to be treated for lead poisoning brought on by his 'safety' demonstration! It would take many more years for governments to recognise the environmental air pollution dangers of lead in petrol and to make us all use lead-free fuel.

If Midgley had not already done enough by creating one environmental problem, he then managed to do it a second time. At Frigidaire, another division of GM, he helped to create chlorofluorocarbon, or CFC. At first 'Freon' – both non-toxic and non-flammable – seemed a perfect refrigerant for air-conditioning and refrigeration, soon also to be used as a propellant in aerosols and even in asthma inhalers. As a result Midgley received another medal in 1937.

Once again it took years for the dangers of CFCs to emerge. They ate ozone, the thin layer of gas that protects the world from harmful sun rays, resulting in a dangerous hole (right). With more prizes and awards, in 1944 Midgley was even elected President of the American Chemical Society.

September 1979   **September 2006**

His career sadly demonstrates two things. First, of course, that we should be extremely wary how carefully how chemicals are foisted on our fragile world. And secondly, that there is a serious flaw in the old business saying, 'What's good for General Motors is good for America'.

Jules **MONTENIER**

'I thought I heard Buddy Bolden shout
Open up the window, let that bad air out.'

That is probably the oldest-known jazz tune, attributed to the legendary New Orleans cornettist, Buddy Bolden.

In fact, some of Bolden's original lyrics were even ruder – *'stinky butt, funky butt, take it away'* – but what he was describing was playing jazz amidst the powerful smell of a New Orleans hall packed with sweaty dancers 'rubbing their bellies together', around 1900, before air-conditioning or deodorants. It became so well-known that even whistling the tune was thought offensive.

Half a century later in London jazz clubs the olfactory atmosphere was no less challenging. Nor, for that matter, was it any better in offices, shops or public transport. Many people smoked, so they noticed it less, but 'B.O', or body odour, was a real social problem, coupled with the embarrassment in that rather more genteel age of telling 'even your best friends' that they were far from fragrant. (As a friend put it, 'Why is it always the people with bad breath who want to confide in you?').

Human sweat is vital for cooling the body and is in fact largely odourless. Indeed, it can even attract the opposite sex. But when it is fermented with bacteria in hot and humid conditions, especially under the arms, it becomes offensive.

The very first commercial deodorant appeared as far back as 1888, even before Buddy Bolden was complaining in *'Funky Butt'*. It was called 'Mum', a cream named

Inspired Chemistry
...makes Stopette the completely dependable anti-perspirant...never harsh, yet never weak and ineffective. And easier than ever to apply. The Stopette formula, created by Dr. Jules Montenier, destroys odor-producing bacteria, safely checks excess perspiration...all with the gentleness of a mist-fine spray. One deft squeeze of the hand-formed, unbreakable bottle envelops the entire underarm, assures positive protection. And you never touch Stopette, hardly know it touches you. Refreshing as the finest cosmetic...harmless to clothes. At all drug and cosmetic counters.

Family size: $1.25 plus tax
Travel size: .60 plus tax
Jules Montenier, Inc.,
Chicago

Poof!
there goes
perspiration

Stopette
THE ORIGINAL
SPRAY DEODORANT

after the slang word to keep silent. Deodorants worked by using alcohol to kill bacteria and could be combined with anti-perspirants that contained aluminium compounds to reduce the sweating in the first place. Aluminium, however, can cause irritation.

It was Dr Jules Montenier in New York who solved this problem chemically, in 1941 producing 'Stopette'. A best-seller, this had the memorable advertising slogan, 'Poof! There goes perspiration' (left). A spray squeezed from a flexible plastic bottle, it was to launch the entire plastic bottle industry.

Montenier decided to sponsor a television show to promote 'Stopette' and his other products, 'Poof! Deodorant Powder' and 'Finesse, the flowing cream shampoo', and in 1950, CBS created the programme 'What's my line?' for him. This became a smash hit (right) The only problem was that, as it spread from city to city, his sponsorship costs soared. However, Montenier refused to have a co-sponsor, and after eight years the show ended up ruining him. Heartbroken, he was forced to sell out, to the beauty company Helen Curtis in 1958.

However, thanks to him and other pioneers, deodorants and anti-perspirants have become a routine part of our lives, and it is easy to forget what a life-changing service they do. As one of the best advertising slogans put it, 'You owe it to the rest of us'.

Annie **MOORE**

Over 120 million Americans owe their presence in the United States to a small island in the middle of New York harbour, Ellis Island. And the very first to arrive there was young Annie Moore from Ireland.

'Give me your tired, your poor, your huddled masses yearning to breathe free, the wretched refuse of your teeming shore, send these, the homeless, tempest-dashed, tossed, to me. I lift my lamp beside the golden door.' The words of the poet Emma Lazarus, engraved on the base of the Statue of Liberty across the bay, welcomed the millions of immigrants seeking a new and better life in the United States.

Ellis Island was originally called 'Oyster Island' by the early Dutch colonists. A merchant, Samuel Ellis, acquired the island, and in 1808 the state of New York bought Ellis Island from his family.

More and more people in poor and strife-torn Europe began to think of America as a golden land of opportunity, and learning from the chaos and unexpected horrors of the Irish 'Famine Ships' arriving in the 1840s, the authorities became well-organised to receive them.. However, by 1890, the original Immigration Station on the tip of Manhattan was no longer adequate to process the mass of immigrants pouring into

New York.

The new Immigration Station on Ellis Island (right) had dormitories, a hospital, kitchens, a baggage station, an electrical plant and a bath house - and accommodation for large numbers of immigration and naturalisation officers, as well as interpreters, guards, clerks, cooks and all important doctors and nurses.

When the immigrants' ships arrived off New York, the first and second-class passengers were inspected on board and went on to Manhattan. It was only the 'steerage' passengers, paying the lowest fares, who had to go to Ellis Island to be processed.

On January 1st, 1892, the Station opened and the very first person to come ashore was Annie Moore from Cork - on her 17th birthday. On board ship she had answered a series of 29 carefully crafted questions. Now, as she entered she was monitored as she climbed to the second floor for any signs of lameness, shortness of breath, a heart condition or mental problems. Once she had passed further medical examinations, including the dreaded 'eye-lid lift' to check for the infectious disease *Trachoma*, she was checked against the 29 questions. After about three hours, Annie was passed, and as the first successful immigrant through the Station, was presented with a $10 gold piece by an official - which must have been a pleasant birthday surprise.

By the end in 1954, over twenty million immigrants had passed through Ellis Island, helping to create the incredible, dynamic melting pot that is the United States.

Annie Moore lived the rest of her life in New York and is honoured by statues both at Ellis Island and at Cobh in Ireland, from whence she made that historic voyage.

James **NAISMITH**

For someone who would create a sport sometimes featuring giants, James Naismith was quite slight - only 5'10" - but he was nevertheless an excellent athlete. A Canadian, born in Ontario, he had represented Montreal's McGill University in Canadian football, lacrosse, rugby, soccer and gymnastics.

In the winter of 1891, Naismith found himself in America, as a physical education teacher at the YMCA International Training School in Springfield, Massachusetts. It was bitterly cold and the young men were confined indoors, irritable and rowdy. Naismith's boss told him to create a new indoor game that *'would not take up too much room, would help the athletes to keep in shape, be fair to all players and not be too rough'*.

To achieve this, James Naismith figured he needed a ball softer than in most sports, to avoid contact between players while retaining the ball and to have goals that could not be defended. So, with 13 rules, he designed a game in which a soft soccer ball should be lobbed into peach baskets fixed ten feet from the floor, with nine players as opposed to today's five-a-side. Within a year, the game was so popular that the Springfield College newspaper featured it in an enthusiastic article called 'A New Game'.

Naismith went on to Kansas University and by 1898 'basketball' was thriving there, and within two years there were inter-college competitions all over the east of the United States.

Two innovations that Naismith had not envisaged then improved and speeded up the game. With safety fears allayed, 'dribbling' the ball was now allowed, and some genius had the simple thought of cutting out the bottom of the baskets. Before that, a man with a ladder laboriously retrieved the ball after every goal!

Although Naismith himself regarded his invention as a bit of a curiosity, he was delighted, aged 74, to hand out the medals for basketball at the 1936 Olympic Games, three years before his death. Women's basketball arrived at the 1976 Olympics in his old stamping ground of Montreal, and now with 300 million participants, the game is enormously popular worldwide.

What Naismith probably did also not foresee was the amazing height of some modern champions, like 7'6" 'Wilt the Stilt' Chamberlain (who reached Naismith's adult height when he was only nine), or that Michael Jordan would be voted 'the most admired athlete in America'.

But he would certainly have been pleased.

Thomas **NEWCOMEN**

Steam power changed our world, decisively and forever. Its impact was huge and its influence universal. It powered an Industrial Revolution, transforming a small island called Britain into a world power, whose steamships then created an Empire.

Steam changed everything in industry, from the mining of raw materials to the cheap production of finished goods. It also propelled manufacturing out from the rural cottage and the remote water-powered mill, and thus created our huge cities.

The steam locomotive, the 'Iron Horse', literally made America, and railways gave us timetables and time zones – indeed a new concept of time. Sadly, steam also powered 'arms-races', railway war 'mobilisations' and started 'global warming'.

Curiously, this all began with a rather unglamorous requirement – to remove water from mines underground.

It took several people, all of them British, quite a time to solve that problem. Back in 1662, the Marquess of Worcester had proposed using steam and its condensation to create a vacuum, making atmospheric pressure actually 'lift' water. Thomas Savery and Denis Papin experimented with such 'fire-engines', or thermic pumps, but it was Thomas Newcomen who created the first practical steam engine. Newcomen's 'atmospheric engines' were soon pumping water out of mines all over Britain, mostly coalmines, but also the tin and copper mines of Cornwall, the world's leading producer.

But the trouble with Newcomen's engine was that 80% of the steam was wasted reheating the cylinder which had just been cooled by a jet of water to condense the steam. (This is what created the vacuum that allowed the pressure of the *atmosphere* to power the machine.).

This inefficiency, and the heavy coal consumption, of 'atmospheric engines' did not matter to coalmine owners who had tons of spare coal or 'slack' hanging about. But in Cornwall, where the coal had to be laboriously delivered by carts or even mules, it certainly did, and it made much of the deep mining virtually uneconomic.

If you said 'separate condenser' to most people, their eyes might glaze over, but that is exactly what James Watt invented – and it changed the world.

A Scottish engineer, Watt had experimented with a model of a Newcomen engine, and soon detected the basic flaw in its design. He resolved to power his machine by 'steam pressure', and condense the steam separately. It was now a true steam engine, economical and much more adaptable to the rotary motion which could power the new textile machines like Arkwright's 'Spinning Jenny' and, of course, lead to the moving steam engine or 'locomotive'.

It also used four times less coal than Newcomen's engine, and Boulton & Watt were able to charge their customers, especially in Cornwall, in a novel way – by how much coal they saved.

For the next century steam power would transform every aspect of our world. Today, our children may hurry past the Newcomen's silent industrial beam engines in museums, but they never cease to be captivated by a panting, breathing, almost living steam locomotive, nor stop loving 'Thomas the Tank Engine'.

Steam's enduring influence on the English language
'He's getting all steamed up' * 'Don't blow your stack' * 'Avoid being side-tracked' * 'A 60 Watt bulb' * 'Full steam ahead' * 'They've given us the green light' * 'It's built up quite a head of steam' * 'Open the throttle' * 'We've been railroaded' * 'Under our own steam' * 'It's a whistle stop tour' * 'Go away and let off steam' * 'I don't want to be steam-rollered into anything' * 'He's all fired up over this' * 'I've been shunted sideways' * 'She's rather posh' ('Port Outward, Starboard Home'; expensive ship cabins shaded from the sun, going to and from India.) * 'Smokestack America' * 'He's off the rails' * 'I think we've run out of steam' * 'Wrong side of the tracks' * 'It's just a water-plug town' * 'They just derailed the plan' * 'It's his only safety valve' * 'A steamy affair' *

And on music, especially in America, where trains are often a metaphor – for lost love, loneliness, religion, hope, restlessness, the future, the past.....
'Chattanooga Choo Choo', 'Rock Island Line', 'Wabash Cannonball', 'Wreck of Old 97', 'Casey Jones', 'Midnight Special', 'The City of New Orleans', 'Orange Blossom Special', 'Life's Railway to Heaven', 'This train is bound for glory', 'King of the Road', 'Train whistle blues', 'Alabamy bound', 'Choo Choo', 'Freedom Train', 'Homeward Bound'. 'Roll on 18 wheeler', 'Choo Choo ch'boogie', 'Atchison, Topeka and Santa Fe', 'Folsom Prison Blues', ' The last Ride', 'John Henry', 'Blues in the night', 'Boxcar Blues', 'Hey, Porter!', 'The Christmas Cannonball', 'Honky-tonk train blues', 'Lonesome Whistle', 'Train of Life', 'Freight Train', 'Yonder comes the train', 'Runaway train', 'Fireball Mail', 'Down Bound Train', 'That old train', 'Night train to Memphis', 'Hobo Blues', 'Ghost Train', 'Life is like a mountain railroad', 'Ride a blue train', 'Freight Train Boogie', 'Railroad Bill', 'Blow your whistle, freight train' 'Tennessee Central Number Nine', 'This Train', 'Last Train to Clarksville', 'Yonder comes a freight train', 'I thought of you','K.C. Moan', 'Tuxedo Junction', 'Take the A Train', 'Homeward bound', and many, many more…

George **NICHOPOULOS**

There are probably several people who contributed to the downfall of the genius that was Elvis Presley, but two stand out. The first, who most of us have heard of, was 'Colonel' Tom Parker, his agent for 22 years, ending up taking 50% of Elvis' earnings, rather than the normal 10 – 15%. Far from being a Colonel, he had actually deserted as a private soldier from the US Army, and was not even 'Tom Parker', but Cornelis van Kuijk, born in Breda in Holland, and thus not a legal US citizen, having jumped ship in an American port.

While Parker did play a major role in making Elvis into a star, he also made some terrible mistakes which damaged his client, not least financially. Because Parker needed to fund a secret gambling habit, he committed Elvis to a series of 27 mediocre but money-making singing films while refusing to let him take more serious parts that were offered to him in films like Thunder Road, West Side Story and Midnight Cowboy.

While the Beatles and the Rolling Stones invaded America, Elvis was never allowed to perform off American or Canadian soil, so he never made it to Britain where his fans were clamouring for him. The reason was simple. Parker, as an illegal immigrant, might not have made it back into the United States. However, even after they quarrelled, their relationship staggered on. Presley's biographer Peter Guralick wrote *'they were like a married couple, who started out with great love, loyalty and respect which lasted a considerable period of time until towards the end of Presley's life they should have walked away. Yet neither had the courage, for a variety of reasons'*.

Far less well-known as an unhelpful influence on Elvis was Dr. George Nichopoulos, his doctor, who first treated Elvis in 1967 for saddle pain and became a friend and business associate as well as his physician. What happened over the next few years was tragic and bizarre. Elvis had visited President Richard Nixon in the White House in 1970 and in a somewhat strange meeting had persuaded Nixon to make him an agent of the Federal Narcotics Bureau, complete with a badge. Elvis affirmed his contempt for the hippie drug culture, even citing the Beatles as a trend of anti-Americanism and drug abuse in popular culture. (Paul McCartney later commented, 'The great joke is that we were taking *illegal* drugs, and look what happened to him').

Indeed, Elvis had convinced himself that prescription drugs weren't really 'drugs' at all, and he gradually became appallingly addicted to them, affecting both his health and his public performances. After his premature death in 1977 at only 42, caused by a drug overdose, 'Dr. Nick' was indicted by the District Attorney on 14 counts of over-prescribing drugs. Nichopoulos got off, but it was revealed that in 1977 alone he had prescribed 10,000 doses of amphetamines, barbiturates, narcotics, tranquillizers, sleeping pills, laxatives and hormones for Presley. The very day he died, 'Dr Nick' had written eight prescriptions. Elvis's body was found to contain no less than 14 different drugs.

10,000 doses in a year

Nichopoulos claimed he had tried to cut Elvis's intake down, but at least four times Elvis had actually threatened him with guns.

As David Stanley, Elvis's friend and brother-in-law pointed out, 'This is Elvis we're talking about, and if he wanted something, he got it. It was that simple'.

Years later things have changed. Michael Jackson's doctor, Dr Conrad Murray, was arrested, tried and sent to jail for over-prescribing drugs. It was a robust new approach that tragically came too late for two great stars.

Robert **NOYCE**

For most of us, there is something truly stupefying about the microprocessor or 'microchip'. The idea that roomfuls of computers, or even deskfuls of them, can be replicated by a tiny sliver of silicon the size of someone's fingernail is truly fantastic – and, of course, fantastically true.

The innovator we have most to thank for the chip is Robert Noyce, dubbed 'the Father of Silicon Valley'. Noyce was born in Iowa, a direct descendant of pilgrims on the Mayflower. His career at Grinnell College was nearly ended when he stole a pig and slaughtered it to feed a student party, but he was luckily saved by a friendly physics professor and went on to the Massachusetts Institute for Technology.

In 1957, he left Shockley Semiconductor Laboratory with his friend Gordon Moore, a chemist and physicist, and they were backed by Sherman Fairchild to create Fairchild Semiconductor. In 1959, Noyce privately filed a US patent called 'Semiconductor Device and Lead Structure', a design to create the first integrated circuit. With another inventor, Jack Kilby, he had effectively created the microchip.

In 1968, Noyce and Moore left to found their own company, and Noyce wrote a three-page business plan so clear and inspired that Art Rock, who had financed Fairchild Semiconductor, was able to raise $2.5 million in just two days, not least because of Noyce's reputation. N.M. Electronics became Intel, 'Integrated Electronics', although they had to license the name Intel from a motel chain.

They made their first commercial product, a random-access memory (RAM) chip in 1969. That same year, Busicom, a Japanese calculator company, asked them to design a dozen custom chips that would run a calculator. However, Intel engineer Ted Hoff suggested they could design one general-purpose programmable chip that could take the place of a number of existing chips. Busicom agreed and helped to fund the project. Intelligence could now be programmed by software and did not have to be burned into hardware. This would change history because programmable intelligence became so cheap that it could power not only sophisticated aerospace and industrial machines, but household appliances – including computers. Delivered in 1971, the 4004 microprocessor, which crammed 2,300 transistors on to a one-eighth by one-sixth-inch chip, had the power of the old giant ENIAC. Several years later, Intel's 8080 became the brains of the Altair for which young Bill Gates provided the version of BASIC – his first steps towards Microsoft.

The chip by 1985 had a hundred times the power of

A modern Intel™ Core™ Processor (actual size) containing 1.4 billion transistors, compared with 2,300 in the first microprocessor

the 4004. By the 1990's Intel's Pentium brand had become a household name, and now there is hardly anything in the world not controlled by the chip; phones, cameras, computers, cars, trains, aircraft, spacecraft, satellites, pace-makers, and of course, the internet.

Honoured by three US Presidents, Robert Noyce died prematurely in 1990. Many feel that, had he lived, he would have shared the Nobel Prize for Physics with Jack Kilby.

His little chips were one of the most phenomenal inventions in history, even though most of us still don't know how they work.

Silicon comes from one of the commonest materials on earth – sand or quartz. Silicon in its pure form is an insulator, but when fractionally impure it can pass current, hence the semi-conductor, the basis of the silicon chip.

Processed silicon bars are sliced into wafers .5 mm thick. Light is shone through a succession of masks as tiny miniaturised circuits are photographically printed and etched on to the wafer. Layers of boron, phosphorus and aluminium are deposited forming transistors, resistors, capacitors and diodes, controlling and guiding the current (Intel's first chip had 2,300 transistors, the latest more than a billion!). Each wafer is cut up ('diced') to form dozens of tiny chips ready to be 'packaged' into their components. The whole extraordinary process can involve 'clean rooms' in several countries and 45 days from wafer, to chip, to market.

William Smith **O'BRIEN**

He was a very unlikely candidate for an Irish revolutionary. William Smith O'Brien, Member of Parliament for Limerick, was a Baronet's brother, and educated at Harrow and Cambridge. But even he could not bear what was then happening in Ireland.

The recent disasters had started with reliance on the potato, brought to Ireland by Sir Walter Raleigh. By 1845, Ireland's population had grown to a massive eight million, compared with England, Wales and Scotland totalling sixteen million. Such a huge number of people could only be sustained by the potato, 'the lazy crop', which could be left in the ground while the men went to work at other jobs, and could be grown on tiny plots of land. No less than three million people had become dependent on this one source of food.

Then a devastating disaster struck, *Phytophthora infestans*, the potato blight, which overnight could turn healthy potatoes into black, evil-smelling, rotting mush. This reduced the 1845 crop by one third; next year it was even worse, with three quarters lost. The removal of a staple food, rich in vitamins, caused immediate starvation, and worse, diseases like typhus, scurvy and dysentery. Millions died. These disasters were quickly followed by mass immigration to escape; to England, the United States, Canada and Australia. Hundreds of 'Famine Ships' lay in North American harbours with their hapless passengers dying on board, or in quarantine stations in sight of freedom. Soon they were re-named 'Coffin Ships'.

By 1847, Ireland had tragically lost over one quarter of her people. Weakened by deprivation and disease, the remainder were in despair. So, with three colleagues, O'Brien hatched the ill-fated 'Young Ireland Revolt' against British rule, to be fought under the French Revolution-inspired tricolor of green, white and orange, now Ireland's flag.

The British government swamped Dublin with troops. Moreover, the conspirators were lulled into overconfidence by the optimistic promises, from all over Ireland, of 5,000 'fully armed men'. But the clergy vigorously opposed the rising, and when a few poorly armed peasants did assemble, they quickly dispersed once they discovered that there was no free food and they were not allowed by the leaders to confiscate private property.

Retreating south into the countryside, the almost farcical and humiliating reality was that the rebels mustered only 32 'fully armed men' and another 20 'prepared to throw stones'. On July 29th 1848, in Tipperary, this trusty band intercepted some mounted constabulary who retreated into a stone cottage near the village of Ballingarry, owned by a widow. 'The Battle of Widow McCormick's Cabbage Garden' was interrupted by the furious lady returning home to find her house under fire and her children trapped inside. Fiercely, she ordered all the combatants to cease fire and go home, which they did rather shamefacedly. O'Brien was arrested by a guard at Thurles railway station – surely the only time that railway staff have arrested a man for High Treason.

He and the other three ringleaders were found guilty, and were among the last people to be sentenced to 'hanging, drawing and quartering.' The young Queen Victoria was horrified to find out what this entailed, and insisted that the sentence be reduced to transportation to Australia. Smith O'Brien refused this clemency, demanding either death or a Royal Pardon. A special act, the 'Transportation for Treason Act', was passed in 1849 – just to be rid of him and his companions.

In the event, his exile had greater political effect than the abortive revolt. In Van Diemen's Land (now Tasmania), O'Brien, as an MP and the best-connected felon to be transported, became the focus of the anti-transportation movement. Curiously, this was Australian-led. Previously transported folk, now respectable with families, wanted to prevent the arrival every few weeks of ships carrying 'disreputable people.'

Smith O'Brien was eventually pardoned and his three companions escaped to America where one of them, Thomas Meagher, became famous as a Union General in the Civil War, leading the Irish Brigade. It would take over six decades before Ireland would achieve her freedom, either by political or military means. But by then, her patriots had learned to plan much further than a scrap in a humble cabbage patch.

Eddie **O'HARE**

Chicago's main airport is one of the world's biggest, and people may wonder why it's called O'Hare (although they probably wouldn't question why it was changed from the more humble 'Orchard Depot Airport'). It is a story full of elements that many associate with 20th century America - courage, opportunism, greed, crime and duplicity.

Edward 'Easy Eddie' O'Hare was born to third generation Irish-Americans in St Louis in 1895. He grew up to be a lawyer and became rich when his most profitable client turned out to be Owen P. Smith, who invented the mechanical rabbit used in greyhound racing. He encouraged his eldest son Edward, known as 'Butch', to be an excellent marksman, and after flying with Charles Lindbergh, became a pilot himself, enthusing 'Butch' with a fascination for planes.

After divorcing his wife, O'Hare moved to Chicago where he fell in with another, but much less respectable client, the notorious gangster Al Capone (left), who dominated the Chicago crime scene – especially the distribution of illegal beer and liquor during Prohibition. Although now even richer because of his association with Capone, Edward O'Hare then did something very strange – he decided to ruin Capone. In 1930, he asked a journalist friend to fix a meeting with the Internal Revenue Service and started his secret alliance with investigator Frank J. Wilson, who later wrote *'On the inside of the gang I had one of the best undercover men I have ever known – Eddie O'Hare'*.

After one year, O'Hare had directed Wilson to the Capone book-keeper, and had helped to break Capone's ledger code. Crucially, he also tipped off the judge at Capone's 1931 trial that the gangster had bribed every member of the jury. So the judge simply swapped them with another jury down the hall. Capone, found guilty of tax evasion, went off to Alcatraz.

Why did O'Hare do it, this dangerous act of treachery? The answer probably lies with 'Butch', whom O'Hare desperately wanted to have a respectable career. He succeeded. The year Capone arrived in Alcatraz, Butch arrived at Annapolis – America's elite Naval Academy – destined for a heroic career.

His father, however, paid the price – gunned down in his car in 1939, a week before Capone was released on medical grounds. The love of his life, Ursula Sue Granata, then married Frank Nitti, Capone's second in command.

'Butch' O'Hare went on to be a fighter ace in the Pacific, the first naval pilot to win the Medal of Honor, presented by President Franklyn Roosevelt, and described as *'modest, inarticulate, humorous, terribly nice and more than a little embarrassed by the whole affair'*. He was just what was needed in 1942, a live American hero, and became famous, soon blessed with a baby daughter.

An inspirational leader and mentor to others, 'Butch' sadly disappeared in night combat in 1943, probably killed by a very lucky shot from a Japanese bomber.

Six years later, in 1949, Chicago's Orchard Depot Airport was renamed O'Hare International after 'Butch', and a F4F Wildcat fighter (right) is displayed in Terminal 2 in his honour.

Few enough of the hurrying passengers probably know about Butch O'Hare and even less about his father 'Easy Eddie' – who was arguably a more significant figure for Chicago – playing a strange but vital role in ridding it of its Prohibition-era crime.

Denis **O'NEILL**

They both came from County Cork. Denis O'Neill, a little-known man, was destined to kill a very famous one 34 years later – something he would deeply regret.

Denis 'Sonny' O'Neill was born in Bandon in 1888. Like so many Irishmen, he joined the British Army, becoming a trained sniper. Thus, in 1916 he was one of thousands of Irishmen in the trenches of World War I when the 'Easter Rising' took place in Dublin.

Michael Collins, two years younger, was born into an intensely Republican family. One of the most attractive, charismatic and tragic figures in Irish history – a mixture of infectious, warm enthusiasm and ice-cold calculation. He arrived from working in England in time for the doomed Easter Rising, fighting at the General Post Office alongside Patrick Pearse.

He surrendered, but luckily the British did not recognise him and he escaped General Maxwell's firing squads (page 144). On his release from prison in England, he returned to Ireland to start his war.

In 1918, he was elected as MP for Cork South, but refused to take his seat in Westminster. Rather, he masterminded the brilliant escape from Lincoln Jail of his colleague Eamon de Valera, who decided to go to America to raise support. Collins' military role set him apart in a sophisticated intelligence war, with spies in the British headquarters in Dublin Castle, where he once spent the night examining British files.

By 1920, 50,000 troops including the notorious 'Black and Tans' and 'Auxiliaries', together with 15,000 policemen battled 15,000 Volunteers. On 'Bloody Sunday', Collins – now called 'the Big Fella' – used his 'Squad' of gunmen to kill the 'Cairo Gang' of British intelligence officers in their beds, and 'Black and Tans' shot 14 people at Croke Park football stadium. Britain now realised the terrible cost of a full-scale guerrilla war in lives, money and international reputation. Peace feelers went out and led to a truce.

De Valera now came back from America. A difficult man, he was plainly jealous of Collins, snarling as he arrived, 'We'll see who's the Big Fella'. When he first went to London, he pointedly excluded Collins. The second time, to shift the blame, he sent Arthur Griffith with Collins as his Deputy. There they were trapped into signing a Treaty that would, because of Ulster's opposition, force the partition of Ireland. Britain's Lord Birkenhead said to Collins, 'I may have signed my political death warrant tonight.' Michael Collins replied prophetically, 'I may have signed my actual death warrant.'

In spite of Collins' best efforts at reconciliation, de Valera rejected the Treaty. The Irish split and a Civil War erupted. To avoid the return of the British, Collins was even forced to borrow field guns from them to shell his anti-Treaty former comrades holed up in the Four Courts. The tragic Civil War lasted eleven months and killed more Irish than the war with Britain ever did.

And so it was that the Irish Free State's Commander in Chief, Michael Collins, feeling confident and at home, decided to do an inspection tour of his native West Cork. After meeting friends and supporters at various pubs,

Collins drove off, supported by an armoured car. On the road from Bandon, at Béal na mBláth (the mouth of the flowers), Collins' column was stopped by the local anti-Treaty IRA, and five ambushers opened fire.

As Commander in Chief, a Minister, and probably the future President of Ireland, he should have taken the urgent advice of his sensible companions and retired to play his role in history. But no. Used to quick decisions, he grabbed a rifle, shouting, 'Let's fight, boys!' Rashly standing away from the cover of his armoured car, he was hit, in the failing light, by a last parting shot from 'Sonny' O'Neill.

500,000 people attended Collin's funeral, an outpouring of grief in Ireland that has never been seen before or since. O'Neill knew that he was now in danger and left his native Cork for ever to live the rest of his days in Tipperary. There he was a popular figure with a love of greyhound racing, who died in 1950 aged 62.

He always regretted that it was he who killed Collins. And not surprisingly. Over the years the Irish people began to feel that the country might have been a better place under Michael Collins than under the colder, fanatic Eamon de Valera.

John Boyle **O'REILLY**

The *Hougoumont* was the last convict ship to go to Australia. One of her reluctant passengers was John Boyle O'Reilly of County Meath in Ireland. He had already served two years in English prisons and was condemned to 18 more in Australia. Indeed, he had been lucky to escape the death sentence, because he was one of the 'Military Fenians'.

The Fenians would provide just another false dawn in Ireland's long struggle for freedom from Great Britain. James Stephens, a veteran of the failed 1848 Rising, had learned that success required arms and military skill. In 1858 he created a new secret society in Ireland and in New York, the Irish Republican Brotherhood, or 'The Fenians'. With Irishmen providing half of all Britain's troops, Stephens hit on the idea of recruiting soldiers in the regiments stationed in Ireland. One of these was Trooper John Boyle O'Reilly (below), who soon recruited 80 members from the 10th Hussars.

By 1865, one third of the regular army and half the militia had been secretly sworn in as Fenians, ready to act on Stephen's orders to rise in armed revolt, stiffened by hundreds of Irish-American officers experienced in the recent Civil War. But James Stephens then fatally hesitated and delayed. John Devoy, who had done most of the Fenian recruiting, wrote bitterly, '*All the risks and sacrifices were thrown away by incompetent, nerveless leadership.*'

Informers got wind of the plot and the British pounced. Hundreds of soldiers were court-martialled and imprisoned. And so in October 1867, a small group of 'military Fenians' found themselves on the *Hougoumont*. After ten weeks, they were paraded in Fremantle and told the prison rules, often including the word 'death' in the routine punishments, and reminded that 'escape was impossible through the cruel desert landscape or the shark-infested sea.'

The British were overconfident. Within a year, O'Reilly had charmed the warder on a road-building detail, becoming a 'probationary' convict constable and messenger, and even falling in love with the warden's daughter. Then the local Catholic priest arranged his escape. He broke away, hid in the bush and was rowed by sympathisers twice out to sea in a tiny boat and finally picked up by an American whaler. It took months for him to reach the US, but O'Reilly, in Boston, became a successful writer, newspaper editor and poet (later John F. Kennedy's favourite).

However, he had not forgotten his comrades languishing in Fremantle. He met John Devoy and suggested a daring plan – to buy a ship, sail it to Fremantle and rescue the six remaining Fenians. They recruited Captain George Anthony who found the 200-ton whaler *Catalpa*. A touch of genius was to send out in advance two Irishmen to plot the operation on land. John Devlin would pose as a wealthy American investor who charmed the little town of Fremantle, as well as the Governor, who even showed him round the prison. Word was passed to the prisoners, who were amazed that escape might at last be possible.

The *Catalpa* arrived after months of difficulties. All seemed ready. The Fenians were now 'trusties', working outside the prison. The steam gunboat HMS *Conflict* had luckily just left. Horses and wagons stood by.

Very early on Easter Monday 1870, the plan swung into action. The men leapt into the wagons and galloped south to the beach at Rockingham, where the *Catalpa's* longboat waited. Desperately they rowed out into the surf, as police bullets splashed around them.

In Fremantle the prison bell tolled the alarm. The wires cut, the *Conflict* could not be recalled, so the Government mail steamboat, the *Georgette*, was commandeered and set off. She caught up the next day, a field gun lashed to her deck and crowded with police and soldiers. The two ships ran parallel, with the police furiously threatening Captain Anthony with attack. Eventually the political dangers of firing on an American ship asserted themselves and the *Georgette* reluctantly turned back.

To the fury of the British, O'Reilly and the rescued men became heroes in America and the daring escape gave fresh heart to the Irish. But it would take five more decades before a well-organised military force would make Ireland became a nation again.

? Ana de **OSORIO**

Malaria has always been a worldwide and deadly scourge, its effect critical at pivotal moments. For instance, it destroyed successive invaders of Rome – Visigoths, Vandals, Huns and Ostrogoths. Even in the colder north, a Roman invasion of Scotland once lost half its 80,000 men. Expeditions, colonisation missions and engineering projects from many nations failed because of malarial fever, and whole armies were often all but wiped out.

The Spanish, in their vast colonies of South America, were all too familiar with the disease, although the way it was spread by mosquitoes was yet to be understood. And it was a Spanish aristocrat who, by chance, would help to save the world from this terrible affliction.

In 1638, Ana de Osorio, the Countess of Chinchón, and the beautiful wife of the Spanish Viceroy of Peru, was close to death, desperately ill with malaria, and racked by its cold rigors and hot fevers as she lay in the Viceregal Palace in Lima. The doctor suggested to the Count that they try using a local remedy, an extract from an Andean bark, *quinquina*. Miraculously, the Countess was saved.

In fact, Spanish Jesuit missionaries had discovered the healing power of *quinquina* four years earlier. But nobody paid attention. As so often, it required the dramatic saving of 'a celebrity' for the medical and botanical world to sit up and take any notice.

When the Countess returned to her estates at Chinchón near Madrid, she used the *quinquina* bark to protect her workers from malaria, turning the swamps into profitable rice paddies. The bark from the tree, which botanists had designated, but misspelled Cinchona, was brought back by her physician and sold in Seville. It was called the 'Countess's bark', and was at first only available to the rich. However, the Jesuits became involved and it became something of a Catholic monopoly, so some Protestants stubbornly and sadly refused to take it. Indeed, Oliver Cromwell called it the 'power of the devil' and died prematurely, after suffering from bouts of malaria all his life, a victim of his own religious prejudice!

Less-blinkered fellow countrymen two centuries later grasped the need for quinine on an industrial scale. With their huge Empire mainly in hot climates, the British knew only too well the devastating effects of malaria, which killed or crippled both colonised and colonisers alike: 'Beware, beware the Bight of Benin. One comes out, where fifty went in'. An enthusiastic amateur botanist, Clements Markham, persuaded the Indian Office and Kew Gardens to finance an expedition to find the original quinquina plants and reproduce them in India. The £10,000 voted proved to be a bargain for the British Empire. Between 1859 and 1862, Markham brought cinchona trees to India and large scale production began, aiming to protect British and Indians at a fraction of the cost of the original 'Countess's' or 'Jesuits' bark'.

Quinine became the world's main protection against malaria, breaking the cycle by killing the reservoir of parasites in humans before they can be re-transmitted by the mosquito. The British ex-colonial habit of drinking 'gin and tonic' becomes logical if you use the American version – 'gin and quinine water'.

While malaria is still a killer, the saving of one influential celebrity life in Peru helped to save tens of millions of lives in the centuries to come.

One of the best examples of mosquito control was over the Panama Canal. Ferdinand de Lesseps, the hero of the Suez Canal, had been ruined by Panama, with yellow fever and malaria killing 30,000 of his workers.

When the United States later stepped in, a decisive figure emerged, American medical officer Colonel William Gorgas. He fully understood that to prevent mosquitoes from spreading yellow fever and malaria, methodical efforts had to be made to cover all stagnant water with oil and insecticide to prevent the insects from reproducing. He also made it compulsory to put screens on all windows, not just to protect the inhabitants, but also to stop them being reservoirs of the diseases. And, of course, Gorgas made them all take 'quinine'.

Only then could construction start under a team from the U.S. Military Academy at West Point. Thirteen years later, in August 1914, the first ship passed from one ocean to another. A tiny enemy was beaten and nearly 8,000 miles of sailing round South America was reduced to a mere ten hours.

Elisha **OTIS**

Most of us know the name OTIS because we often see it above the buttons in lifts. Indeed the company that bears his name is now the largest maker of elevators and escalators in the world.

But it was not only for manufacturing elevators that Elisha Otis is important, but for making them possible at all – and, with them, all high-rise buildings – the 'skyscrapers' that dominate our cities and which we now take for granted.

The need to hoist things up into the air is nearly as fundamental as the need for the wheel to move them on the flat. Man devised ropes and cables, block and tackle, capstans, winches and buckets. So, why not also lift people in the buckets or cages? There was, of course, an excellent reason – the very real fear of the ropes breaking with fatal results. It was because of that fear that most cities continued to have buildings about seven storeys high – as much as one could reasonably expect someone to puff up the stairs.

Elisha Otis was born in Halifax, Vermont, in 1811, and after building mills, started constructing wagons and carriages. A skilled and imaginative craftsman, he went on to make bedsteads, later turning his hand to inventing a train brake and then an automatic baking oven.

In his bedstead factory in New York, he needed to lift heavy material to the upper levels. As a result he created a hoisting platform, but decided to make it safer. What he looked for was a device to stop the elevator platform falling if the cable broke, leading him to create a safety brake in the form of a strong steel wagon spring that would bend and mesh with a ratchet, catching and holding the platform. But how was he to publicise his new and safe elevators?

The 1854 New York World's Fair gave him his opportunity, and Otis decided on a touch of pure theatre. In front of a large and curious audience, he was hauled high into the air on an open platform. Suddenly, a man stepped forward and cut through the rope with an axe. Clunk! The elevator fell a few inches and held fast. The crowd gasped. Otis was safe, and so was the future of elevators. The orders poured in.

Now it became possible to lower miners ever deeper into the earth, while urban dwellers could be swished to the top of 'skyscraper' offices and ever-taller apartment buildings, changing our world forever.

William **PARKER**

William Parker, 4th Baron Monteagle, was very fortunate in marrying Elizabeth Tresham – and it proved a stroke of luck for several hundred others. It was a letter written to Lord Monteagle by her father that saved all their lives in the 'Gunpowder Plot', whose failure the British celebrate every November 5th.

The plot, hatched in 1605, was to blow up the Houses of Parliament, killing King James I, his government and the whole ruling aristocracy. Had it succeeded it would have been the political and social equivalent of 9/11, Kennedy's assassination and the French Revolution all rolled into one.

The plot was hatched by provincial Roman Catholic landowners who were bitterly

disappointed with James's unexpected crack-down on Catholicism, and planned to replace him with his infant daughter Elizabeth. The ringleader, Thomas Catesby, turned to Guy Fawkes (left) because of his military and explosives expertise. A cellar was rented under the Houses of Parliament, and 36 barrels of gunpowder, nearly 3 tons, were smuggled in and hidden behind piles of wood.

The State Opening of Parliament was delayed time and again, and more people were brought into the conspiracy. Finally, it was announced that Parliament would sit on 5th November 1605. All was ready. However, one of the newcomers was Sir Thomas Tresham, who knew that his Catholic son-in-law, Lord Monteagle, was due to attend, and for family reasons got cold feet about the intended carnage. Tresham wrote him a letter on 26th October warning him not to attend because *'They shall receive a terrible blow, this Parliament, and yet they shall not see who hurts them.'*

Monteagle, who had been treated well by the government, did not burn the letter, but had it read aloud by a friend to one of the main conspirators, a way of giving them a week to know they were betrayed and should call off the plot and escape. He then went and showed it to Robert Cecil, James's Secretary of State, an anti-Catholic spymaster. Writing the letter was a bad enough mistake, but the real blunder was that, knowing it had been sent so foolishly, the conspirators still decided to carry on with the plot.

Lord Monteagle then accompanied the Earl of Suffolk, the Lord Chamberlain and his soldiers on a raid the night before the Opening, and Guy Fawkes was caught, arrested and tortured. Many of the plotters galloped north, and were caught at Holbeche House in Staffordshire. Their defence against the King's troops was weakened because several of them had been injured trying to dry out gunpowder in front of an open fire (they were plainly missing Guy Fawkes' explosive skills).

All the conspirators were hanged, drawn and quartered – except one, the letter writer, Sir Francis Tresham. He was locked up alone in the Tower of London and died in mysterious circumstances six weeks later.

King James ordered that bonfires be lit every 5th November, topped by an effigy of the Pope – later replaced by Guy Fawkes. Of the plotters, his name is the only one we remember. And starting in America, 'Guy' slowly became changed from a 'person of grotesque appearance' to just another man's name. Nobody remembers Parker.

John Stith **PEMBERTON**

Both sides in the American Civil War used morphine to treat the pain of their wounded, without realising the dangers of addiction. Indeed, the twenty years after 1865 saw the worst addiction rate – in proportion to the population – in American history. One of these veterans and blameless morphine addicts was John Stith Pemberton.

After the war, Pemberton became a respected member of Georgia's medical establishment, and his laboratories are still in operation 125 years later. As a practical pharmacist and chemist, Pemberton also wanted to do something about his own drug dependence. He experimented with coca-based wines in what he called 'Pemberton's French Wine Cola'. The leaves of the coca trees of South America had long been known as a stimulant, either chewed or drunk. Reflecting public anxiety about depression, alcoholism and drug addiction among veterans, and 'ladies with nervous prostration and irregularities of stomach, bowels and kidneys', his coca wine was advertised as a medicinal product that also happened to be 'a pure, delightful, diffusible stimulant' (There was still cocaine in the mixture).

However, Atlanta and the county in 1885 brought in temperance laws, so Pemberton now produced a non-alcoholic version of his wine. His bookkeeper, Frank Mason Robinson, came up with the alliterative name 'Coca-Cola', and the script still used in the famous logotype. The name reflected the then quite high dose of coca leaf, combined with the caffeine stimulant provided by the Kola nut. It was advertised as 'a cure for headache, exhaustion and poor nerves'.

Sadly, morphine addiction had not gone away for John Pemberton, and as a result, a marketing genius, Asa Candler, obtained control of the company and its brand in 1892. Candler set up a franchised bottling system, still in use today, whereby Coca-Cola provides the 'secret' syrup concentrate to the bottlers who mix the syrup with filtered water and sweeteners and then carbonate it to sell in their appointed market.

In 1915, Coca-Cola ran a competition among its bottle suppliers to *'create a unique bottle shape that a person could recognise even if they felt it in the dark, and so shaped that, even if broken, a person could tell at a glance what it was'*. Bottle designer Earl R. Dean, found inspiration from a cocoa pod in *Encyclopaedia Britannica* and roughly copied it. It is essentially the bottle used a century later all over the world.

Coca-Cola, 'the pause that refreshes', went from strength to strength. During World War II, the company's image was hugely boosted by its nightly radio show 'The Victory Parade of Spotlight Bands', featuring all the popular big bands. On Christmas Day, 1942, Coca-Cola sponsored the spectacular 'Uncle Sam's Christmas Tree of Spotlight Bands' of 43 famous bands, each playing for 15 minutes from East to West, the largest musical marathon ever.

Such imaginative marketing has paid off over the years, with Coca-Cola's advertising always iconic, including the original image of the red-coated Father Christmas. People used to say, 'As American as apple pie', but today far fewer people eat apple pie, whereas Coca-Cola is enjoyed all over the world. Indeed, the product itself has become in many ways a symbol of America – for good or bad.

Coca-Cola is now sold in 200 countries, with 1.8 billion bottles and cans drunk every day. John Pemberton could never have imagined where his drug cure would lead.

Tom **PENDERGAST**

In a corner of Case Park in Kansas City stands the statue of a man whose dubious influence would reach all the way to the White House. Today, Tom Pendergast is only a faint memory, but his career certainly had implications for the United States and beyond.

The Pendergasts arrived from St. Joseph, Missouri, and one son, Jim, soon went into Kansas City politics, bringing in the family to help. His youngest brother, Tom, showed local brilliance. 'I know all the angles of organising and every man I meet becomes my friend. I know how to select ward captains and I know how to get to the poor. Every one of my workers has a fund to buy food, coal, shoes and clothing. When a poor man comes to old Tom's boys for help we don't make one of those damn fool investigations like these city charities. No, by God, we fill his belly and warm his back and vote him on our way'.

The brothers soon decided that they could control Kansas City and important neighbouring Jackson County, achieving this by complex moves to divide and conquer their competitors. When the Republican Governor of the state sent in a representative to 'curb city corruption', the Pendergasts merely joined forces with him to defeat their erstwhile Democrat allies. When Jim died, Tom grasped at every chance. A new reform movement in 1916 was successfully hijacked to give him overall control over the city, which he would hang on to as its Mayor for over 20 years.

Dubious methods included giving out 6,000 jobs to Pendergast's supporters, 2,000 of which required no work to be performed. Social 'welfare' programmes cemented their control, while taxes were even biased in favour of his supporters.

As 'Prohibition' tried to ban drinking in the rest of the country, the Pendergast machine gained control over the police department. Kansas City now became a 'wide-open' city, with gambling, prostitution and saloons booming. It was as if Prohibition did not exist, and a by-product was a boom in music, especially jazz. Everything seemed to be going swimmingly for Tom Pendergast.

Unfortunately he was getting in far too deep with the underworld, and a merely corrupt political machine became gangster-controlled – with a mobster, Johnny Lazia, as his lieutenant. Tom's gambling losses made him ever more dependent on Lazia, who soon dominated Kansas City's slot machines, numbers racket, bootlegging and speakeasies. The Federal authorities now began to take a real interest in both Lazia and Mayor Tom Pendergast.

Nevertheless, Tom was able to exert his influence in one decisive manner. Since

1922 he had backed Harry Truman (pictured left with him) in nearby Jackson County, which the 'machine' controlled. In 1934, Tom supported Truman for the Democratic nomination for Senator for Missouri. Truman, tainted by his association with Tom's machine, was 96,000 votes behind until Jackson City announced its votes – 137,000 for Truman and a suspiciously paltry 1,500 for his competitor! Thus Truman was to win the nomination and was later elected Senator.

But things now turned bad for Pendergast. Johnny Lazia was gunned down, and Tom was caught taking a gigantic bribe. Jailed in 1939, he was released after a year on the condition that he left politics.

But he lived to see Harry Truman become Vice-President of the United States, and when Tom died in January 1945, Truman attended his funeral, stating loyally, 'He was always my friend, and I have always been his'. Just three months later, President Franklin Roosevelt died and Harry Truman became President. Today few people remember the shady friend who propelled him to the White House.

Nikolay **PIROGOV**

Mention 'Crimean War' and 'nursing', and one name would come to most people – Florence Nightingale – the famous 'Lady with the Lamp'. But there should be three; not only Florence Nightingale, one of the most famous women in history, but also Mary Seacole, relegated until recently to undeserved obscurity, and Nikolay Pirogov – of whom most of us have never heard, despite being a giant of medical innovation and a Russian national hero.

Florence Nightingale hated the 'tyranny' of the drawing room and defied both convention and her parents to take up nursing. Shaken by the news from the Crimea, she first achieved fame when, in 1854, with 38 women volunteer nurses, she arrived in the huge, dark, dirty, over-crowded and disease-filled hospital at Scutari, in what is now Istanbul. She immediately set to work, bombarding her political friends for money and supplies. Contrary to what was then reported, she did not reduce the death rate, mostly from disease, at the hospital. It actually rose until the blocked sewers and hidden cesspit underneath were flushed out by a Sanitary Commission six months later. Indeed, it wasn't until years later that she acknowledged the deadly effect of germs. But what she did do was to bring a new level of management and caring to nursing. On her return, Florence (right) was feted by society and became the second most respected woman in Britain after Queen Victoria.

By contrast, Mary Seacole was very shabbily treated. The daughter of a Scottish army officer and a free Jamaican Creole 'doctress', Mary took over Blundell Hall in Jamaica, a hotel much respected by European officers, and helped with a major cholera epidemic. Then, moving to Panama, she established a reputation for helping to treat

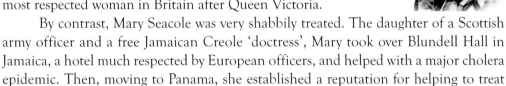

the sick in another devastating cholera outbreak.

Hearing that cholera was devastating British troops in the Crimea, she sailed to Britain to try to join Florence Nightingale's nurses, but was rejected by the War Office, perhaps on racial grounds. However, as William Howard Russell of *The Times* wrote, she then became '*both a Miss Nightingale and a chef*', as well as '*a warm and successful physician, who doctors and cures all manner of men with extraordinary success.*'

When the war ended 'Mother Seacole' was stuck with now unwanted provisions and she returned to Britain penniless, only to be rescued by the fundraising of many of the prominent people who knew of her work, including, anonymously, Florence Nightingale. Despite all her extraordinary achievements, Seacole died in obscurity and has only recently been properly recognized.

The third medical hero of the Crimea is largely unknown, because he was on the 'enemy' side. Nikolay Pirogov, (below) son of an army major, started his medical training

at just 14, later training in Germany. As Professor of Surgery at St Petersburg's Military Medical Academy, he pioneered the use of ether as an anaesthetic and compiled a complete anatomical 'atlas'. He is also considered to be the founder of field surgery, and routinely used anaesthetics during surgery – in contrast to the British, who often preferred a man to 'bellow lustily with pain than die in silence.'

Pirogov also invented 'triage', the method of deciding in a battlefield or civilian disaster how to prioritise the treatment of injury, now used all over the world. Moreover, he pioneered several kinds of surgical operations and the use of plaster casts for broken bones. What is more, when it came to female nurses, he had none of the prejudices that bedevilled the snobbish British. He had hundreds of female nurses under his command, dwarfing Florence Nightingale's little group.

But, typically, only in Russia has Nikolay Pirogov been granted the acclaim that he deserves.

Eugene **POLLEY**

Just recently a research study in Britain revealed that one third of its young people suffer from back pain – amazingly the same proportion as pensioners – with kids slumped for hours in front of television cited as one of the reasons for this very new phenomenon. And television is also recognised as one of the reasons for modern obesity. The emergence of the 'couch potato' has been attributed to one man, Eugene Polley, who created the first TV 'zapper', whereby for the first time viewers didn't even have to indulge in the minimal exercise of getting up to turn over the channels.

Eugene Polley was born in Chicago in 1915 and twenty years later found himself at Zenith Electronics. After World War II, when he worked on radar, television really took hold, and in America more and more channels became available. The inconvenience of getting up and making changes on the actual set led to a device called, appropriately, 'Lazy Bones' – but this was attached to the set by a long wire. Something 'wireless' was needed.

Eugene Polley created the 'Flash-Matic' that looked like a ray gun. It needed to, because you had to point a visible beam of light accurately at photocells on the four corners of the TV screen, thus turning the picture or sound off or changing the channels.

Zenith gave him a $1,000 bonus and advertised the Flash-Matic, somewhat curiously, as 'a TV miracle, absolutely harmless to humans'. Polley was equally proud, stating 'The remote control is the next most civilised invention after the flush toilet. It's almost as important as sex'.

Unfortunately, his new device, which cost $149 (an incredible £2,000 today), had other drawbacks. Sunlight could change the channels and viewers found they couldn't remember which part of the TV to point at. So Zenith decided to back an invention of a colleague, Robert Adler. His 'Space Command' was an ultrasound clicker with small hammers that struck rods to produce high-frequency sound signals. What is more, it was no cheaper, and it also suffered from the flaws of interference, this time from sounds like jingling keys and even rattling coins.

While both men won prizes jointly for their devices, Polley was always annoyed that he never received sole recognition for his invention. In fact, he was proved right in the end, and today's versions of his zapper are the low-frequency infra-red remotes we now use to control our TVs and DVD players, even though as 'couch potatoes' we find it harder and harder to control our weight.

Henry **POOLE**

In the 1930s, the dress sense of the elegant David, Prince of Wales, soon briefly to be King Edward VIII, was followed assiduously by 'society' and the fashion world – he even left us the 'Prince of Wales check'.

However, much more long-lasting was the influence, sixty years earlier, of his predecessor as Prince of Wales, Queen Victoria's son 'Bertie'. Forced to wait in the wings for decades as his mother ruled on and on, he became both, an enormous man and a huge influence on fashion. He created a great fashion change that lasts to this day.

During the nineteenth century the only proper dress for a gentleman in the evening was 'white tie and tails'. Wonderfully elegant, this could also be stiff and hot, easy to soil and, without a servant to help, quite elaborate to assemble.

Because of these shortcomings, in 1865 the Prince of Wales called in his tailor, Henry Poole, a founder of Savile Row and also the official Court Tailor. He asked Poole to design for him a short smoking jacket to be 'worn privately at home'.

And there, as the Prince intended, the 'dinner jacket' as we now call it, might have remained. However, twenty-one years later in 1886, the Prince met the American financier James Brown Potter and his wife Cora, and invited them to come and stay for the weekend. He added that at Sandringham 'they always wore short coats in the evening'. So Potter rushed round to Savile Row to ask Henry Poole to make up such a garment quickly in time for the great weekend.

When he returned to New York, Potter was sufficiently emboldened by his brush with royalty to decide to wear the new short coat to the Tuxedo Club in Tuxedo Park, defiantly commenting that 'if it was good enough for the Prince of Wales, it is probably good enough for the Tuxedo Club!'

Other brave pioneers would follow, who all happened to be customers of Henry Poole. Griswold Lorillard, the tobacco heir, also wore it at the Tuxedo Club – and so, for Americans, the 'Tux' was born. However, in more staid Saratoga, Evander Berry Wall, 'King of the Dudes', was ejected for wearing one at a grand ball. Back in London, the Prince's friend 'Duppy', Viscount Dupplin, helped to make the short coat slowly fashionable.

It took a long time. The elegance of 'White tie and tails', or full evening dress, does live on – usually on grand occasions like banquets at the Mansion House, for City Livery Companies and Royal Warrant Holders – and even TV's *Strictly Come Dancing*. But the rest of the world wears dinner jackets.

The Prince and his tailor certainly started something.

Alfonso de **PORTAGO**

The Mille Miglia was undoubtedly the most dramatic and dangerous of motor races. Its creation in 1927 was an act of revenge by the Auto Club di Brescia, which had seen the Italian Grand Prix – which they had pioneered in 1921 – 'stolen' from them the next year by the Automobile Club of Milan and held at Monza. With the help of the Fascist Party, a dramatic new race would now bring prestige back to Brescia.

The Mille Miglia was driven round a thousand miles of Italian roads, closed to traffic but not to people. In the dark of the evening, starting with low-powered sports cars driven by virtual amateurs, a car would roll down the ramp at Brescia every minute, with the fastest cars leaving at dawn.

Over the years the race, mostly dominated by Italians, would have some strange moments. Gianni Marzotto once won in a smart double-breasted suit, and another winner's car was found full of cigarette ash and empty brandy bottles. The German Rudolf Caracciola sneaked up behind three Alfa Romeos with his lights off and became the first foreign winner.

By the 1950's, superfast works teams from Maserati, Ferrari and Mercedes were screaming down the country roads, blasting past the slower cars. It was dangerous enough driving along narrow roads and through typical Italian towns and villages. And for the drivers, it was doubly terrifying because the uncontrolled spectators crowded on to the road, only leaping back when the cars came through. So it often seemed that they were driving at 170mph straight at a solid wall of people.

In addition, it was almost impossible to memorise the thousand mile course. The most successful method of knowing what on earth lay beyond the crowd was devised by Dennis Jenkinson, who acted as navigator for Stirling Moss (right) in his Mercedes in 1955. After a careful reconnaissance drive, he created an 18 foot scroll, like a loo roll, on which every corner, bridge or bump on the route had been noted, and for a thousand miles he shouted instructions in Moss's ear, 'Second gear, hump-back-bridge, saucy one left, dodgy one right...'

This intrepid pair would break the tradition that 'he who leads at Rome never wins at Brescia.'

But inevitably, a much less careful and attentive character was to put paid both to himself and the race. In 1957, running fourth, Spain's glamorous sportsman and playboy, Marquis 'Fon' de Portago, pulled in to refuel. He had hit a bank and his Ferrari mechanics shouted to him that a wheel was damaged and needed changing. Impatiently, he waved them away and howled back into the race, only to skid to a halt after fifty yards for a passionate kiss with his beautiful girlfriend, the Hollywood actress Linda Christian.

His romantic and Latin sense of priorities had tragic results. 10 miles down the road his tyre burst and his car ploughed into the crowd, killing him, his navigator and ten spectators.

Under pressure from the Vatican, the Mille Miglia was never run again

Juan **PUJOL**

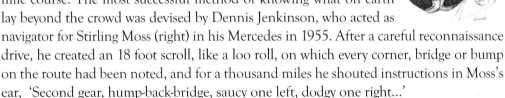

Juan Pujol had three names, his real one and two code names, GARBO and ARABEL, reflecting the fact that he was one of the most effective double agent spies in history – and the only man to be decorated by both sides in World War II.

Pujol was born in Barcelona in 1912 and was caught up in the Spanish Civil War, serving on both sides whilst avoiding actual combat, an experience that taught him to hate Communism and Fascism equally, meaning Russia and Germany.

When World War II started, he wanted to help Germany's enemy, Britain, but initially turned down by the British, managed to get himself recruited as a German spy. His German minder in Madrid thought Pujol was in Britain, whereas he was actually in Lisbon, cleverly using British travel guides, books and magazines, newsreels and railway timetables to convince the Germans that he was in London and had, moreover, recruited a team of sub-agents. Gradually the British realised that someone was successfully feeding false information to the Germans, and at the instigation of the Americans they brought him to London, giving him the code name GARBO. But it was as ARABEL that he began to overwhelm the Germans with a mountain of false information from his 27 entirely fictitious sub-agents. Indeed the Germans trusted him so much that they did not even bother to recruit any more spies in Britain and handed over $340,000 ($4.5 million today) in wages for his 'team'.

ARABEL's apparently valuable stream of information was sometimes pure fiction, some of it useless and some accurate, but delivered late. His report of ships leaving for the invasion of North Africa was airmailed to Madrid, but deliberately just too late.

 Pujol's great triumph was his pivotal role in the vital 'Operation Fortitude' deception, in which his hundreds of messages reinforced the German belief that the Normandy invasion was just a feint and that the real attack was coming to the Calais area from General George Patton's fictitious 'First US Army Group'. Thus Hitler, who received some of Pujol's messages directly, refused to let Rommel unleash his Panzer divisions and left huge, useless forces in the Calais area for weeks.

In July 1944, Pujol (above) was, ironically, awarded the Iron Cross by the Führer and a few weeks later the British, perhaps embarrassed, made Pujol a Member of the Order of British Empire.

After the war Pujol faked his own death and went to live quietly in Venezuela. Only in 1984 was his name revealed, and he was welcomed by Prince Philip at Buckingham Palace before visiting the Normandy beaches which he had done so much to help liberate.

Pyotr **RACHOVSKY**

Probably very few people have ever heard of Pyotr Rachovsky, and almost certainly none of the millions of Jews being shot by the Nazis in the fields of Russia or being herded into the gas chambers would have ever recognised his name. If they had, they would have cursed him. It was his forgery that sealed their fate; used to propel and justify what is often considered the greatest crime in history, the Holocaust, Hitler's attempt to annihilate the Jewish people.

The '*Protocols of the Elders of Zion*' were purported to be the sinister written records of a secret meeting during the first Zionist Congress in Basel in Switzerland in 1897, revealing that the Jewish leaders were plotting to take over the world.

In fact, the *Protocols* were written that year by Pyotr Ivanovich Rachovsky, an agent of the Russian Czarist secret police. He had copied them from a satirical novel attacking Napoleon III by Maurice Joly called '*A dialogue in Hell between Montesqieu and Machiavelli.*'

They were indeed anti-Semitic, but also had the purely domestic purpose of trying to discredit the modernising Jewish Russian Minister of Finance, Sergie Witte. Their twenty-six chapters range from the sinister, '*use violence and intimidation*' to the slightly silly, '*make the people unhappy by banning drinking.*' Whatever the limited Russian purposes of the forgery, the *Protocols* became a 'Pandora's box' when published in 1905. After the Russian Revolution in 1917, Russian royalist exiles spread the *Protocols* as proof that the Jews were responsible for the fall of the Czar. One of these encouraged American Henry Ford in his brand of anti-Semitism. Ford's newspaper, *The Dearborn Independent*, serialised the Protocols in 1920 under the banner *'The International Jews: The World's foremost problem'*, while Ford used his wealth to reproduce the series in half a million books and several foreign languages. More and more countries were flooded with copies.

Having at first been taken in, *The Times* in London then exposed the *Protocols* as complete forgeries in August 1921. Most sensible people now dismissed them as forgeries. Indeed, when Hitler was shown them, he knew perfectly well that they were not authentic. But he also knew that they ideally suited his own purposes and subsequently used them for the philosophy of his 1923 book *Mein Kampf*, (My Struggle), linking economic hardship to a secret Jewish plot and ultimately to Bolshevism. The *Protocols* became the chief weapon in the Nazi hate campaign against the Jews master-minded by Joseph Goebbels, the Propaganda Minister, who printed millions of copies in dozens of languages. A Swiss judge in 1933 was to rule, *'For all the harm they have already caused and may yet cause, they are nothing but ridiculous nonsense.'* But Hitler had also written in *Mein Kampf* his cynical view: *'The broad mass of a nation will more easily fall victim to a big lie than to a small one.'* He now had his big lie.

Without the *Protocols*, it is unlikely that the German nation could have been whipped up into such a frenzy of anti-Semitism, based on the strange double position that Jews were somehow 'subhuman', but also dangerously clever. It solves the mystery of how hundreds of thousands of previously decent people could willingly participate in the methodical extermination of Jews. The Holocaust would arguably have been impossible, and we might never have heard of Auschwitz, or all those other atrocious camps.

Amazingly, the *Protocols* are still being used as factual truth by those who want to continue the myth of a Jewish conspiracy, including fanatical sects in the United States. Furthermore, in case anyone thought they were no longer causing trouble, there are 50 books in the Middle East based on the *Protocols*. Indeed, extreme Muslim groups have embraced their veracity to justify everything from 9/11 to suicide bombings all over the world.

What an appalling legacy for a bit of internal political 'spin' over a century ago.

Mary **READ** and Anne **BONNY**

Mary Read and Anne Bonny were extraordinary women with five things in common. Both were born under the stigma of illegitimacy, both became brave fighting pirates, both ended up on the same ship under the same pirate captain, becoming firm friends, and both avoided the noose by pleading pregnancy.

Mary Read was born in 1690 in Plymouth, and her mother disguised her as her legitimate brother who had died, in order to continue to receive money from Mary's grandmother. Growing up still dressed as a male, Mary worked as a footman, a sailor and eventually a cavalryman fighting in Flanders, only reverting to female dress when she fell in love and married a Flemish soldier. When he died, she sailed to the West Indies. But her ship was taken by pirates and she eventually met the notorious Captain 'Calico Jack' Rackham and his lover Anne Bonny.

Anne Bonny's mother, Mary Brennan, was the housemaid to William Cormac, a lawyer in Kinsale in Ireland, and when Anne was born they avoided disgrace by sailing for America where we first hear of Anne as a tomboy tearaway in Charleston. She married James Bonny – a fortune-hunting sailor – and her father, who was now rich, disinherited her. So she moved to the pirate-invested Bahamas and met 'Calico Jack', becoming his mistress and getting rid of James Bonny.

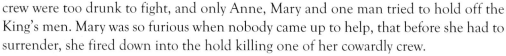

When Anne (right) first met Mary Read, she rather fancied her – because Mary was dressed as a handsome young man. Indeed, 'Calico Jack' became seriously jealous until the secret was revealed. Mary and Anne soon became good friends. Sailing with Rackham in a stolen ship, the *Revenge*, the two women fought alongside the men and were successful pirates, indeed notorious enough for both to be listed as 'wanted' in America's only newspaper, *The Boston News-Letter*.

Many ships were then seized and plundered, but the highly profitable partnership did not last long before disaster struck. In October 1720 their ship was attacked in the middle of the night by a sloop commissioned by the Governor of Jamaica. Most of the pirate crew were too drunk to fight, and only Anne, Mary and one man tried to hold off the King's men. Mary was so furious when nobody came up to help, that before she had to surrender, she fired down into the hold killing one of her cowardly crew.

When Rackham and his captured crew were sentenced to hang, Anne snarled to her erstwhile lover, 'If you had fought like a man, you need not have been hanged like a dog!' However, 'Calico Jack' had done Anne one last favour. Pregnant, she 'pleaded the belly'. English law allowed a stay of execution for pregnant women that luckily applied to both to Anne and Mary.

Mary died in prison during childbirth, but Anne's rich father at last used his money and influence and she was brought back to Charleston. There she married, had ten more children and died as the respectable Mrs Burleigh at the grand old age of 80.

Louis **REARD**

Today we take skimpy bikinis for granted. Beaches round the world are full of them. It is now hard to remember that, as a product, it was a failure until rescued by the beautiful shape of a young French film star – Brigitte Bardot.

Soon after World War II, Louis Réard faced a problem. A car engineer, he had agreed to help his mother with her swimwear business, and in 1946 discovered that their biggest, rival Jacques Heim, planned a tiny two-piece bathing suit, *'L'Atome'*, and was going to advertise it as 'the smallest bathing suit in the world'.

In fact, two-piece bathing suits were nothing new. Ancient Sicilian mosaics depicted them, and during the recent World War II, the US Government had positively and patriotically encouraged them as a reduction in fabric.

Louis Réard realised he needed something extra – or at least extra small – 30 square inches, and he planned to beat Jacques Heim by launching his miniature sensation on July 5th, 1946. However, he needed a name and a model. The name came just four days before the launch. In the Pacific, the Americans had tested two atomic bombs against old ships, from submarines to battleships. The place was called Bikini Atoll. So now he had his 'explosive' name.

However, the model presented a problem. Not one of the usual Paris models would contemplate wearing the tiny garment. So Réard hired Micheline Bernadini – quite relaxed because she was normally a nude dancer at the Casino de Paris.

Launched at the Molitor swimming pool on the Seine in Paris, the 'Bikini' was a brief sensation and Micheline received 50,000 fan letters. But as a product it faced an immediate wave of conservative reaction. Three Catholic countries banned it outright – Italy, Portugal and Spain. Beauty contests like 'Miss World' now also banned it, as did Hollywood, one of the great arbiters of fashion. Esther Williams, America's swimming film star, vowed never to wear something that was only for 'disgusting old voyeurs'. America's beaches and pools remained 'Bikini-free' for years, with women following the advice of *Modern Girl* magazine, *'It is hardly necessary to waste words over the so-called Bikini since it is inconceivable that any girl of tact and decency would ever wear such a thing.'* The Bikini seemed destined to be an embarrassing failure and a fashion dead end. It took ten years – until 1956 – for rescue to arrive in the lovely shape of 'sex kitten' Brigitte Bardot in the controversial

film *And God Created Woman* – exactly the sensation the bikini needed. More established and courageous stars like Marilyn Monroe and Jayne Mansfield now followed, and in 1960 Brian Hylands finally persuaded America's teenagers with his pop hit *'Itsy Bitsy Teenie Weenie Yellow Polka Dot Bikini'*. Then, Raquel Welch (left) was propelled to stardom by her fur bikini in *One million Years BC*, and Ursula Andress (above) set the tone for all Bond girls as she emerged bikini-clad from the sea in *Dr No*.

As for Louis Réard, he always claimed that nothing was a true Bikini 'unless it was small enough to be pulled through a wedding ring.'

Alves **REIS**

Artur Alves Reis was a young, balding, penniless businessman of 26 when he arrived in 1916 in backward, poor Angola with an up-market bride and an impressive but phoney diploma from 'The Polytechnic School of Engineering at Oxford University.' After some success as an engineer, he returned to Portugal where he was jailed for embezzlement. While serving his sentence, he planned to create a perfect crime. He would make Portugal forge millions of her banknotes and give them to him.

Reis discovered that most of Portugal's banknotes were printed by Waterlow and Son, one of the world's great security printers. On 4th December 1924, the Chairman, Sir William Waterlow, received a Dutch visitor, Karel Marang van Ysselveere, who explained that he was a member of a Dutch syndicate 'coming to the aid of Portugal's colony of Angola.' It was to advance Angola $5 million, and the Bank of Portugal would permit them to print banknotes, later to be overprinted 'ANGOLA'. Marang handed over an impressive contract – a complete forgery, the brilliant creation of Alves Reis.

Marang and Sir William agreed that the Vasco de Gama 500 Escudo note was the most suitable, because Waterlow's already had the plates. Sir William insisted on confirmation from the Bank of Portugal in writing. Reis quickly went to work on a modified contract, together with a forged letter from the bank's Governor, Camacho Rodriquez, confirming an initial order of 200,000 notes and stating that for political reasons all arrangements and correspondence should be through Marang.

Sir William did some checking of his own. He investigated Marang, who seemed respectable, but broke the agreement and sent a letter of confirmation direct to Governor Camacho. But by bad luck, the letter was lost in the mail. Reis's luck was holding. Soon the 200,000 notes were printed, collected by taxi, and sent by train to Portugal. They never went near Angola, nor were they overprinted 'ANGOLA'. An elaborate system of 'money-laundering' swung into action, mainly by black market currency dealers in Oporto. Reis became rich, buying farms and companies, and lavishing money and jewels on his wife.

So much money was soon in circulation that the Bank of Portugal itself was forced to quell rumours of forgery. Reis even created the Bank of Angola & Metropole, making huge investments in Angola, where he became a hero. Then, to eliminate the risk of the Bank of Portugal discovering his ruse, he tried to buy it. As the share price began to rise, a suspicious newspaper, O Seculo, began to investigate. 'WHAT'S GOING ON?' was the first headline.

Reis was returning from Angola by ship when things started to unravel. In Oporto, a currency dealer almost jumped to the right conclusion, going to the local Bank of Portugal office claiming that the notes were counterfeit. Police surrounded the Bank of Angola & Metropole and its manager was jailed. But when the Bank of Portugal's counterfeit expert arrived, he was forced to declare the notes genuine – which, in a sense, they were.

Red faces and recriminations all round. But not for long. Next day, an alert official noticed a bank note number was the same as one on another note. Then many more.

Alves Reis's luck had run out. On 6 December 1925, he was duly arrested on the ship's gangplank.

Reis would stay in jail for nineteen years, his friends for lesser terms. Sir William became the Lord Mayor of London, but was soon ousted from his printing firm, dying in 1931 tainted by the scandal. The most serious result was for Portugal herself. Antonio Salazar, as Minister of Finance, after clearing up the mess, then became the longest ruling dictator in Europe.

Rick **RESCORLA**

There were many American heroes and heroines during the horrific 9/11 aircraft attacks on the Twin Towers. But Rick Rescorla was a special and unusual hero.

First of all he was British-born, from Cornwall, who at only four years old during World War II became so entranced with the American troops waiting for D-Day that he resolved to become a soldier.

Rescorla was to fulfil his military ambitions not once, but twice. First, in 1957 he enlisted in Britain's crack Parachute Regiment. Later serving as a Police Inspector in Africa, he became very friendly with Daniel J. Hill, an American, and under his influence enlisted in the U.S. Army in 1963, soon graduating from Fort Benning as an officer and being assigned to the 6th Cavalry. In Vietnam, 'The Cornish Hawk' was also nicknamed 'Hard Core' for his personal bravery and inspiring leadership, and described by one senior officer as 'the best platoon leader I ever saw.' He eventually left the army as a Colonel (right) with a silver and bronze star, and became Security Director at Morgan Stanley – based in the World Trade Center.

With his lifetime of military training and general alertness, in 1992 Rick Rescorla warned the owners of the World Trade Center that the buildings, and especially the iconic Twin Towers, were vulnerable to an attack by a truck bomb left in the basement parking area. He was ignored. The very next year, the then little-known Al-Qaeda did just that. Rescorla helped evacuate the smoke-filled buildings and was the last man out.

He then warned both the building owners and Morgan Stanley that the next attack might come from aircraft. His warnings were disregarded again, as was his advice to Morgan Stanley to move from such symbolic buildings to somewhere safer. When they argued that their lease still had five years to run, he decided to at least prepare for the worst, drilling everyone from top to bottom in strict evacuation procedures. Thus when his prophecies were tragically fulfilled in 2001, and big, fully-fuelled airliners hit each tower, Rescorla ignored the building officials' advice to stay put, and helped 2,700 Morgan Stanley employees to climb down the stairs to safety. He then re-entered Tower 2 and was last seen on the tenth floor still climbing to see if he could rescue anyone else. After the tower collapsed, only nine Morgan Stanley employees were found to have died. Sadly Rescorla was one of them, aged sixty two, a true hero.

Harold **RIDLEY**

If the lens in an eye becomes cloudy or opaque, the image is progressively blurred and indistinct and the eye loses sight – a condition known by the ancient term 'cataract'. It is by far and away the commonest cause of blindness in the world with many millions affected, and the only solution is the surgical removal of the whole lens.

Refined techniques and new instrumentation made this surgery more sophisticated and safer from the 19th century onwards, but the restoration of sight by spectacles always had drawbacks. An operated eye does not link satisfactorily with an un-operated eye as everything it sees is nearly twice as large and the ability to focus is lost. Although this can be partially remedied by the patient wearing a contact lens, in the elderly and in developing countries where the cataract problem is greatest, this is not really a satisfactory option.

At the height of the Battle of Britain on August 14th 1940, a pilot from Tangmere took off in a borrowed plane and forgot his goggles. His Hurricane was hit and the cockpit's Perspex canopy shattered into fragments, some of which penetrated his eyes. The pilot parachuted to safety and was transferred to Moorfields Eye Hospital in London for surgery. Over the next few years Harold Ridley, one of the surgeons, examined the pilot several times, noting that the Perspex in the eyes did not seem to be causing any foreign body reaction. A medical student, while watching Ridley performing a cataract operation, asked 'Why not replace the extracted lens with another one?'

For a long time Ridley had been considering doing just that. Now with the knowledge of the safety of Perspex within the eye, he decided to answer this simple question. With the co-operation of the optical firm Rayner and ICI, a lens was designed of material similar to Perspex and on November 29th 1949, at St. Thomas's Hospital, Ridley inserted the first intra-ocular lens (IOL). It was intended to keep this a secret to gain experience for about two years, but the news came out in the close-knit ophthalmic community in London. What followed was not the deserved praise for the success of this pioneering operation, but a great deal of antagonism, perhaps because of genuine concern about complications or just professional envy. Harold Ridley, for a time, was ostracised by many of his colleagues and refused opportunities to publish or speak about this new operation at national and international meetings. However, he continued to refine the surgical technique and soon a few eye surgeons in England and abroad started to carry out similar procedures.

It took nearly thirty years for 'intra-ocular lens' implantation to become accepted as the procedure of choice in cataract removal and the accolades began to pour in from all over the world. Awarded numerous medals, in 1986 Ridley was elected a Fellow of the Royal Society, and finally in 2000 at the age of 94 he received a knighthood.

Today, millions of operations with intra-ocular implants (above) are performed each year throughout the world. Countless numbers of patients have had their sight restored since that day in November 1949 when a single brave and farsighted surgeon altered the whole face of eye surgery with one of the most important advances in medicine in the 20th century.

Wilhelm **ROENTGEN**

Not so long ago, children would relieve the boredom of shopping with their parents by going off to play with shoe stores' X-ray machines, installed to check the fit of shoes. For minutes on end, as late as the 1950s, while mothers and shop assistants were distracted, they giggled with delight at the ghostly shape of bones revealed by the magical machine. In those days radiation dangers were not recognized.

A picture of a hand startled the world in 1895, beginning the process that made X-rays one of the most important discoveries in history. In Munich, Wilhelm Konrad Roentgen (left), German but with a Dutch mother, was one of many scientists investigating the rays emanating from the Crookes experimental discharge tubes being used to research the streams of electrons called 'cathode rays'. Several had noted the mysterious images projected on to photographic plates.

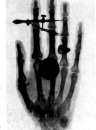

Indeed, by accident, Roentgen discovered an image of a key he had left on top of a photographic plate. However, it was *Hand mit Ringen* (right), a photograph of his wife's hand, plainly showing her bones and wedding ring, which electrified the world. Roentgen would give us the name 'X-rays', meaning 'unknown rays'. He was also the first scientist to study the rays methodically, receiving the very first Nobel Prize for Physics.

It was in the field of medical diagnosis that the ability of X-rays to penetrate solid objects was first used, and which has given us the whole science of radiography. Not only can bones be scanned for fractures and abnormalities but also soft tissues – in the chest for pneumonia, lung cancer or pulmonary oedema, and in the abdomen for intestinal problems including gallstones and kidney stones, let alone man-made objects like bullets. US President William McKinley begged Thomas Edison to send an X-ray machine to find his assassin's second bullet. For the blood system, a 'contrast compound' like iodine is injected into the veins and arteries; for the intestines it is barium. X-rays are also used to combat diseases, notably cancer, in the treatment now known as radiotherapy.

The use of medical X-rays has become more and more sophisticated. Photographic glass plates gave way to film and then digital and computed radiography which crucially require much less exposure for the patient.

The use of X-rays has spread way beyond medicine, from quality control in welding and metallurgy, to airport security systems and then on to measuring the vast distances of astronomy, down to tiny dimensions of microscope research. They even played a role in the discovery of DNA.

But it is undoubtedly in medicine that most of us realise the most powerful and beneficial effects of X-rays, and for which many owe their lives. And you can be sure that the experts operating the rays do not fool about like we did as children. They not only protect themselves with lead shielding but, rather intimidating for the patient, even rush off to another room before pressing the button.

Margherita **SARFATTI**

Nobody could accuse Benito Mussolini of being inhuman. Indeed, in many ways he was all too human, a man of considerable charm with a hypnotic personality. An excellent writer and journalist, the Italians flocked to hear him speak, and he brought them many practical and social improvements to Italian life ('the trains ran on time'). But he could be weak, lacking in judgement, bombastic and only too able to fool himself.

Mussolini was also passionate, over-sexed and very attractive to women, which ultimately helped to lead to his downfall. In 1910, he had married Rachele Guidi, a domestic servant who was to remain a faithful and supportive wife in spite of his many affairs. But two other women were to dominate Mussolini's life. One was beneficial, and the other a disaster.

In 1915, Mussolini became Editor of the newspaper *Il Popolo d'Italia*, where he fell under the influence of Margherita Sarfatti, one of Italy's leading art patrons and political journalists. A striking redhead, she was highly intelligent and, importantly, Jewish. She was also pro-British, pro-French and anti-Nazi. She hated violence and became a hugely important moderating influence on Mussolini, both at home and abroad for nearly twenty years.

Time and again it was Margherita's sensible advice that won the day for the headstrong Mussolini – from the timing and style of his Fascist seizure of power in 1922 to his forceful blocking of Hitler's first attempt to take over Austria. Britain and France both approved of Mussolini and joined his 'Stresa Front' to contain Hitler. Austen Chamberlain, Britain's Prime Minister Neville Chamberlain's brother, was a personal friend, and even Winston Churchill was an admirer (Indeed, we now know that Britain's secret service had financed Mussolini's early forays into politics).

However, Margherita had her enemies, who described her as 'greedy, calculating, arrogant and opinionated'. Her reputation for intrigue and 'boudoir influence' infuriated those not in her favour.

And suddenly she was over fifty, and her influence based on sexual attraction was waning. In September 1933, Mussolini noticed a pretty girl driving with her fiancé. She smiled and waved, and Mussolini stopped his car to talk to her. All too soon Claretta Petacci became the dictator's mistress, and Margherita lost her power and influence. Thus, in 1935, when Mussolini tried to create his own empire with his foolish invasion of Abyssinia, he did not listen to Margherita's advice against 'a dangerous adventure.' In vain, she wrote to him: *'If you go into Ethiopia, you will fall into the hands of the Germans and then you will be lost.'*

Prophetic words. Italy lost the respect of the world, and the friendship of France and Britain. And after Abyssinia, Mussolini was indeed pushed into the arms of Hitler, whom he disliked and feared, but whose ruthless will and ambitions he would now have to support.

Margherita Sarfatti, in despair at her former lover's foolishness and seeing the first signs of anti-semitism against Italy's Jews, left for South America. 'Her deep love for Mussolini became a boundless hatred'. As predicted, Italy was sucked by Germany into a disastrous World War and then invaded by the Allies. Mussolini was deposed by his King, but then rescued by the Germans to live out a powerless half-life as the Allies closed in.

To be fair to his pretty but empty-headed pro-Nazi mistress, Claretta remained loyal to the bitter end. She paid the price, shot alongside her lover by Communist partisans, and then hung upside down with him in Milan.

It was a tragedy for them, for Italy, and the history of the whole world that twelve years earlier, she and Mussolini just happened to be on the same road.

Robert **SHORT**

In March 1932, a huge funeral took place in Shanghai – then, as now, one of China's most vibrant and important cities. 500,000 wailing mourners lined the streets. But this funeral was not for some respected Chinese leader, but for a young American pilot – Robert Short. He had the dubious honour of being the first American to be shot down in aerial combat with the Japanese – and nine years before Pearl Harbor locked the two nations officially in war.

Japan had attacked China in January 1932 and was now using its mastery of the air to bomb and terrorize the civilian population. Boeing had decided to give the Chinese an experimental fighter, the Boeing XP925A, to try it out in combat conditions, and it was being delivered by a young pilot working for Boeing's importer, Robert Short, who was also a 2nd Lieutenant in the US Army reserve.

On February 19th 1932, Japanese planes appeared. Short had his fighter armed, took off alone and flew straight at three Japanese fighters. He shot down one, killing the pilot, Lt Kidokoro. Three days later, again all alone, he intercepted three bombers and three fighters attacking a refugee train. This time the odds were too great, and after killing the Japanese leader, he was himself shot down.

The Chinese were so deeply moved by his brave gesture in trying to protect them that they invited Robert Short's parents to come from Tacoma, Washington, to his funeral, with the Chinese Commander-in-Chief, writing *'The name of Robert Short will live long in the scroll of honour of great men, and his meritorious service will ever be in the memory of all Chinese'*.

Indeed it has, because more than half a century later, in 1986, the citizens of Suzhou erected a monument (right) in his memory. Not even the anti-American sentiments of a Communist regime could dim the grateful emotions of the local people for a long-dead hero.

? Fred **SMITH**

One of the essential tasks of a well-organised society is to move information quickly. Relays of horse riders served the Roman Empire well, as they did Genghis Khan's Mongol Empire. In the 19th century in London, you could send a letter in the morning and get a reply 'by return of post' before lunch, because there were, amazingly, 11 deliveries and 9 collections a day. The famous 'Pony Express' was quickly overtaken by the railways, which became the normal and quickest way to distribute mail, while at the same time spawning the whole mail-order industry.

However, in the United States after World War II, the mail lost this transport system because express passenger trains began to disappear, ruined by competition from the cars, buses and trucks on new Interstate Highways and faster, more reliable flying services. And it was aircraft that gave Fred Smith his big idea.

Fred Smith's father was a rich man, owning part of Greyhound Bus, so Fred could have relaxed into a life of leisure. However, after four years flying in Vietnam as a Marine officer, he returned to study economics at Yale. There he wrote a dissertation envisaging an airport hub – into which parcels could be flown in, sorted and flown out again overnight. Shortsightedly, Yale was unimpressed and gave him a modest C.

But when he graduated he decided to risk all on his idea, and he had carefully calculated the economics. Freight had been a sideline for passenger airlines, and if there were no direct flights, parcels had to be reloaded several times – expensive and slow. But with Fred Smith's system, planes would only need to be reloaded once. Most importantly, only relatively few aircraft would be needed to cover a huge network. If you wanted to link 100 locations directly with one another, you needed 4,950 routes. But by adopting Fred's approach, only 99 were required.

His local airport in Arkansas, Little Rock National, showed little enthusiasm (how it must rue that decision!). So Fred Smith now opted for Memphis, Tennessee, an airport roughly in the middle of the country. In 1973 'Federal Express' began flying a tiny fleet of Dassault Falcon 20s to 25 U.S. cities, marketing itself as *'The freight service with 550 miles an hour delivery trucks'*. Even so, its pioneering efforts led to financial difficulties and its undaunted founder personally rescued it. He flew to Las Vegas, won at blackjack and kept the company afloat.

By 1976, Federal Express was in profit, restrictions were lifted on all-cargo airlines and the first big aircraft arrived. FedEx went from strength to strength, helped by iconic advertising –'Absolutely, positively, overnight.' FedEx even became part of the language.

You 'FedExed' a document after you had 'Xeroxed' it, so to speak. In 2000, the wheel came full circle with FedEx the carrier for express mail for the U.S. Postal Service, just as the railroads had been. FedEx now operates hubs all over the world, with a huge fleet of 658 aircraft and 30,000 ground vehicles.

Fred Smith lives on what he calls a 'fun farm' just outside Memphis, with ten children and many grandchildren; a contented man. He even played himself in the film *Castaway*, welcoming back Tom Hanks, a FedEx man stranded on a desert island who manages to survive and return to civilisation – and to deliver his parcel.

Richard **SORGE**

Author and historian Frederick Forsyth summed up Richard Sorge perfectly: *The spies in history who can say from their graves, 'The information I supplied to my masters altered the history of our planet' can be counted on the fingers of one hand. Richard Sorge was in that group.*

Sorge was always likely to be a split personality, with a German father and a Russian mother, born in Russia, and then educated in Germany. He fought for Germany in World War I, was wounded, fell for his nurse and was influenced by her Marxist father. He went to Moscow and became a Soviet spy – arguably the most influential spy in history.

In 1929, he was in England, instructed to lie low. Returning to Germany, Sorge joined the Nazi Party as a cover and started a career as a journalist – also as a cover. Under the guise of writing for *Frankfurter Zeitung*, he now moved to Shanghai and then began to construct his spy ring. He was always attractive to women. Agnes Smedley, a left-wing journalist, wrote *'He's a he-man. Never have I known such good days'*. Agnes introduced Sorge to Hotsumi Ozaki, writing for the Japanese *Asahi Shimbun*, who joined his spy ring.

In May 1933, Moscow decided he should form a spy ring in Japan, and there his network soon included Ozaki, two other Comintern agents, and Max Clausen, a successful businessman. Together they cultivated many military and political contacts, Ozaki especially, with Prime Minister Fumimaro Konoe.

Sorge, as an 'ardent Nazi', cosied up to the German Ambassador in Tokyo and the Military Attaché, Eugen Ott. Ott became Ambassador in 1938 and trustingly allowed Sorge access to secret information and cables. Moscow was very clear. *'We need detailed information concerning changes in Japanese foreign policy. Reports that follow events are not enough. We must have advance information.'*

Sorge's advance information was fantastically valuable: prior knowledge of the Anti-Comintern Pact in 1936, the German-Japanese Pact of 1940 and the Japanese attack on Pearl Harbor. Sorge now expected that his next coup would be welcomed and acted upon. He revealed the precise date, June 22nd 1941, of *Operation Barbarossa*, Hitler's treacherous attack on his 'ally'.

Moscow thanked him, but in fact Stalin had sneered, 'There's this bastard who's set up factories and brothels in Japan and even deigned to report the date of the German attack as 22nd June. Are you suggesting I should believe him too?'

Stalin was ignoring mountains of evidence – from other spy **Stalin ignored** rings, diplomats and deserters, even Roosevelt and Churchill, who **all warnings** had obtained it from the breaking of the Enigma codes.

On June 22nd, precisely as predicted, the Germans launched three million men,

3,600 tanks, and 2,500 aircraft. Stalin's refusal to listen to Sorge, or anyone else, resulted in catastrophe. 3,000 Soviet planes were destroyed in the first three days and three million men were soon encircled. While the front collapsed, so did Stalin. But he recovered, and gradually the Russian weather and the stubborn bravery of the Russian soldiers wore down the German advance.

On 14th September, Sorge sent another vital message, revealing that the Japanese were not going to attack the Soviet Union. Now Stalin did believe his spy, and 400,000 fresh, winter-prepared troops and a thousand tanks were rushed by rail to Moscow, which the Germans were now approaching.

But even as they rolled westwards, Sorge was arrested. As he was questioned, five thousand miles away, the freezing, exhausted Germans were stalled, in sight of Moscow. The troops that Sorge's message had released were unleashed, hurling the Germans back 200 miles. The Soviet Union and its ungrateful leader had been saved.

After the war, General Tominaga, who had been Japan's Vice-Minister of Defence, revealed that they had proposed three times to the Soviets that Sorge be exchanged. Three times they replied: 'Richard Sorge is unknown to us'.

Because of Stalin's guilty conscience, Richard Sorge died – unrecognised until years after the monstrous dictator's death. Only in 1964 was his story revealed. He was made a 'Hero of the Soviet Union', with his sardonic face put on a stamp.

Not really much of a tribute to the man who stopped Hitler ruling the world.

Louise **STARKEY**

Their student friends thought the sketch so entertaining that they urged the three young creators to try to get it on the radio. So in June 1930, the three unknown girls from Northwestern University approached WGN in Chicago and even offered to perform for no pay. Louise Starkey, ('Clara'), Isobel Carothers ('Lu') and Helen King ('Em') were about to make history. The trio had created the very first 'soap opera'.

Clara, Lu and Em, with storylines around three women living in a small-town duplex, was soon sponsored by Super Suds of the giant Colgate–Palmolive company and ran for 15 years.

Many such radio shows followed, aimed at housewives during the afternoons. Their main sponsors were detergent companies – hence 'soap operas'– and they soon transferred to television. The longest running soap was *Guiding Light*, mostly focused on marital problems, lasting an incredible 72 years. Then the oldest TV soap became Britain's *Coronation Street*. Britain also boasts the longest-running radio soap, *The Archers*, curiously started as an agricultural advice series to help the British cope with post-war rationing and food shortages.

While both American and British soaps used to be low budget and with working class, everyday situations, in the 1970s there was a divergence. Britain's huge successes were *Coronation Street* and *East Enders*, both revolving round the local pub. However, after the risqué success of *Peyton Place*, with events like unwanted pregnancy, the Americans began to favour much frothier soaps. They brimmed with rich, big business moguls, beautifully dressed and glamorous women and were spiced with promiscuous villains like 'J.R.' Ewing in *Dallas* and elegant bitches like Joan Collins as the scheming Alexis in *Dynasty*.

Australia's *Neighbours* and *Home and Away* are set in sunny suburbia in the middle ground between the fantastical American soaps and the grittier British ones.

The soap format extends to all sorts of situations: urban living and working with *Friends*, *Frasier*, *Mad Men* and *Sex in the City*; hospitals, with *General Hospital*, *Dr Kildare*, *ER*, *Casualty*, *House*, *Grey's Anatomy*; lifesaving and ogling at babes in *Baywatch*; schools with *Beverly Hills 90210*, and plenty of crime and punishment with *Cagney & Lacey*, *Hawaii Five-O*, *Hill Street Blues*, *The Bill*, *Z-Cars*, *The Sopranos*, and, more recently, the *CSI* and *NCIS* phenomena. And that doesn't include the home-grown soaps in every language.

One wonders if Louise and her friends, having a bit of a laugh, knew what they were unleashing on the world.

? STARS' REAL NAMES

Among the remarkable people we've never heard of are a huge number of film and television stars, musicians and celebrities who we actually do know very well – but under different names. Whether their real names were too ethnic, foreign, unsexy, ordinary, boring, strange or just unpronounceable, they changed them, and here are just a few:

Alfred Jones - **Ray Milland**
Allen Konigsberg - **Woody Allen**
Archibald Leach - **Cary Grant**
Arnold Dorsey - **Engelbert Humperdink**
Asa Yoelson - **Al Jolson**
Barry Alan Pincus - **Barry Manilow**
Benjamin Kubelsky - **Jack Benny**
Bernard Schwartz - **Tony Curtis**
Betty Joan Perske - **Lauren Bacall**
Camille Javal - **Brigitte Bardot**
Carlos Irwin Estevez - **Charlie Sheen**
Caryn Johnson - **Whoopie Goldberg**
Cassius Clay - **Muhammad Ali**
Charles Carter - **Charlton Heston**
David Kaminski - **Danny Kaye**

David Robert Jones - **David Bowie**
Demetria Guynes - **Demi Moore**
Diana Fluck - **Diana Dors**
Dino Crocetti - **Dean Martin**
Doris Kappelhof - **Doris Day**
Douglas Ullman - **Douglas Fairbanks**
Ehrich Weiss - **Harry Houdini**
Eleanora Fagan - **Billy Holiday**
Elias Bate - **Bo Diddley**
Ernest Evans - **Chubby Checker**
Frances Gumm - **Judy Garland**
Frank James - **Gary Cooper**
Frederick Austerlitz - **Fred Astaire**
Gordon Sumner - **Sting**
Greta Gustafsson - **Greta Garbo**

Harlean Carpentier - **Jean Harlow**
Hedwig Kiesler - **Hedy Lamarr**
Henry Deutchendorf - **John Denver**
Issur Danielovitch - **Kirk Douglas**
Jerome Silberman - **Gene Wilder**
Joan Sandra Molinsky - **Joan Rivers**
Larry Zeigler - **Larry King**
Leslie Hornby - **Twiggy**
Lucille Le Sucus - **Joan Crawford**
Madonna Louise Ciccone - **Madonna**
Maria Von Losch - **Marlene Dietrich**
Marion Michael Morrison - **John Wayne**
Maurice Micklewhite - **Michael Caine**
McKinley Morganfield - **Muddy Waters**
Melvin Kaminsky - **Mel Brooks**
Michael Dumble-Smith - **Michael Crawford**
Michael Shalhoub - **Omar Sharif**
Natasha Gurdin - **Natalie Wood**
Nicholas Coppola - **Nicholas Cage**
Norma Jean Baker - **Marilyn Monroe**
Raquel Tejada - **Raquel Welch**

Richard Starkey - **Ringo Starr**
Robert Zimmerman - **Bob Dylan**
Roy Schere, Jr. - **Rock Hudson**
Rudolpho D'Antonguolla - **Rudolph Valentino**
Seth Ward - **James Dean**
Shirley Schrift - **Shelley Winters**
Sophia Scicolone - **Sophia Loren**
Steveland Hardaway - **Stevie Wonder**
Terry Jean Bollette - **Hulk Hogan**
Thomas Mapother IV - **Tom Cruise**
Truman Person - **Truman Capote**
Tula Ellice Finklea - **Cyd Charisse**
Virginia McMath - **Ginger Rogers**
Walter Matuschanskayasky - **Walter Matthau**
William C Dukenfield - **W.C. Fields**
William Beedle, Jr. - **William Holden**
William Henry Pratt - **Boris Karloff**

Seth Ward

Norma Jean Baker

Maurice Micklewhite

Camille Javal

Leslie Hornby

Archibald Leach

Marion Morrison

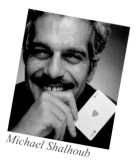
Michael Shalhoub

In recent years, more stars seem to be content with the names they were born with, however ethnic, foreign, unsexy, ordinary, boring, strange or just unpronounceable: Arnold Schwarzenegger, Al Pacino, Robert De Niro, Harrison Ford, Tom Hanks, Sean Connery, Peter O'Toole, Jack Nicholson, Matt Damon – all seem proud of their names.

Gideon **SUNDBÄCK**

All over the world we use them – on clothes, luggage, sleeping bags, shoes, tents, even body bags. They slide open and closed with a noise that goes 'zip', which is exactly what we call them.

The 'zipper', or 'zip', had several inventors. The first was Elias Howe, who in 1851 patented his 'Automatic, Continuous Clothing Closure'. However, he had also just invented the sewing machine, which took up most of his time, with little left to pursue his 'Clothing Closure.'

It took another 44 years for a Chicago inventor, Whitcomb Judson, to create and patent his 'Clasp Locker' in 1893 – a complicated hook and eye shoe-fastener. But at that year's Chicago World's Fair, it attracted little attention – let alone sales.

However, working at the Canadian plant of Judson's Universal Fastener Company was Gideon Sundbäck, a Swedish-American engineer who had married the plant manager's daughter and become chief designer. A few years later, Gideon decided to improve the 'Judson C-curity Fastener', including increasing the number of teeth from 4 to 11 per inch. Patenting his own 'Separable Fastener' in 1917, he also designed the machinery to make it. He is therefore the true father of the modern 'zipper'. However, it took 6 more years for that name to arrive.

It was only when B.F. Goodrich made a new type of rubber boot and referred to its Sundbäck fastener as 'the zipper' that the name stuck.

Curiously, while zippers were used extensively for boots and shoes, it took another 20 years for the clothing industry to catch on. In the 1930s, children's clothing companies began to promote zippers as an aid to children dressing themselves. Then the French noticed, and raved about the zipper for trousers – thus ensuring the victory of zippers over buttons in the 'Battle of the Fly'. Today, Gideon Sundbäck's zippers are found everywhere, with some so sophisticated they can be watertight – or even, on NASA-designed space suits – completely airtight.

Gustavus **SWIFT**

The beef industry in America was always destined to be big business. After the Civil War, the plains of Texas were swarming with cattle with no market, scarcely worth a dollar a head. But in the hungry cities to the north, such cattle were worth many times more.

The first entrepreneur of the industry was Joseph McCoy, who arrived in Abilene, Texas, 'a small dead place of a dozen log huts', and bought 480 acres to build stockyards, because crucially the railroad had just arrived. He then persuaded the Texas ranchers to drive their cattle in huge herds up the legendary Chisholm Trail, 'for hundreds of miles, a chocolate band amid the green prairies'. The 'Cowtowns' were filled with the noise of cattle and locomotives by day, and by night with the sound of gunfire and the racket of drunken cowboys. Abilene became famous, as did Wichita, Dodge City and Kansas

City. And most of the cattle were shipped to the huge Union Stockyards of Chicago, helping it to become one of America's greatest cities.

Another visionary now intervened. Gustavus Swift had spent his early life on a New England farm and then as a butcher. He moved west and by 1875 was one of the 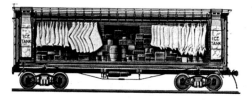 dominant figures in 'The Yards' of Chicago. However, he became dissatisfied with the inefficiency of shipping cattle as livestock 'on the hoof', realising that 60% of a cow's weight was inedible. He reasoned that it would be much better to slaughter in Chicago and send out processed beef. But to do this, he would need refrigeration. Swift and others had experimented with refrigerated railroad boxcars, or 'reefers', but it was not until 1878 that Swift's engineer, Andrew Case, came up with the perfect design, with ice and salt hoppers at each end with open roof hatches distributing cold air across the hanging meat.

Swift then tried to interest the railroads that served Chicago, but they all turned him down. Why? They had too much invested in stock cars and cattle pens. So he built his own fleet of 'reefers', eventually totalling 7,000.

Gustavus Swift became a giant in the industry. Employing 21,000, he processed two million cattle, four million pigs and two million sheep a year. And his assembly line (or rather disassembly line) methods inspired Henry Ford to adopt the conveyors and fixed workstations that made him a legend in mass production.

By the time Swift died in 1903, thousands of 'reefers' in high-speed trains, re-iced at intervals with the speed of pit stops, were given priority over crack passenger expresses. Gustavus Swift's invention had changed the food industry forever.

Nikola **TESLA**

Thomas Edison was a great man and a great inventor. But there was one incident in his life over which he behaved with all the greed, immorality and deceit worthy of the worst of the 'robber barons' of America. This was called 'The War of the Currents'.

Undoubtedly one of the most useful of the 1,340 inventions of the 'Wizard of Menlo Park' was Edison's 1879 creation of the incandescent light bulb. He soon went on to create generators, a distribution system and electricity meters, and famously lit up the Wall Street district with the backing of America's legendary banker, J. Pierpont Morgan. But there was a flaw in this apparent miracle, this liberation from oil and gas lighting. He had used 'direct current', or DC, and this could not be transmitted over long distances, needing not only power stations every mile or so, but thick copper wires that made downtown cities look like spider's webs. Such was Edison's reputation, however, that most people simply accepted the poor situation.

But then a young man arrived from Europe where great strides had been made with 'alternating current' or AC, including new transformers, motors and meters. Rome

was to be the first city to use AC. Nikola Tesla, (left) aged 28 and born in Croatia, was shocked by what he saw in America. Visiting Edison he promised he could solve the shortcomings, and Edison was so confident that his own system could not be improved that he offered Tesla a large financial reward.

When Tesla quickly announced that he had solved the problem – including a new design for an AC motor – Edison refused to pay up, claiming that '*the offer had been an American joke!*' A furious Tesla resigned on the spot, and his genius and his patents were snapped up by others, notably George Westinghouse who had been investing time and money on AC.

The huge advantage that AC could be generated in large remote power stations, then distributed cheaply at high voltage and stepped down by local transformers to low voltage should have been obvious. But Edison had invested heavily in his DC patents, and he and General Electric were quite looking forward to the profits from building lots of little power stations, even if communities could ill afford them.

Thus the 'War of the Currents' broke out – with Edison and General Electric with DC on one side and Tesla and Westinghouse on the other with AC. Edison then behaved badly – using his public relations people to imply that AC was more hazardous, even staging shows in which dogs and horses were electrocuted and organising the first use of AC on a bungled execution of a murderer in an electric chair. He even tried to popularise the term 'Westinghoused' for being electrocuted.

However the tide was turning. At the Columbian Exposition in 1893 in Chicago, both systems were used and AC proved much more efficient, with Tesla also featuring in an amazing show of lightning, even passing current through his own body. As more and more communities turned to AC, the directors of General Electric, accepting the situation, overruled Edison and his pride and embraced the new technology. However, this did not stop Edison's people indulging in one last and tasteless propaganda exercise – the filmed electrocution of 'Topsy', an elephant that had killed three men (now on YouTube).

AC swept the world while DC systems dwindled. A last few remnants like Helsinki changed in the 1940s, and Stockholm in 1970. One holdout was in London, Bankside Power Station, which supplied DC for the huge printing presses in Fleet Street. When Fleet Street disappeared as a newspaper centre in 1981, so did Bankside, and today of course, we know it as Tate Modern.

? Paul **TIBBETS**

On February 23rd, 1915, Enola Gay Tibbets gave birth to a son. Her own first two names had been rather casually chosen after a character in a novel that her father was reading when she was born. Little was she to know that those forenames would become indelibly associated with the greatest destruction and loss of life the world had ever seen.

The deliverer of that destruction, her son Paul, first became hooked on flying at twelve years old when he went up with a barnstorming pilot. At university he contemplated becoming a surgeon, but the lure of flying won, and in 1937 he enlisted in the US Army Air Corps. By 1942, he was one of the very best bomber pilots, leading his squadron on the first American Flying Fortress raid into Europe and was often requested by General Eisenhower as his personal pilot.

But his abilities were soon to be put to an even more serious purpose. Chosen to test the huge B-29 Superfortress for a year, he was moved to Utah and was then briefed on the mission to drop the atomic bomb on Japan. 'I will go as far as to say that I knew what an atom was', he later said about his ignorance.

Having had to pretend to his wife that the many civilian scientists on the base were 'sanitary engineers', she one day asked one of them, Professor Alan van Dyke, to unblock a drain, which he did with a smile.

Paul Tibbets then recruited into the 509th Composite Group the very best pilots, navigators, bombardiers and support teams – 1,800 of them. Soon they were moved for final training to Tinian in the Marianas Islands. Back in New Mexico, on July 15th 1945, an atomic bomb was successfully exploded. Eleven days later, the cruiser Indianapolis delivered a second one to Tinian.

President Truman was faced with a truly appalling dilemma between invading a ferociously defended Japan, which might cost a million American lives, or using the bomb.

The Japanese were warned that they were threatened by 'a new and terrible weapon' unless they gave in, but had little concept what the message really meant, and did not respond. Before dawn on August 6th 1945, Tibbets' B-29 with 'Enola Gay' emblazoned below his cockpit, lifted off from Tinian. Six and a half hours later, he was 31,000 feet above Hiroshima, whose inhabitants stared unconcerned at the lone aircraft, assuming it was a reconnaissance plane. The atomic bomb 'Little Boy' fell away and 43 seconds later, at 1,850 feet, exploded, its vast fireball killing over 80,000 people and destroying all in its path. After the blinding flash, the crew of 'Enola Gay' stared transfixed as the blast nearly knocked them from the sky and a fiery red mushroom cloud rose 30,000 feet above them.

The pilot who had literally led Japan into war at Pearl Harbor, Captain Fuchida, landed in Hiroshima safely the next day, in spite of silence from the control tower. In his immaculate white uniform he walked towards the devastation past a stumbling procession of thousands, blackened and naked, who 'seemed to have come out of hell'. He may have reflected that surprise attacks can be two-edged weapons.

Indeed that is what Paul Tibbets said after Japan surrendered a few days later. 'I viewed my mission as one to save lives. I didn't bomb Pearl Harbor. I didn't start the war, but I was going to finish it'.

Albert **TROTT**

While it can never rival soccer in terms of popularity, cricket is still one of the world's great sports. The British Empire ensured that it spread, particularly in India, and it now embraces a variety of international matches including 5-day Test Matches, One-Day 50-overs and Twenty 20 matches. In England and Wales there are inter-county 4-day matches, 1–day matches of 40 overs per team and Twenty20 matches of 20 overs per team. Women's cricket has also boomed recently, with England doing very well.

Cricket's heroes are well-known enough: the bearded W.G. Grace; Gilbert Jessop; Australian Don Bradman – regarded as history's greatest batsman – and Harold Larwood, who sought to tame him with 'bodyline' bowling; the great English batsman Len Hutton; Denis Compton, also unusually a star footballer (playing for Arsenal); controversial Yorkshireman Geoffrey Boycott, and more recently, the equally controversial South African Kevin Pietersen.

However, there is one Test player who is less well-known but still regarded as remarkable. Born in Victoria, Australia in 1873, Albert Trott burst onto the Test scene in 1895 in the 3rd Test, when he took 8 English wickets for only 43 runs, and scoring 38 not out and then 72 not out. Having then scored 85 not out in the 4th Test he was, very curiously, left out of the Australian team to tour England in 1896 – so he headed for England at his own expense and started playing for MCC. He then also played for Middlesex between 1898 and 1910 and played two Test matches for England in South Africa in 1899.

On July 31st, 1899, Trott achieved the feat that made him briefly famous. He is the only man to hit a ball over the Lord's Pavilion, landing in the Groundsman's garden. At the time such a massive hit only earned 4 runs, not the 'six' introduced in 1910. (Although, curiously, if the ball had been hit clean out of the whole ground, it would have earned a six). In sweet revenge, this famous hit was made playing for MCC against the very Australian team from which he had been dropped.

By now he was regarded as one of cricket's greatest all-rounders, with a curious round-arm bowling style that could be deadly. He could be fast, or rely on a guileful spin, and was dangerously unpredictable – seldom bowling the same ball twice.

But after 1901, this colourful and eccentric player began to put on weight, perhaps because of his jovial habit of drinking beer on the boundary with the spectators. He thus lost some of his agility and much of his earning power. But he was always popular, and in 1907 there was a benefit match to raise money for him. Memorably, he bowled an amazing double hat-trick, taking four wickets with four balls, shortly followed by another hat-trick. The match ended so quickly that it did not raise enough money, prompting his ironic remark 'I've bowled myself into the poorhouse!' A few years later, in 1914 aged only 41, Trott was penniless. One day he wrote his will on the back of a laundry ticket, leaving his clothes and £4 to his landlady. Tragically, he then shot himself.

MCC paid for his funeral, but his headstone was not erected until 1994. No wonder he is now only a vague memory.

Jethro **TULL**

We may recall the bible story about sowing seed and its problems – 'and some fell on stony ground'. Since agriculture first started, men have attempted to raise crops by scooping seeds from a bag and throwing them around. Such 'broadcast' sowing is bound to be wasteful and haphazard. Indeed, we bemoan young men 'scattering wild oats'!

What was plainly needed was a much more methodical system – placing the seeds in well-ordered rows, at a specific depth and spacing – and then covering them up, thus giving each young plant an equal chance to flourish.

The Sumerians, in what is now Iraq, had created a single tube seed 'drill' as early as 1,500 BC and the Chinese followed seven hundred years later with multi-tube drills, pulled by oxen. Indeed, China's huge population may well not have been possible without the crop yields created by this innovation.

The contact with the Chinese brought the drill to Italy hundreds of years later, in 1602, and it was in Italy that Jethro Tull encountered it. Tull was travelling in Europe both to seek a cure for an illness and to indulge in his passion for agricultural advances. He realised just how valuable the increase in crop yields achieved by a drill could be – up to eight times that of broadcast sowing.

In his improved machine, the seeds fell from what was quaintly called the 'penis' of the drill into a mechanical metering device which distributed the seeds down the tubes, carefully set at the correct distance apart, where they dropped into a the furrow created by the 'coulters' or mini ploughs, which also had the beneficial effect of weeding ahead of the seed; weeding being another of Tull's passions.

As with many such mechanical innovations of that era, it took some time for the seed drill to be adopted. Indeed, Tull's own workhands resisted it, because they could readily see that it would replace many of them when inefficiently 'broadcasting'. Nevertheless, Tull's seed drill, together with his other farming inventions, played a crucial role in Britain's 'Agricultural Revolution', almost as important as her Industrial Revolution.

Today, faced by food shortages, the world is desperately struggling to find solutions, (some of them controversial), that might increase yields even marginally – fertilisers, pesticides and genetically modified crops. Something that today increased yields eight times would be a miracle.

Jethro Tull died in 1741 aged 66, at his home called 'Prosperous Farm'. He has made a great many farmers prosperous since then.

Andrew **VOLSTEAD**

Excessive drinking has been a social problem for many countries. In Britain, drunken men of the upper classes beat their wives and gambled away their estates, and drunken men of the working classes beat their wives, beat up other men and drank away the family's wages. In the United States, the Women's Christian Temperance Society was

Some might prefer the liquor!

formed in 1874, and women were to play a major role in the American temperance movement because saloons were (often correctly) equated with brothels.

Then, in 1919, the powerful Anti-Saloon League persuaded Congressman Andrew Volstead (below) from Minnesota to push through the 18th Amendment or National Prohibition Act. Known as the 'Volstead Act', this prohibited the manufacture, distribution and sale of alcohol.

The legislation, however, had consequences unforeseen by the well-meaning Representative from Minnesota and his friends. Legitimate bars were now replaced by thousands of illegal 'speakeasies' and control of drink distribution was soon dominated by gangsters; first the Irish and then increasingly Sicilians and Italians – the beginning of the power of the Mafia.

The trouble was that most American citizens liked to drink. In one Detroit police raid, the local Mayor, the Sheriff and Congressman were caught . And there was so much money generated that the police and the judges could normally be 'bought' anyway.

The blatant and public gang warfare culminated in 1929 in Chicago's 'Bootleg Battle of the Marne' with a cavalcade of cars full of O'Bannion/Weiss gangsters machine-gunning Al Capone's headquarters with 5,000 bullets, and soon after that the notorious 'St. Valentine's Day Massacre', Capone's revenge.

After the 1929 'Wall Street Crash' and with the gloom of the Depression, Americans began to fall out of love with the spurious glamour of the speakeasy and especially the brutal behaviour of the bootleggers. In 1932, the end of Prohibition was made into an election-winning promise by the Democrats, and the Volstead Act was duly repealed the next year. Its legacy, unfortunately, was organised crime – now powerful and rich enough to turn to other profitable and much nastier products like drugs.

One wonders what Andrew Volstead, who died in 1947, thought of it all.

? Thomas **WAKLEY**

The campaigns of many newspapers and magazines have influenced history: *The Times* in the Crimea War, *Harper's Weekly* destroying New York's corrupt 'Boss' Tweed, *L'Aurore* with Emile Zola's 'J'accuse!' over the Dreyfus affair, *The Washington Post* with Watergate and recently *The Daily Telegraph*, revealing the scandal of the expenses of Britain's Members of Parliament, and *The Guardian* toppling the *News of the World* over phone-hacking. But one of the most consistent in its impact must be *The Lancet*, the world-famous medical journal.

This respected organ was the brainchild of Thomas Wakley, a dynamic and pugnacious man who had become a surgeon at the precocious age of twenty-two. Only three years later, in 1820, he founded *The Lancet*, deliberately naming it after the instrument used to lance a boil, as well as the pointed lancet arch – to indicate 'the light of wisdom'. Wakley's colleagues included the reformer and essayist William Cobbett, and a libel lawyer – whose skills would be in much demand – because, as Wakley wrote in the first edition, 'We shall be assailed by much interested opposition. We hope that the age of 'mental delusion' has passed, and that mystery and concealment will no longer be encouraged'. He then proceeded to 'lance' into medecine's corruption, nepotism and malpractice. *'We deplore the state of society which allows various sets of mercenary, goose-brained monopolists and charlatans to usurp the highest privileges. This is the canker-worm which eats into the heart of the medical body'.*

Again not mincing his words, he took particular aim at the The Council of the College of Surgeons *'which remains an irresponsible, unreformed monstrosity in the midst of English institutions – an antediluvian relic of all that is most despotic and revolting, iniquitous and insulting, on the face of the Earth'.*

He tried to launch a rival London College of Medicine but failed against the combined opposition of 'interested' parties, but his efforts eventually led to much-needed reforms.

In 1835, Wakley became the Radical Member of Parliament for Finsbury and resolved to campaign with this added strength. He fought strenuously against the Poor Laws, police bills and Lord's Day Observance. He also backed the Chartist Movement, the 'Tolpuddle Martyrs', Free Trade, as well as Irish Independence and continuous medical reform.

Some of his successes included the setting up of medical coroners, the eradication of flogging in the British Army and the elimination of the fraudulent and widespread adulteration of basic foods like sugar, coffee, pepper, bread and tea.

The Lancet kept up the innovative pressure, announcing vital new medical advances like blood transfusions, Caesarian sections, Lister's antiseptics, intravenous fluids, and later, the phenomenon of 'shellshock' in World War I, as well as the use of penicillin.

Still controversial, *The Lancet* has not only influenced medicine, but the politics of medicine. The creation of just one man just ten years after Waterloo, there has never been a journal that has so consistently fought its ground for nearly two centuries.

Fred **WARING**

In December 1936, the musicians were packing up their instruments at New York's Vanderbilt Theatre. A live radio show by one of the most popular bands in America had just ended. Fans crowded around, but one visitor was not really interested in the music. Fred Osius, a kitchen appliance businessman, knew that the leader of the band loved gadgets and inventions. So he talked his way into the dressing room of Fred Waring.

The musician that Fred Osius was so determined to meet had enjoyed a very interesting career. In 1918, at Pennsylvania State University, Fred Waring had formed the curiously-named 'Waring-McLintock Snap Orchestra', later 'Fred Waring's Banjo Band'. So successful did this become that he abandoned his engineering studies and went on tour with what was now called 'Fred Waring and his Pennsylvanians', becoming one of the Victor record label's best-selling bands, sponsored by Ford, Old Gold, Chesterfield and General Electric.

However, Fred Waring had never lost his interest in machinery, and that is exactly what Fred Osius was counting on when he cleverly inveigled himself into that dressing room. He told Waring that he had acquired a blending machine to mix soda fountain drinks, made possible by the invention of small motors that had revolutionized the appliance industry. The electric blender had a tall container, which had blades to chop and purée food and drinks. All that was needed to perfect it in the difficult times of the Depression, explained Osius, was 'a little more money.' Waring agreed to help, not least because he thought he could purée raw vegetables for his own ulcer diet. However, six months and $25,000 later, the machine was still not performing properly, so Waring decided to take it over and have it redesigned.

The result was his 'Miracle Mixer' (right), launched to wide acclaim at the 1937 Chicago National Restaurant Show. The next year he changed the name to 'Waring's Blendor', the curious spelling to give it a little more distinction.

His efforts to get his blender adopted were supplemented by a one-man sales campaign to all the hotels and restaurants he visited on tour all over America with the band. 'This mixer is going to revolutionise American drinks', he told a St Louis reporter. It did a great deal more than that. The blender or food processor was soon an essential in most kitchens and bars. Producing food for babies was transformed, and today blenders churn out health foods and 'smoothies'.

Less well-known has been its vital role in hospitals and science laboratories. Indeed, Dr Jonas Salk used a Waring blender in the process of developing his polio vaccine.

Long after Fred Waring's splendid, happy music has been relegated to music archives, the company he founded is still churning out these now indispensable machines.

Harry **WASYLYK**

You have to be quite elderly to remember the problems of getting rid of household waste – or 'trash', as Americans call it. The heavy metal dustbins of old were crammed with stinking, unhealthy food waste, and the job of a 'dustman' both unpleasant and unhealthy. Nor do many of us recall the dirty clothes and faces of the dustmen on their weekly visits, or their lowly status in society compared with today's 'refuse collectors', picking up carefully sorted rubbish bags from light plastic bins, rather than lugging them over their shoulders to the dustcart. Few men wanted to be 'on the dust' – except perhaps at Christmas when tips were due. One man was to change all that.

Harry Wasylyk was born in 1925 in Canada in the city of Winnipeg. With the improvements in plastics, he worked with Larry Hansen to create green, disposable polyethylene garbage bags. Their first idea was to sell them to the local Winnipeg General Hospital. But Larry Hansen worked for the Union Carbide Company in Canada, which saw the potential of a much wider use for the bags, not just for commercial use but for the huge domestic market. Union Carbide was a highly innovative company that had started by making carbide mining lamps and was famous for many brands including Ever Ready Batteries. (Unfortunately, the company became infamous in 1984, perhaps unfairly, for the chemical leak disaster in Bhopal, India).

Union Carbide brought the innovation from Harry Wasylyk and Larry Hansen and launched 'GLAD' bags in 1963 which then became a best-selling brand.

Now we use such plastic bags all the time, and not just to put in our rubbish bins, which remain clean and clear of flies. Sometimes made of thicker plastic for construction waste, they can also have handles and drawstrings and be oxo-biodegradable. They are used in the street, in offices, hospitals and factories – and of course the home, where millions of us could not imagine life without them.

? Chaim WEIZMANN

All over Britain each Autumn, children pick up shiny brown horse-chestnuts, drill holes in them, attach them to string and then try to smash the 'conkers' wielded by their friends.

The conker, which arrived in Western Europe from Turkey in 1576, appears a harmless enough fruit. Its handsome tree – the horse chestnut – has become an evocative icon of the countryside, parks and streets, providing the ammunition for innumerable 'conker fights.' Yet few know that the fruits have had an unexpected influence on world affairs via the munitions factories of World War I. And, by a strange irony of history, the Islamic world might rue the day they reached the West.

In 1916, the tragic Battle of the Somme had revealed to the Minister of Supply, David Lloyd George, a desperate need to source more and better munitions, and especially cordite, the propellant of artillery shells, of which Britain would eventually fire off 258 million. For this, he needed a large quantity of acetone, a solvent essential for its manufacture, of which there was then a serious shortage.

Lloyd George, and Winston Churchill who, in charge of the Navy, was equally anxious about shell quality, turned for help to a 'boffin.' Zionist and chemist, Professor Chaim Weizmann of Manchester University took up the challenge. He used his process of bacterial fermentation on maize starch to yield acetone. However, Britain's imports of maize from North America were running low because of the German U-boats' campaign against merchant shipping. Weizmann needed a new source of starch – and suggested conkers, free and plentiful. In the autumn of 1917 an extraordinary national collection campaign went underway, with children from all over Britain gathering sacks of the precious fruits for processing factories in Dorset and Norfolk, sending their conker parcels to Government offices in London for secrecy. Acetone was now available, cordite production assured, and in November 1918, Germany surrendered to the victorious Allies.

A grateful Lloyd George, by now Prime Minister, wanted to reward Weizmann. He asked the Professor if there was anything he could do for him, no doubt thinking along the lines of a knighthood or a peerage. Yes, there was. Weizmann would 'like help to establish a homeland for the Jews in Palestine'. He was sufficiently persuasive that the Prime Minister introduced him to the Foreign Secretary, Arthur Balfour, to take the matter forward. And that, wrote Lloyd George, 'was the fount and origin of the Balfour Declaration' that established, in principle, the modern state of Israel and 'left a permanent mark on the map of the world.'

It did, because the fledging state of Israel, the product of an almost casual gesture about conkers, then grew too slowly. In vain did Weizmann appeal in 1920, 'Jewish people, where are you?' Few Jews in Europe, especially in Germany where they were prominent, wealthy and influential, had any intention of abandoning their successful lives for some poor, hot, barren settlement. So, tragically, most were later trapped and perished in the Holocaust. Meanwhile Israel, growing slowly, became the focus of resurgent Arab nationalism.

Since 1948, when Chaim Weizmann duly became Israel's first President, the apparently laudable concept of Israel's 'promised land' has sadly spawned wars, refugee camps, terrorism, oil crises, suicide bombers, Al-Qaeda, 9/11 and terrible conflict in Iraq and Afghanistan.

Few can imagine when the conflict will ever end.

George **WELCH**

There are two good reasons why we should know more about George Welch. Twice he should have won America's top decoration, the Medal of Honor.

The first happened on December 7th, 1941, a beautiful Sunday morning at Pearl Harbor, where rows of proud battleships rode peacefully at anchor, at a low state of readiness and where fighter planes were crowded in neat rows to make it easy to guard against sabotage. Most people were still asleep, despite America and Japan being plainly on a collision course, and intelligence about impending war flooding in.

At 06.30 the destroyer USS *Ward* depth charged and sunk a midget submarine trying to enter the harbour, but nobody reacted to the *Ward* report. Then, at 07.02, an inexperienced young Lieutenant Kermit Tyler, at the new Information Center, decided that the very large, fast-moving blip reported by radar operators was just some B-17s arriving from California, and in one of the most memorable lines in warfare, told them 'Don't worry about it'. Pearl Harbor's last chance to avert disaster was gone.

At 08.00, the band on the battleship *Nevada* began to play for the 'Colors' ceremony.

Suddenly the music was drowned by the snarl of aircraft and then explosions.

Many of the fighter pilots had been up all night dancing and playing poker. A plane roared past. 'The damned Navy, buzzing us again to hurt our hangovers'. Then an explosion. They rushed outside. The sky was full of planes and those neat rows of American fighters were being totally demolished by strafing Zeros.

Second Lieutenants George Welch and Kenneth Taylor were not asleep. In fact, they had just decided to have a nightcap after an all-night party. They took in the horrific scene at a glance. Their own planes were luckily parked at a little auxiliary grass airstrip at Haleiwa, ten miles away.

While Welch ran for Taylor's new red Buick, Taylor, without authority, shouted down the phone to Haleiwa, 'Get two P40's ready. No, it's not a gag – the Japs are here!'

They drove at breakneck speed, dodging Japanese planes, leaped into their warmed-up fighters and thundered down the runway. Over the marine base at Ewa, they caught up with twelve 'Val' dive bombers and each shot one down. Taylor then chased another and it plunged into the ocean. Deadly, agile Zeros homed in on the American pair. Welch's P40 was hit, he dived into cloud, decided the damage was not serious and emerged to shoot down another 'Val'. Both pilots then landed in the burning chaos of Wheeler Field to re-arm and re-fuel.

Just as they were about to take off, senior officers actually started to lecture them on unauthorised behaviour! But the next wave of Japanese scattered the crowd and the two young pilots roared off straight at the enemy.

A handful of other pilots had managed to get into the air, and if just a little more time had been gained, the battle might have been less one-sided. The Japanese lost just 29 aircraft, the Americans 188 with 159 damaged, while 19 ships were sunk or damaged.

Welch and Taylor were designated the first American heroes of the war, both with four 'kills'. Both were nominated for the Medal of Honor supported by their Air Force commander, General 'Hap' Arnold. But other officers, perhaps smarting from being caught out so badly, downgraded the awards to the Distinguished Service Cross – for the ridiculous reason that 'They had taken off without proper authorisation'.

George Welch, like his friend Taylor, survived the war. After clocking up another 12 victories in the Pacific, he retired because of malaria and became a test pilot for North American Aviation, famous for creating the superb P-51 Mustang.

Flying the experimental version of the Sabre, the XP-86, it is claimed that Welch broke the 'sound barrier' two weeks before 'Chuck' Yeager in the Bell X-1 (page 129). This could be neither verified nor announced, because, first of all, Secretary of the Air Force, Stuart Symington, had forbidden North American to break the barrier before the X-1, and second the P-86 was about to be an operational fighter and its performance had to remain secret. Yeager got the glory and the Silver Medal of Honor.

Three years later Welch was in Korea, where in his F-86 Sabre he shot down several MIG-15s while 'supervising' his Air Force students. But his 'kills' had to be distributed among them – as once again he was 'under orders'. By now, he was surely used to *not* getting the credit he deserved.

George Welch died in 1954, still doing what he loved most – piloting a plane to its limit – and still largely unlauded and unrecognised. To 'welch' on someone is a common enough phrase. Whatever its origin, it certainly applied to him.

Horst **WESSEL**

If you want three years in prison in today's Germany, either sing or hum in public the 'Horst Wessel Song' – once the Nazi's unofficial National Anthem. The words were written by a 22-year old nonentity called Horst Wessel, with the title '*Der Unbekannte SA-Mann*', 'The Unknown SA-Man', which was exactly what he was.

Horst Wessel was born into a family of Lutheran pastors living, ironically, in Berlin's *Judenstrasse* or 'Jew's Street'. As a teenage gang leader fighting the Communists in the streets, he attracted the attention of Dr Joseph Goebbels, Berlin's Gauleiter, who sent him to Vienna to study Nazi agitation methods. At 22 (right), he was the leader of his local troop of the *Sturmableilung*, or S.A., one of millions of the Nazis' thuggish 'Brownshirt' enforcers. Based on his daily experiences, he wrote a *Kampflied* or fighting song, and Goebbels' newspaper *Der Angriff* published it. Here is the rather banal first verse:

> The banner high, ranks tightly closed
> The S.A. marches with silent steady steps
> Comrades shot by the Red Front and reaction
> March in spirit with us in our ranks.

A year later, someone then shot Horst Wessel himself, on his doorstep. Nobody quite knows who or why. A fight with local Communists, a quarrel over his unpaid rent – or even over his prostitute girlfriend? Whatever, it seems a grubby, inglorious incident of little significance. But, once again, in stepped Joseph Goebbels, now Hitler's brilliant propaganda chief. A huge funeral with 30,000 people was orchestrated with Goebbels himself making a passionate graveside oration.

The 'Horst Wessel Song', now set to the tune of an old naval marching song, became the Nazi's 'Song of Consecration' and, once they had achieved power, it was sung as the second half of '*Deutschland, Deutschland über alles*'. Streets, squares and railway stations were named after Horst Wessel, along with ships, panzer divisions and fighter squadrons. Horst Wessel must surely be one of the most undeserving icons in history, propelled there by one of Dr Goebbels' 'Big Lies': '*If you tell a lie big enough and keep repeating it, people will eventually come to believe it!*'

Goebbels was the master of the lie. He boasted about the blond Aryan ideal, while he himself was a clubfooted dwarf. Extolling family life, he indulged in innumerable affairs. My father, Toby O'Brien, then helping to run Britain's own propaganda, made up a song in his bath, to the tune of *Colonel Bogey*. It became immediately popular, but was plainly inaccurate about Goebbels' sexual abilities.

'Hitler has only got one ball,
Goering's so very small,
Himmler's so very similar,
And Goebbels has noebbels at all'.

To justify his hatred of the Jews, his organisation of *Kristallnacht* and participation in the Holocaust, Goebbels perpetuated the lie about the Jewish conspiracy to rule the world, using the forged and discredited *Protocols of the Elders of Zion* (Page 178). He even had the nerve to pretend that the Poles had attacked Germany first. And on a lighter note, having banned Germans from listening to jazz 'from Jews and Negroes', he created a rather good jazz band, 'Charlie and his Orchestra' to beam swing and jazz with racist propaganda lyrics to the British and Americans troops in England.

This clever, cool, cynical, witty and evil man ended up in the Berlin bunker, and after the suicide of his beloved Führer, poisoned his own six children before shooting his wife Magda and then himself. Even he could not lie or 'spin' his way out of that grisly death.

And now we are left with that haunting and illegal song from one of his very first inventions – Horst Wessel.

Stuart **WHEELER**

One of the fastest-growing forms of wagering is 'spread-betting', and financial 'spread-betting' has become a huge force, with over a million gamblers in the UK alone. Spread-betting operates by wagering on the outcome of an event and the accuracy of the prediction above and below 'the spread'. If you say the outcome will be higher than the figure quoted by the bookmaker, the more right you are, the more you win. Conversely, the more wrong you are, the more you lose. Together with the price of stock exchange indices, it now extends to commodities, individual shares and even sporting results. It can be very profitable and very risky. As the man who developed it in Britain, Stuart Wheeler is a rather unlikely figure.

Stuart was not born lucky, both abandoned by his mother into an adoption society in 1935, and with a clubfoot. His luck changed when Betty Wheeler came to visit. About to adopt a really pretty child, her sister Joan then noticed 'a boy standing up and making a nuisance of himself. He looked more interesting'. It was not the last time that Stuart would be noticed for being a nuisance.

> **'A boy standing up and making a nuisance of himself'**

While his new family appeared well-heeled, his American-born father, Alexander Wheeler, was actually a non-working, sporting, 'country gentleman'. When he died, by carefully husbanding their remaining meagre resources, Betty managed to give Stuart an excellent education at Eton and Oxford. But after National Service in the Welsh Guards, he had a lacklustre career as a barrister and a banker.

However, he had a razor-sharp mind for numbers and had been an enthusiastic gambler since childhood, playing bridge with Omar Sharif and gambling at the Portland Club with Lord Lucan two nights before he disappeared.

Wheeler noticed that while foreign exchange restrictions made it impossible to actually buy gold, you could bet on its price – and any profits would be tax free. He put  the idea to Cyril Stein of Ladbrokes who turned it down. So in 1974, he created IG Index with £200 of his own money and £29,800 from others, including Selim Zilkha of Mothercare, who provided it 'as a favour to a friend'.

When the company went beyond betting on the prices of gold and then commodities and into stock exchange indices, it began to flourish. In the first months of 1987, it made £700,000 profit, but the 'Crash' wiped that out in days. Luckily, 'The Financial Services Act' of the previous year meant spread-betting debts were legally enforceable. The punters paid up and IG Index survived.

Until 2000 Stuart Wheeler (left) – a quiet, principled and unassuming man – was virtually unknown to the general public, unlike his photographer wife Tessa Codrington and three beautiful daughters. However, he did hit the financial headlines when IG Index went public and his £200 investment turned into £44 million, allowing him to buy and restore Chilham Castle in Kent.

Then in 2001 he gave £5 million to the cash-strapped Conservatives, and when William Hague realised that there were no strings attached – no titles, no influential position – he exclaimed, 'You must be the perfect donor – like Father Christmas!'

As the single biggest political donor in British history, Wheeler's influence did begin to show in 2003, when he appeared on the BBC *Today* programme to argue that Iain Duncan-Smith was not a suitable leader. Michael Howard took over, but resigned in 2005, to be followed by David Cameron.

However, Wheeler's views on the encroachment of Europe led him to back the United Kingdom Independence Party with £100,000 for the 2009 European Elections. Unsurprisingly, the Tories expelled him.

For such an unknown, self-effacing 'numbers' man, Stuart Wheeler has wielded huge influence. He created one of the great new financial sectors. He altered the fortunes and direction of the Conservative Party. He helped UKIP to keep going and, in 2010, UKIP took enough vital votes from the Tories in marginal seats to create the need for the Conservative/Liberal Democrat coalition that has changed the political landscape.

UKIP continues to have a major influence on Britain's political scene.

Lulu **WHITE**

A memorable jazz number, 'Mahogany Hall Stomp', was first performed by Louis Armstrong. And it is the last memory of Lulu White's 'Mahogany Hall', (right of picture) the most magnificent brothel in New Orleans, and listed at 235 Basin Street in the 1910 *Blue Book*, the 'Guide for Gentlemen'. This praised its delicious food, fine wines and spirits and its sumptuous décor with glistening chandeliers, Tiffany stained-glass windows, expensive oil paintings and its distinctive mahogany staircase.

Lulu White had originally arrived from Alabama and was of mixed race herself, employing 40 beautiful, light-skinned 'Octaroons'. For many years Mahogany Hall boomed, as did most of the brothels of New Orleans, which had built up a robust reputation for vice since the French had first settled there. Puritan morality in the rest of America only served to boost the city's main attraction.

From the 1870s, whole blocks were filled with brothels, ranging upwards in style from Clip Joints, Cribs, Whorehouses, Bordellos, Houses of Assignation, Sporting Houses and Mansions. Enthusiastic visitors from all over the country had only to walk off the trains and straight into Basin Street.

In 1898 Alderman Sidney Story stepped into history. He hated prostitution, but his theory was: 'If you can't eliminate prostitution, at least you can isolate it'. He therefore persuaded the city's Board of Aldermen to define a 'District' that legalised brothels, and outside of which prostitution became illegal. At a stroke he succeeded in creating the world's ultimate 'red light district.' Unfortunately for him, the obscure politician's name would forever be attached to 'Storyville', as the District was cynically dubbed.

More infuriating for Story was that he had another pet hate – jazz – and the brothels and dance halls of Storyville became the perfect places for jazz musicians. Even the tunes sounded like a street map – *Burgundy Street Blues, Dauphin Street Blues, Bourbon Street Parade, Basin Street Blues, Canal Street Blues, St Phillips Street Breakdown, Perdido Street Blues.*

To entertain the punters, ragtime was played by piano players like 'Jelly Roll' Morton (you can probably guess what a jelly roll was). Indeed, jazz itself was used as a word for sex. Musically, jazz was an amalgam of black work songs (the Blues), New Orleans marching music and Creole sophistication. The names of those who learned their trade in Storyville echo with us years later: Kid Ory, Bunk Johnson, Sidney Bechet, 'King' Oliver and, of course, a little kid on a cart delivering coal to the brothels called Louis Armstrong.

But the reason we know their names is because when America entered the Great War in 1917, New Orleans became a major naval base, and the Navy, fearful of

Storyville's potential health or crime effects on its young recruits, persuaded the city to close the 'District' down. Thousands of girls were forced to go north to Chicago, no doubt to fill the brothels run by gangsters like 'Big Jim' Colisimo, Johnny Torrio and Al Capone. Much more lasting in its influence was the similar migration of the jazzmen, who then began to put on record the wonderful music the world calls 'New Orleans Jazz'.

Even with Mahogany Hall closed down, Lulu stayed in New Orleans and died in obscurity in the 1940s, probably unaware of the musical miracle she had helped to release.

Eli **WHITNEY**

It is not often that someone has been in a position to create unwittingly the reasons for a civil war and then devise one of the ways of ending it.

Eli Whitney was born in Massachusetts in 1765, and by the time he was fourteen was involved in manufacturing, operating a nail-making factory. He then studied at Yale and was accepted to be a private tutor in South Carolina. But sailing south, he decided to go to Georgia instead. Also on the ship was a widow who invited Whitney to visit her plantation. Her fiancé, Phineas Miller, would become Whitney's business partner.

On the Georgia plantation, Whitney noticed a serious problem. Cotton, once picked, had to be cleaned of its seeds. Doing this by hand took a whole day just to clean one pound, making the crop scarcely profitable. Pondering this obvious bottleneck, Whitney was inspired by watching a cat trying to pull a chicken through a fence and getting only feathers, and fabricated a simple device in a wooden box – an 'engine'. His 'cotton gin', as it was soon called, had a wooden drum armed with hooks that pulled the cotton fibres through a mesh, leaving the seeds behind. With this device, a man or woman could clean fifty times more cotton in a day. Cotton production, now hugely profitable, soared in volume. Vast areas were cleared and planted with easy-to-grow cotton, including those deemed unsuitable for other crops. 'King Cotton' had arrived, and millions of tons of cotton were shipped each year to factories in New England and Europe. Indeed, Manchester in England was soon called 'Cottonopolis'.

However, while Whitney's 'gin' was beneficial for Southern wealth, the plantations now needed ever more workers to pick cotton – which meant ever more slaves. Thus the moral arguments against slavery as an institution, which had been gathering strength, were now weakened. Tragedy was in the making. Eventually, the South would grow so confident economically that it defied the North and precipitated the Civil War.

Ironically, Eli Whitney made no money from his revolutionary 'cotton gin'. A simple device, it was so easy to copy that his patent was useless and litigation to protect it nearly ruined him. So, virtually bankrupt by 1798, he grasped at a very different opportunity. He responded to a War Department public offer to make muskets for the US government – despite the fact that he had never made a gun in his life. Incredibly, he won a contract and luckily was sent a foreign pamphlet on *'arms manufacturing techniques'*. He quickly espoused the concept of 'interchangeable parts', which, coupled with power machinery, became the basis of mass production, and not only for weapons. At last, he became a rich man.

Whitney's methods would ensure that the North would become an industrial powerhouse. The South that he left behind, still dependent on cotton and his gin, became a rural backwater, far too reliant on one crop. Three decades after Eli Whitney's death, the two halves of the country would be locked in war. But 'King Cotton's' over-confident assumption that Europe, and especially England, would intervene to help the South were dashed. Europe, disapproving of slavery, stood aside and turned to Egypt for its cotton, and after four years of agony and sacrifice, the Confederacy was defeated by a Union equipped by a massive arms industry pioneered by the same Eli Whitney that had made 'King Cotton' possible.

Bob **WILLS**

During the Rolling Stones' 'Bigger Bang Tour' in 2005, Mick Jagger stepped forward on the stage in Dallas, 'We've never sung this music before, and maybe we never will again! A bit of Country music from Waylon Jennings.' Then, to rapturous cheers, Jagger sang about Texas, 'It's the home of Willie Nelson, the home of Western Swing, And he'll be the first to tell you, Bob Wills is still the King.' Jagger was referring to 'Bob Wills and his Texas Playboys', a star of five decades earlier who in that part of the world would have even been more famous than the Rolling Stones.

James Robert Wills was born on a Texas Panhandle cotton farm, into a very musical family. Jim Rob worked the cotton fields alongside African-American pickers, hearing for the first time the songs that would influence his music. He 'jig' danced with the children, a precursor to his later stage antics.

In 1913 the family moved to Turkey, a Texas fly-speck. There, in 1915, 10 year old Jim Rob Wills played his first public dance, because his father was too drunk to play. Wanting to see more, he hopped freight trains from town to town trying to eke out a living. Deciding on barbering, he landed a job at Hamms Barber Shop, while fiddling at night. In 1929, Jim Rob moved to Fort Worth, playing in a minstrel and 'medicine show'. There was already a 'Jim' in the show, so the manager began calling him 'Bob'. Now he would be known as Bob Wills.

At Fort Worth he had his first break because Wilbert 'Pappy' O'Daniel, later Governor of Texas, but then working for Burrus Mills, set up Bob Wills in 'The Light Crust Doughboys'. From this 'Bob Wills and his Texas Playboys' evolved, together with Western Swing – a mixture of Country, jazz and minstrel shows.

The Playboys appeared in smart cowboy dress. Bob's look was that of a well-dressed bandleader, but one from Texas, with cowboy hat, cigar, and fiddle being all part of his trademark. Over the years, hundreds of musicians would be 'Playboys' with trumpets and saxophones, and female vocalists. The band's makeup changed frequently, growing into a veritable western symphony, or shrinking to a tight little fiddle band. The Playboy rhythm would influence other music with a powerful pulse, like Rock 'n' Roll. Indeed,

Chuck Berry's 'Maybelline' was an adaptation of Wills' 'Ida Red,' folk tune.

From 1934 to 1942, KVOO radio in Tulsa, Oklahoma, was key to the Playboys' lives. They would travel for nighttime dances in towns hundreds of miles away, but be back for a live noon broadcast every weekday and a gospel radio show on the weekend. Their grassroots popularity spreading, recording artist Don Walser remembers walking home from school, the entire neighborhood picking up the Tulsa broadcasts. 'You could hear a Bob Wills song from start to finish walking by those windows.'

By 1945, they were famous enough to play at Nashville's prestigious Grand Ole Opry. A drum set was unheard of in the world of Country music back then. Opry staff insisted his drummer couldn't play, so Bob agreed to let the drums be hidden behind curtains. But as they started to play, he hollered, 'Move those things out on stage!' Bob Wills would leave a permanent mark. There would forever be a beat in country music. (But they were not invited back!)

Two songs became standards. Bob's 'Spanish Two-Step', written in the 1930s, became 'San Antonio Rose'. Bob's hypnotic hollers of 'San Antone!' would literally be heard all over the world in 1969, as the Apollo 12 astronauts sang it, looking back at the earth from a lunar orbit. It has sold 14 million copies. The mournful instrumental 'Faded Love' started out as a simple fiddle tune by Bob's father, John Wills, since recorded by over 300 artists.

Bob Wills was married six times. Years of hard travelling and drinking had taken their toll on his health. So after a second heart attack in 1964, he 'sold' the management of the band for ten thousand dollars, and his 'Bob Wills Ranch House' to Jack Ruby, notorious for shooting Lee Harvey Oswald.

Bob Wills died on May 13th, 1975 at the age of 70. His headstone bears the epitaph 'Deep Within My Heart Lies A Melody.'

It certainly did.

Zhao ZHENG

With her huge size, massive population, work ethic and grasp of technology, China is poised to become the greatest power on earth. And the fact that she is one unified country – rather than competing states – can be put down to one remarkable man – Zhao Zheng, later to be called the Emperor Qin Shi Huangdi ('First Sovereign Emperor of Qin').

Qin was just one small state in the north-west, but its strong central administration, strict legal codes and excellent army enabled it to subdue the 'Warring States' and the remnants of the Zhou dynasty which had lasted seven hundred years. From 221 BC, Emperor Qin ruled his country with an iron grip, burning Confucian books lest they give people ideas of not obeying his rigid laws. He created provinces ruled by governors and imposed uniformity of language, law, coinage and weights and measures.

He also built canals and roads, and most dramatically, the Great Wall of China. His first 3,000 miles of this were built in just ten years at a cost of a million lives – 300 dead for every mile. The Wall was not just a barrier but effectively a military road, with watch-towers every few hundred yards, garrison towns and a signalling system of smoke fires to summon sufficient troops depending on the danger. It was fully manned and operational for 2,000 years, and still remains a truly impressive, even beautiful, monument to man's ingenuity to this day.

Perhaps even more extraordinary is Emperor Qin's tomb, first discovered in 1974 under a vast mound by astonished farmers digging a well. Started soon after Qin's accession as a teenager, the tomb complex took 700,000 men 36 years to construct. The actual tomb, hermetically sealed, has never been opened, but it is guarded by formations of more than 7,500 terracotta soldiers. Life-sized, these were mass-produced and then assembled – with each face carved with unique features. There are also horses, chariots, and high ranking officers, together with civilians including entertainers and civil servants.

The soldiers' weapons are not only real but still sharp – thanks to the chromium oxide plating that the West did not discover and replicate for another 2,000 years. In addition, the Emperor was buried with a vast amount of valuables, and to keep this a secret he had the last workers buried alive, with hair-triggered cross-bows then positioned as booby traps. In recent years a number of objects and terracotta soldiers from his tomb featured in a travelling exhibition that created spectacular interest in museums in Europe and in North and South America.

The Qin dynasty effectively died with the man himself, but the disciplined and unified nation that he created certainly lives on.

Arthur **ZIMMERMANN**

On January 16th, 1917, Arthur Zimmermann, Germany's good-humoured and naive Foreign Minister, sent a coded telegram to his Embassy in Mexico City – arguably the most stupid and momentous such message in history.

Zimmermann was equally naive over both America's attitudes and Britain's ability to break German codes. In reality, London's brilliant, top secret 'Room 40' cracked 15,000 German messages during World War 1. There, the unlikely grey-haired figure of the Reverend William Montgomery studied Zimmermann's telegram. He realised that, even partly decoded, it was crucial, and took it to the legendary Captain William Hall, RN, whom America's Ambassador Walter Page described to President Woodrow Wilson as 'a clear case of genius. All other secret service men are amateurs by comparison.'

One glance told Hall that here were words hinting at something cataclysmic, with phrases like *'unrestricted submarine warfare'*, *'war with the USA'*, *'propose an alliance.'*

Both Britain and Germany were exhausted from three years of bloody trench warfare. Zimmermann had been persuaded by the generals that an all-out U-boat war was Germany's only chance, and persuaded himself that Mexico might actually side with Germany against the United States, her powerful neighbour to the north.

Room 40 struggled to recreate a perfectly complete telegram, because, while it had  to convince the Americans, it must not reveal that the British had deciphered it. Since Germany's trans-Atlantic cables had been cut by the British, her telegrams went indirectly. One route went through Washington, but a British agent also stole a copy of the Western Union cable (left) that reached Mexico via the German Embassy in Washington, complete with its different headings and number. Now the leak could *look* as if it had come from Mexico, not London.

Soon Hall's decoding was complete, and revealed a proposed alliance with Mexico, to be rewarded with several US states. The British held an explosive propaganda coup. But would they have to use it? The Americans had broken diplomatic links with Germany, but had gone no further.

After all, President Wilson had been re-elected on the slogan, 'He kept us out of the war'. Finally, on February 22nd the anxious British could wait no longer. Arthur Balfour, the Foreign Secretary, handed the telegram to the astounded Ambassador, Walter Page, in 'as a dramatic a moment as I remember'.

President Wilson was forced to act. The Press Association was secretly given the story, and on March 1st it broke in every US newspaper. A few suggested a 'British forgery', and the Mexicans, Japanese and Germans quickly denied it all. But then Zimmerman blundered again by admitting: 'I cannot deny it. It is all true.'

Now, American public opinion swung. Texans imagined German and Mexican troops marching in to take away their state. The West Coast envisaged a Japanese invasion.

On April 2nd, President Wilson went to Congress to ask for war, citing the now infamous cable. National fervour mounted (right), and soon American fresh troops poured into Europe to tip the scale against Germany – and the US became a world power.

Before he resigned (because of the telegram), in August Zimmermann sent Lenin to St Petersburg in a sealed train, thus launching the blight of Communism on the world.

Poor Arthur Zimmermann. Always a little too confident in his ill-thought-out actions, he was a disaster for Germany and the world.

INDEX